"THIS BOOK IS A NECESSARY PURCHASE."

—*Library Journal*

"Del Martin is emerging as the nation's Number One authority on the battered wife."

—*San Francisco Examiner*

"**BATTERED WIVES is recommended to all those who, whatever their disciplinary background or degree of activism, want to see the relations between men and women raised to a high level of civility.**"

—*Contemporary Psychology*

"A shocking but necessary and believable study"

—*Booklist*

Battered Wives

(Updated)

Del Martin

PUBLISHED BY POCKET BOOKS NEW YORK

To Phyllis, my partner in life and work, who made it possible for me to write this book—

To Ruth, my publisher and friend, who first got me involved with its subject—

And to the network of sisters around the world who are striving to solve the problem—

POCKET BOOKS, a division of Simon & Schuster, Inc.
1230 Avenue of the Americas, New York, N.Y. 10020

Copyright © 1976, 1981, 1983 by Del Martin

Published by arrangement with Volcano Press, Inc.
Library of Congress Catalog Card Number: 81-12985

All rights reserved, including the right to reproduce
this book or portions thereof in any form whatsoever.
For information address Volcano Press, Inc., 330
Ellis Street, #518, Dept. B., San Francisco, Calif. 94102

ISBN: 0-671-49591-7

First Pocket Books printing November, 1977

10 9 8 7

POCKET and colophon are registered trademarks
of Simon & Schuster, Inc.

Printed in the U.S.A.

CONTENTS

INTRODUCTION

Many different ways have been devised for keeping women subordinated to men in patriarchal societies. Footbinding was used by the Chinese to cripple women for over 1,000 years. Purdah, the practice of secluding women from contact with men outside of the immediate family, frequently accomplished by making women prisoners in their own homes, is still widespread today among the Muslim populations of the Middle East, North Africa, and Asia. Clitoridectomy (excision of the clitoris) is still practiced on millions of pre-puberty girls in Egypt, Sudan, Somalia, Kenya, Yemen, Saudi Arabia, Iraq, Guinea, and Ethiopia. Rape and assault, both within the family and outside of it, are two of the most crude and brutal ways in which Western patriarchal societies seek to maintain the sexual status quo. (These methods are, however, not confined to the West, but appear to be common to all patriarchal societies.) Del Martin's book focuses on assault within the home—particularly when it takes an extreme form, referred to as wife-*battery* rather than mere wife-beating.

It is quite remarkable how much attention has been given to the issue of rape in the United States in the past few years, and how little to the problem of woman-battery. In January 1975 I announced to various groups that the college where I teach would be showing a BBC-made movie on the topic of wife-battery called "Scream Quietly, or the Neighbors Will Hear." I got the distinct feeling that people thought I was being morbid and a little crazy—the reaction I had experienced when telling people I was doing research on rape four years before. Only about ten people came to see the movie. In England, on the other hand, there has been considerable attention to the problem of woman-battering over the past few years, but only recently to rape. Why the difference is an interesting question. I doubt very much that it is because there is more woman-battery in England than in the United States. Whatever the reason, Martin has undertaken the tremendously important task of trying to educate the U.S. public about the extent and seriousness of wife-battery and wife-beating in this country, the many causes of the problem, as well as the solutions. In spite of the paucity of available data, particularly on the men who batter their wives, Martin gives us as accurate a picture as can be constructed at this time on these matters, and she does so in a highly readable manner. While she admits that it is impossible to know the exact prevalence of wife-beating and battery in this country because no satisfactory large-scale prevalence study has been undertaken to date (this is true for rape and the molestation of female children too), she makes it clear that we know enough to realize that there is an enormous problem which is being ignored. With the publication of this book, the continued neglect of this problem will be inexcusable.

Battered Wives is written not only for those working to change the law, reform social agencies, provide housing for battered women, or affect policy-making in general. It is written for all women—not only the victims of this form of male violence, but every single one of us who needs to understand this phenomenon lest those fortunate enough not to have been victims participate unwittingly by our silence in the perpetration of this crime. When the victim is a woman, she is invariably held responsible and stigmatized for what she has suffered, hence, the silence. As Martin emphasizes, this silence must stop. Battered women must speak up, and this book should make it easier for them to do so, and easier for all of us to hear and respect what they have to say.

Hopefully the women's movement will make the battering of women, both within the family and outside of it, as central an issue as they have made of rape. These two forms of violence against women are so clearly related, and the fear of men each instills in women has similar political consequences. In both instances there is often an agonizing fear of death, which sometimes results in actual womanslaughter or femicide (a word invented by Carol A. Orlock to refer to the killing of girls and women by men).

At the International Tribunal on Crimes Against Women, held in Brussels March 4-8, 1976, and attended by over 2,000 women from 33 countries, there was considerable testimony about the battering of women. For example, 49-year-old Mary McCormick from Ireland testified that she had tried three times to leave her home because of constant beatings, but that she had been unable to support her nine children on her $25 a week salary as a washer-up in a hotel. When she tried to leave, her husband signed her into a mental hospital. The signature of a husband is all that is needed under Irish law. The police forcibly removed her and her family from the train she was fleeing on. They detained her at a police station for a day, refusing to tell her what was happening or why. She was then taken, bound, to a mental hospital where she was given Valium and encouraged to accept shock treatments. Three months and a hunger strike later, her 21-year-old daughter was able to sign her out, but only with the aid of a lawyer.

An Englishwoman who had been severely beaten by her husband testified that she had gone through ten different agencies before finally finding a refuge for battered wives, "with one cooker with one ring working and a grill for 12 families and 25 children. We lived there with no windows, no heating, no playground or clothes for the children. But anything would've done for me then; I wouldn't have cared where I'd gone."

The workshop on battered women proposed the following resolution, which was greatly applauded when presented to the plenary session on the last day: "The women of Japan, Netherlands, France, Wales, England, Scotland, Ireland, Australia, USA and Germany have begun the fight for the rights of battered women and their children. We call for urgent action by all countries to combat the crime of woman-battering. We demand that governments recognize the existence and extent of this problem, and accept the need for refuges, financial aid, and effective legal protection for these women." This resolution, along with all the others, was sent to the governments of all countries. More important is the motivation aroused in those present to do something about the problem when they return to their countries.

One of the great strengths of Martin's book is that she shows how male violence against women, including the battering of wives, rape, and femicide, is a natural consequence of women's powerless position vis-a-vis men in patriarchal societies and the sexist values and attitudes that accompany this inequity. Male violence towards women cannot be eradicated without also eradicating the unequal power relationships between the sexes. And, as Martin rightly emphasizes, this means a complete restructuring of the traditional family. Until the division of labor in the family is transformed into one of equal responsibilities for rearing children, caring for the home, and providing for the family financially, women will be relatively powerless both in the family and outside of it, and violence against women will continue to be a problem. This is not to say that there are no ways of checking men's abuse of their power short of this revolutionary change. Another strength of Martin's book is precisely the thoroughness and thoughtfulness with which she deals with the many different levels of what-is-to-be-done about the problem of wife-battery.

Martin has written an excellent book on an extremely important and heretofore neglected topic. Hopefully it will be widely read by the public at large and used by schools for such courses as marriage and the family, the sociology of oppression, and the psychology of aggression and violence. *Battered Wives* is a tremendous step towards our finally confronting this problem in the United States. It is up to all of us to take the next steps.

Diana E. H. Russell
Coordinator of the U.S. Delegation to the
International Tribunal on Crimes Against Women

PREFACE

Throughout this book I have used the term "battered wives," although most of what I have to say applies equally to unmarried women who live with violent men, and many of the examples cited involve unmarried cohabitants. I hesitate to call these women "common-law wives," since many have chosen, for a variety of reasons, not to classify themselves as wives in any sense of this word. No adequate term seems to exist for the man in such a relationship either. "Lover" hardly seems appropriate. Still, the book *is* about men and women who share or have shared a home, not about women and men in general. Therefore, in the interest of underscoring the shared-household factor, I have chosen to use the words "wife" and "husband" liberally. The term "battered wife," therefore, usually refers to any woman who is beaten by her mate, whether legally married or not, and the word "husband" applies to the man in the couple.

Exceptions to these general uses of the terms do occur throughout the book. Obviously, the material on the nature of the marriage contract and divorce applies only to married couples. And there may be differences in the way representatives of the criminal justice system respond to calls for help from unmarried women who have been beaten by their mates. I suspect that the difficulties an unmarried woman experiences differ in subtle ways from those a wife/victim must endure. But for the most part, attitudes toward both—as victims and as women—are more alike than different.

A year ago I knew that wife-beating was a problem in some marriages. But I had no idea of the prevalence of marital violence, nor of its tacit acceptance as a part of life in so many families. Information on the subject was not readily accessible. When I spoke to people about my projected book on battered wives, they swiftly changed the subject or twisted it around to a safer, more socially acceptable topic—child abuse. Men put up their guard at the mention of battered wives, though a few feigned mild curiosity to cover their embarrassment. Women, too, were reticent about discussing the issue. Many, however, when they were later able to talk to me privately, revealed that they were or had been battered wives. To my amazement I learned that "some of my best friends" are among those who had experienced violence at one time or another in their intimate relationships with men. They spilled out their stories as if they had waited for years to find someone who would listen and take them seriously.

Wife-beating, I soon learned, is a complex problem that involves much more than the act itself or the personal interaction between a husband and his wife. It has its roots in historical attitudes towards women, the institution of marriage, the economy, the intricacies of criminal and civil law, and the delivery system of social service agencies. Blame is not easily fixed, nor are the causes of marital violence readily identified.

Working on this book was a consciousness-raising experience for me. People from many parts of the world influenced my growing awareness of the multitude of issues that come into play when addressing the problem of family violence. Child abuse, which is every bit as deplorable as wife-beating, is already an issue. People do not hesitate to express righteous indignation when children are victimized or brutalized. But somehow they become strangely silent when the victim is a woman—a wife and mother. Why? This book explores various avenues in an attempt to answer that question.

Already I have been swamped with letters and phone calls from people who are concerned about family violence and want to know what to do, how to start a refuge for battered wives, and where to obtain funding. I have no magic answer or blueprint. My advice is to start at the local level; form coalitions and task forces; research applicable state laws and city ordinances; investigate policies and procedures of law enforcement (police, district attorney, and the courts); gather statistics from every conceivable source; canvass emergency housing and note admission policies; determine what services are already available and which need to be established; draw up proposals based on that information; make funding agencies aware of the need; lobby for remedial legislation at every level of government; demand a re-ordering of priorities in government and foundation spending; and don't stop until all necessary programs are realized.

The economic and social structure of our present society depends upon the degradation, subjugation, and exploitation of women. Many husbands who batter their wives in anger and frustration are really striking out against a system that entraps them, too. In a peculiar way they, too, are expressing a desire for change in attitudes towards husband-wife roles and the institution of marriage. Social change is inevitable. The question is whether it will be accomplished by violent or peaceful means. As citizens we must assume the responsibility for the answer.

Battered Wives includes the collective thoughts and concerns of a great many people. I am deeply indebted to Betsy Warrior, a feminist activist in Massachusetts, for her help in putting me in touch with people who are either conducting research on marital violence or establishing refuges for battered wives. Previously we had been working in isolation. Today we have a tremendous international communications network which hopefully, through combined efforts, will enable us to find solutions to stem the violence that takes place in the privacy of our homes.

The Women's Litigation Unit of the San Francisco Neighborhood Legal Assistance Foundation, staffed by attorneys and interning law students, began researching the legal ramifications of wife-abuse after two of their clients were killed by their husbands. I am most grateful to these women for opening their files to me. Attorneys Susan Jackson and Mary Vail were particularly helpful in answering my questions about the law and the procedures of the legal system. Marjory Fields, of the South Brooklyn Legal Services, graciously made her files available to me also. Further, she contributed another valuable dimension from her vast esperience as a divorce lawyer for the poor.

Sue Eisenberg and Patricia Micklow, of the University of Michigan Law School, did a monumental piece of work entitled "The Assaulted Wife: 'Catch 22' Revisited," which will be published in the *Women's Rights Law Reporter*. I am grateful to them not only for granting me permission to quote from their research, but for their efforts in publicizing their findings and bringing public attention to this social problem. I have also drawn from excellent papers produced by two other law students: Lois Yankowski, of Washington, D.C., and E. Lehman, of New York.

Richard Gelles, author of *The Violent Home*, Suzanne Steinmetz and Murray Straus, editors of *Violence in the Family*, are sociologists who have contributed greatly to our knowledge of wife-beating as a social phenomenon in the United States. In addition to their published works, they have pooled their resources to make their unpublished papers available to the public. Another sociologist who understands the role of research as an agent for social change is Rebecca Dobash, of the University of Stirling in Scotland, who was my source of information on the British scene. For the 1976 meeting of the American Sociological Association she has organized a working session of twelve members who have some working knowledge and experience with marital violence. The participants, who come from various countries and cultural backgrounds as well as diverse academic and occupational fields, will each submit a paper in advance. The purpose of the session is to bring together a few highly motivated people to exchange ideas and theories, discuss research findings, and explore solutions.

Morton Bard, a police officer turned psychologist who is now at City College of the City University of New York, and Donald Liebman and Jeffrey Schwartz, psychologist-consultants in San Francisco, pioneered the family crisis-intervention training programs now being instituted in police departments across the country. These men generously contributed their published articles, research papers, and course materials. Also most helpful was Commander James Bannon, of the Detroit Police Department, who has conducted a sociological study on domestic social conflict. His analysis of the problems shows a high degree of feminist consciousness and a keen awareness of the victim's predicament that is generally lacking in police attitudes.

Because the list is so long and is ever-growing, it is impossible to include here all those who work in existing refuges for battered wives or who are trying to establish emergency shelters for abused women and their children. So many have sent me brochures, pamphlets, funding proposals, clippings, and other vital information, for which I am most grateful. I would like to give special mention and thanks, however, to Marta Ashley, Sue Critchfield, Jackie Eubanks, Jackie Griswold, Sharon Vaughn, Lynda Weston, and the staff at the National NOW Action Center for their assistance in the information-gathering process.

As for the mechanics of getting this book together, I am indebted to the Glide publishing team: Ruth Gottstein for acting as the catalyst; Suzanne Lipsett who played a major role in shaping the book by helping me to organize the mass of material I received, giving it perspective and form; Noah Phyllis Levin who did the final editing; Geri Davis for designing the cover jacket; and Deborah Johansen for handling public relations.

Finally, I wish to express my appreciation to Erin Pizzey, author of *Scream Quietly or the Neighbors Will Hear,* who conducted such an aggressive publicity campaign on behalf of battered wives in England that it reverberated around the world.

The efforts of all these people and the groups they represent—the vast communications network which now exists—assures us that active steps will be taken to put a stop to wife-beating. After centuries of victimization, feminists all over the world are joining in protest against this crime against women. There is no turning back.

1

A LETTER FROM A BATTERED WIFE

A friend of mine received the following letter after discussing wife-beating at a public meeting.

I am in my thirties and so is my husband. I have a high school diploma and am presently attending a local college, trying to obtain the additional education I need. My husband is a college graduate and a professional in his field. We are both attractive and, for the most part, respected and well-liked. We have four children and live in a middle-class home with all the comforts we could possibly want.

I have everything, except life without fear.

For most of my married life I have been periodically beaten by my husband. What do I mean by "beaten"? I mean that parts of my body have been hit violently and repeatedly, and that painful bruises, swelling, bleeding wounds, unconciousness, and combinations of these things have resulted.

Beating should be distinguished from all other kinds of physical abuse—including being hit and shoved around. When I say my husband threatens me with abuse I do not mean he warns me that he may lose control. I mean that he shakes a fist against my face or nose, makes punching-bag jabs at my shoulder, or makes similar gestures which may quickly turn into a full-fledged beating.

I have had glasses thrown at me. I have been kicked in the abdomen when I was visibly pregnant. I have been kicked off the bed and hit while lying on the floor—again, while I was pregnant. I have been

1

whipped, kicked and thrown, picked up again and thrown down again. I have been punched and kicked in the head, chest, face, and abdomen more times than I can count.

I have been slapped for saying something about politics, for having a different view about religion, for swearing, for crying, for wanting to have intercourse.

I have been threatened when I wouldn't do something he told me to do. I have been threatened when he's had a bad day and when he's had a good day.

I have been threatened, slapped, and beaten after stating bitterly that I didn't like what he was doing with another woman.

After each beating my husband has left the house and remained away for days.

Few people have ever seen my black and blue face or swollen lips because I have always stayed indoors afterwards, feeling ashamed. I was never able to drive following one of these beatings, so I could not get myself to a hospital for care. I could never have left my young children alone, even if I could have driven a car.

Hysteria inevitably sets in after a beating. This hysteria—the shaking and crying and mumbling—is not accepted by anyone, so there has never been anyone to call.

My husband on a few occasions did phone a day or so later so we could agree on the excuse I would use for returning to work, the grocery store, the dentist appointment, and so on. I used the excuses—a car accident, oral surgery, things like that.

Now, the first response to this story, which I myself think of, will be "Why didn't you seek help?"

I did. Early in our marriage I went to a clergyman who, after a few visits, told me that my husband meant no real harm, that he was just confused and felt insecure. I was encouraged to be more tolerant and understanding. Most important, I was told to forgive him the beatings just as Christ had forgiven me from the cross. I did that, too.

Things continued. Next time I turned to a doctor. I was given little pills to relax me and told to take things a little easier. I was just too nervous.

I turned to a friend, and when her husband found out, he accused me of either making things up or exaggerating the situation. She was told to stay away from me. She didn't, but she could no longer really help me. Just by believing me she was made to feel disloyal.

I turned to a professional family guidance agency. I was told there that my husband needed help and that I should find a way to control the incidents. I couldn't control the beatings—that was the whole point of my seeking help. At the agency I found I had to defend myself against the suspicion that I wanted to be hit, that I invited the beatings. Good God! Did the Jews invite themselves to be slaughtered in Germany?

I did go to two more doctors. One asked me what I had done to provoke my husband. The other asked if we had made up yet.

I called the police one time. They not only did not respond to the call, they called several hours later to ask if things had "settled down." I could have been dead by then!

I have nowhere to go if it happens again. No one wants to take in a woman with four children. Even if there were someone kind enough to care, no one wants to become involved in what is commonly referred to as a "domestic situation."

Everyone I have gone to for help has somehow wanted to blame me and vindicate my husband. I can see it lying there between their words and at the end of their sentences. The clergyman, the doctor, the counselor, my friend's husband, the police—all of them have found a way to vindicate my husband.

No one has to "provoke" a wife-beater. He will strike out when he's ready and for whatever reason he has at the moment.

I may be his excuse, but I have never been the reason.

I know that I do not want to be hit. I know, too, that I will be beaten again unless I can find a way out for myself and my children. I am terrified for them also.

As a married woman I have no recourse but to remain in the situation which is causing me to be painfully abused. I have suffered physical and emotional battering and spiritual rape because the social structure of my world says I cannot do anything about a man who wants to beat me. . . . But staying with my husband means that my children must be subjected to the

3

emotional battering caused when they see their mother's beaten face or hear her screams in the middle of the night.

I know that I have to get out. But when you have nowhere to go, you know that you must go on your own and expect no support. I have to be ready for that. I have to be ready to support myself and the children completely, and still provide a decent environment for them. I pray that I can do that before I am murdered in my own home.

I have learned that no one believes me and that I cannot depend upon any outside help. All I have left is the hope that I can get away before it is too late.

I have learned also that the doctors, the police, the clergy, and my friends will excuse my husband for distorting my face, but won't forgive me for looking bruised and broken. The greatest tragedy is that I am still praying, and there is not a human person to listen.

Being beaten is a terrible thing; it is most terrible of all if you are not equipped to fight back. I recall an occasion when I tried to defend myself and actually tore my husband's shirt. Later, he showed it to a relative as proof that I had done something terribly wrong. The fact that at that moment I had several raised spots on my head hidden by my hair, a swollen lip that was bleeding, and a severely damaged cheek with a blood clot that caused a permanent dimple didn't matter to him. What mattered was that I tore his shirt! That I tore it in self-defense didn't mean anything to him.

My situation is so untenable I would guess that anyone who has not experienced one like it would find it incomprehensible. I find it difficult to believe myself.

It must be pointed out that while a husband can beat, slap, or threaten his wife, there are "good days." These days tend to wear away the effects of the beating. They tend to cause the wife to put aside the traumas and look to the good—first, because there is nothing else to do; second, because there is nowhere and no one to turn to; and third, because the defeat is the beating and the hope is that it will not happen again. A loving woman like myself always hopes that it will not happen again. When it does, she simply hopes again, until it becomes obvious after a third beating that there is no hope. That is when she turns outward for help to find an answer. When that help is denied, she either resigns herself to the situation she is in or pulls herself together and starts making plans for a future life that includes only herself and her children.

For many the third beating may be too late. Several of the times I have been abused I have been amazed that I have remained alive. Imagine that I have been thrown to a very hard slate floor several times, kicked in the abdomen, the head, and the chest, and still remained alive!

What determines who is lucky and who isn't? I could have been dead a long time ago had I been hit the wrong way. My baby could have been killed or deformed had I been kicked the wrong way. What saved me?

I don't know. I only know that it has happened and that each night I dread the final blow that will kill me and leave my children motherless. I hope I can hang on until I complete my education, get a good job, and become self-sufficient enough to care for my children on my own.

In the preceding story one woman tells her secret. It is a secret shared by many women who daily fear for their lives. These women bear the brutality of their husbands in silence because they have no one to turn to and no place to go. They are married women; as such they are untouchables in our society. In the traditional Christian marriage ceremony, the minister warns, "Whom therefore God has joined together let no man put asunder." These words stand between the battered wife and any help she may seek. No one dares to interfere in the intimate relationship between husband and wife, even when the husband's violence and the wife's danger are apparent.

Often the battered woman is completely isolated. She feels she cannot discuss her problem with anyone—she is too embarrassed and humiliated. Besides, who would understand? Alone, in pain and fear, she wrestles with questions of what to do and where to go. Often she wonders whether she should do anything or go anywhere. If she has children she may feel particularly trapped. She might fear for her children's safety and emotional health but be unsure as to how to provide for them alone. When the battered woman becomes desperate enough to reach out for help, she often meets with subtle, and sometimes even hostile, rejection. Her problem may seem insolvable to her. At least with regard to the help and support she can expect from society, she may be right.

The isolation of the battered wife is the result of our society's almost tangible contempt for female victims of violence. Until very recently, rape victims were believed to be guilty of precipitating the crime against them until proven innocent in a court of law. The rapist had been tantalized, led on, teased, played with until—who could blame him, the argument went—he lost control and forcibly took his temptress. Thanks to efforts growing out of the women's movement, these attitudes are being slowly chipped away. Hopefully, all rapists will soon be looked upon as sex offenders rather than victims of seductive women.

When a woman is a victim of violence in her own home, however, social attitudes as to who is at fault and who deserves help are still very much against her. The woman is often seen as a nagging wife who has driven her husband past all endurance. Having reached the limit of his patience, he "pummels" her into blessed silence. In the stereotyped version of this archetypal scene, words such as "pummel" and "throttle" actually stand for "beat," "assault," "injure," and sometimes even "murder." The violent husband is hardly ever pursued and dealt with as a criminal, and the welfare of the victim has up to now been so far beneath the official concern of society that her needs were simply not acknowledged. Not only did her needs go unmet, they were usually not even considered to be real.

Today, however, women are taking a stand in various parts of the world to liberate themselves. Together they are addressing the problems they face as women. They are seeking solutions by making their issues public and by taking action that will effect social change. The women's movement has made progress in changing attitudes towards rape. Now women are turning their attention to violent crimes within the home.

The fact that wife-battering has become a social issue arousing international interest can be credited in large part to the pioneering efforts of Erin Pizzey. Pizzey had long been aware of the isolation suffered by married women in trouble, and in 1971, with the help of a small group of supporters, she established an "advice center" in London. The center was meant to be a place where women and their children could come together and meet their peers, escape loneliness, and discuss mutual concerns. Pizzey had hoped that the center would become a base for political action.

But an overwhelming majority of those who showed up at the center were battered women. Until the center was established, these women had had nowhere to go. Thus, the need for a sanctuary was obviously of the first priority, and the center developed into Chiswick Women's Aid, more popularly known as the Battered Wives' Center. In 1974, Pizzey published *Scream Quietly or the Neighbors Will Hear*,[1] the first book on the subject of battered wives. At the time of this writing, Pizzey faces arrest for harboring 110 women and children in a house legally suitable for 36 people.[2]

Interest in the problem of battered women has gradually increased since the publication of Pizzey's book. In 1975, by unanimous vote at its national conference, the National Organization for Women proclaimed marital violence a major issue and established a National Task Force on Battered Women/Household Violence.

Two years before the national action a Pennsylvania NOW State Task Force on Household Violence had been formed by Nancy Kirk-Gormley. After enduring ten years of beatings because she felt trapped by economic needs and lack of child care and job training, she fled her home and ended up in a cemetery by her father's grave above the mills in Pittsburgh. Sitting there alone, thinking, crying alone, Kirk-Gormley began to realize that there must be a better way to deal with this problem in her life. As a member of NOW for almost a year, she had seen addressed almost every women's problem but wife-abuse. The seed of an idea, formed in a graveyard, that victims of household violence should have a place to go and someone to talk with, led to the formation of a self-help group and eventually to the state task force. Today Nancy Kirk-Gormley is divorced and supports herself and her two children through fundraising skills she developed in NOW. As co-coordinators of the newly formed National Task Force on Battered Women/Household Violence, she and I are in touch with countless groups interested in taking action to reduce marital violence in this country.

The International Tribunal on Crimes against Women, held in Brussels in 1976, was a marked departure from the 1975 United Nations meeting in Mexico where, as Simone de Beauvoir said in her message to the tribunal, women had been mandated by their parties and nations to limit discussion to the integration of women into male society. In Brussels women gathered to denounce their oppression in that society and make the world conscious of the scandal of their condition. During the five-day tribunal women from around the world testified to their victimization and analyzed the social, sexual, economic, and political implications of wife-battering, rape, persecution of Lesbians, prostitution, pornography, and other crimes against women. Similar tribunals also took place in cities such as New York and San Francisco.

As a result of these efforts, wife-beating has begun to surface in newspapers, on radio, and on television as a social problem. Slowly, victim counseling centers are acknowledging that battered wives are victims in need of help. Some police departments are beginning to train officers in family crisis intervention. State and city hearings are being held to measure the prevalence of wife-battering and to consider such remedies as legislation, funding for emergency shelters, and the coordination of social services for wife/victims.

Emergency refuges are a chief concern. The overwhelming response by abused wives to Chiswick Women's Aid was by no means a purely English phenomenon. Wherever help is offered, in the form of emergency phone lines or refuge programs, women who have been isolated in their misery and frightened for themselves and their children respond. Battered women need refuges from their family situations where they can begin to think realistically about themselves. Every community in the United States should provide a place where women who are isolated by their secret beatings, as the woman in this chapter was, can make contact with people who will believe their stories and place the blame where it belongs. One of the most chilling side-effects of wife-beating is that it often destroys the beaten woman's self-respect and paralyzes her will. Her physical weakness and inability to defend herself can become metaphors for her inability to live in the world at large. A woman who believes that living with a violent man is preferable to living alone needs help. We must start by providing refuges where battered women can nurse their wounds, reassure their children, and begin to feel their own strength.

The purpose of this book is to investigate the problems of battered wives and to suggest some possible solutions. Any lasting solution to this complex problem should come from the collective thinking of researchers in government and private social agencies, the institutional religions, and political action groups. Such cooperative and constructive thinking will continue to be impossible, however, unless men as well as women come to realize that violence in the home is not a private affair but a grave social problem. Like all violence, domestic violence is a symptom of a greater flaw in our society. As a first step to putting things right, we must see the problem for what it is.

2

VIOLENCE IN THE HOME

Violent solutions to social problems have been incorporated into the mainstream culture of the United States. Violence is not the only reaction; nor is it the most common one. But, whether or not violent behavior is illegal, certain situations exist in which it is expected and almost inevitably occurs. One terrifying aspect of this fact of American life is that both the expectation and the incidence of violent behavior increase every year.

In 1974, serious crime rose 17 percent across the nation —the sharpest annual increase since the Federal Bureau of Investigation started recording crime statistics in 1930.[1] In the final three months of 1974, crime increased at a 19 percent rate; compare this rate to 16 percent in the first nine months and 6 percent for the whole of 1973. Many families have moved to the suburbs and to rural areas to escape the savage environment of the cities, but emigration from the inner city no longer guarantees safety. Crime was up 20 percent in suburban areas and 21 percent in rural districts in 1974.

During the five-year period from 1968 to 1973, murders per year in the United States jumped from 13,720 to 19,510. Some 100,020 persons were killed during that period— twice the number of Americans killed in the Vietnam War.[2] Nearly half of all American households have at least one gun—a pistol, shotgun, or rifle.[3] These types of firearms are used in 67 percent of all murders committed in the United States.[4] Guns in the home may give some people a sense of security, but the danger exists that family members will use them on each other during a heated quarrel. An alarming number of them do.

Descriptions or enactments of violent acts intrude into the American home many times each day by way of newspapers and television. Surveys show that acts of aggression take place every three and one-half minutes on children's Saturday morning shows.[5] The Federal Communications Commission has made moves to regulate the sexual content of family prime-time programming, but claims it has no jurisdiction over other content. As long as portrayals of violence remain popular, advertisers will continue to sponsor violent programs. As the situation stands now, during the prime-time evening hours Americans have their choice of endless depictions of death on the operating table or death on the streets.

Advertisers' use of violence is getting more subtle and thus more insidious. For example, the December 1975 issue of *Vogue* carried a fashion layout in which a couple was shown alternately fighting and caressing each other. In one photograph the male model had just walloped the female model (his arm was raised in the follow-through) and her face was twisted in pain. The caption made no mention of the sado-masochistic theme of the photographs. It merely noted that the woman's jumpsuit could "really take the heat."[6] And, reported in the "No Comment" section of the July 1973 *Ms.* magazine was this ad for a bowling alley in Michigan: "Have some fun. Beat your wife tonight. Then celebrate with some good food and drink with your friends."

Because of the increase in the crime of rape (62 percent in the five-year period ending in 1973),[7] American women are often advised to "stay at home where they won't get hurt." But people who would impose such a curfew on women's freedom of movement might change their tune if they had access to local police reports on domestic violence, which suggest that women may be even less safe in their homes than they are in the streets.

The Incidence of Domestic Violence

Accurately determining the incidence of wife-beating per se is impossible at this time. Obvious sources of information are police reports, court rosters, and emergency hospital admittance files, but wife-abuse is not an official category on such records. Information on the subject gets buried in other, more general categories. Calls to the police for help in marital violence, for instance, are usually reported as "domestic disturbance calls," or DDs. If the police respond to these calls but decide that everything is under control, they may not file a report. If serious injury has been sustained by a wife, or if a wife has been killed by her husband, the incident is reported as assault and battery, aggravated assault, or homicide; wife-abuse is not necessarily specified. Sometimes written complaints registered by wives against their husbands are the only source of statistics available. But who is to say how many abused women do not register complaints?

Emergency rooms in hospitals are not reliable sources of statistics either. For a variety of reasons, women are often reluctant to tell the truth about how they sustained their injuries. Doctors often accept explanations such as "I ran into a door" or "I accidentally fell down the stairs." Even if they suspect that a woman's injuries are due to a beating, they seldom want to risk personal involvement by asking questions.

Statistical evidence on wife-battering must therefore be culled from the more general statistics available on domestic disturbance calls, complaints, hospital emergency rosters, and crime reports. Here follows a random sample of such information from some American cities:

- In Chicago, a police survey conducted between September 1965 and March 1966 demonstrated that 46.1 percent of all the major crimes except murder perpetrated against women took place at home.[8] The study also revealed that police response to domestic disturbance calls exceeded total response for murder, rape, aggravated assault, and other serious crimes.[9]
- A study in Oakland, California, in 1970 showed that police there responded to more than 16,000 family disturbance calls during a six-month period.[10]
- The 46,137 domestic disturbance calls received by Kansas City, Missouri, police represented 82 percent of all disturbance calls received by them in 1972.[11]
- In Detroit, 4,900 wife-assault complaints were filed in 1972.[12]
- In New York, 14,167 wife-abuse complaints were handled in Family Court throughout the state during the judicial year 1972-73.[13] "Legal experts think that wife-abuse is one of the most underreported crimes in the country—even more underreported than rape,

12

which the FBI estimates is ten times more frequent than statistics indicate. A conservative estimate puts the number of battered wives nationwide at well over a million," states Karen Durbin.[14] Using the New York court statistics and the "ten times" formula to account for the cases that dropped by the wayside or were never reported, 141,670 wife-beatings could have occurred in New York State alone. If we can take this kind of guesswork a step further and consider that wife-battering is probably even more underreported than rape, and that there are fifty states in the Union, Durbin's estimate of "well over a million" could be conservative.

- In 1974, Boston police responded to 11,081 family disturbance calls, most of which involved physical violence.[15] At the end of the first quarter of 1975, 5,589 such calls were received—half the previous year's figure in one-quarter the time. (As an aside to these figures, Boston City Hospital reports that approximately 70 percent of the assault victims received in its emergency room are known to be women who have been attacked in their homes, usually by a husband or lover.[16])

- In Atlanta, Georgia, 60 percent of all police calls on the night shift are domestic disputes.[17]

- The Citizen's Complaint Center in the District of Columbia receives between 7,500 and 10,000 complaints of marital violence each year. Approximately 75 percent of the complainants are women.[18]

- In New Hampshire, for his study *The Violent Home*, Richard Gelles interviewed forty neighbors of known violent families as a means of establishing a nonviolent control group with which the violent group could be compared.[19] Of these supposedly nonviolent neighboring families, 37 percent had experienced at least one incident of violence, and for 12 percent violence was a regular occurrence.[20]

- Trends in domestic violence are similar in city after city. But the problem is not just an urban one; it is to be found in rural areas as well. For example, the police chief in a small Washtenaw County (Michigan) town of 6,000 reports that family assault calls come in every day.[21] And another police official with extensive rural experience estimates that police calls for "family fights" are exceeded only by calls relating to automobile accidents.[22]

The figures cited here were randomly selected from a variety of sources. No attempt has been made to adjust them with respect to population or to compare them and discern regional trends. The point here is that a great many domestic-violence cases come to the attention of the authorities. The raw numbers themselves make it obvious that domestic violence is a social problem, and a serious one. Just how serious is anyone's guess, since no one knows how many cases of domestic violence go unreported.

Still, the terms "domestic violence" or "domestic disturbance" are not synonymous with "wife-battering." But you don't need a degree in criminology to realize that the police are not called into a domestic situation unless the weaker person(s) involved need help or are perceived to need help by witnesses. If the involved parties could control and resolve a domestic disturbance, no doubt they would do so without inviting the police to interfere. It can be assumed that someone in most reported cases of domestic disturbance was being overpowered or, at the very least, frightened, or that neighbors or passersby thought that was the case.

Two other commonsense factors will help clarify the relationship between domestic-disturbance figures and wife-battering. First, many households are composed of conventional heterosexual marriages or relationships; and second, in most such relationships the woman is physically weaker than the man. We can assume that a good many of the domestic disturbance calls that do not involve juveniles concern women being intimidated, frightened, or assaulted by men to the point where someone decides that help is needed from the police. This assumption is borne out by statistics. Of the figures available on complaints, 82 percent in New York,[23] 75 percent in Washington, D.C.,[24] 85.4 percent in Detroit,[25] and 95 percent in Montgomery County, Maryland,[26] were filed by female victims.

By looking at another random sampling of police statistics, we can get an idea of just how serious a "domestic disturbance" can be:

- In 1971, Kansas City police found that one-third of the aggravated assaults reported were due to domestic disturbance.[27] Police had been called previously

14

at least once in 90 percent of these cases and five or more times in over half of them.[28] Also during 1971, 40 percent of all homicides in Kansas City were cases of spouse killing spouse.[29] In almost 50 percent of these cases, police had been summoned five or more times within a two-year period before the murder occurred.[30]

- Almost one-third of all female homicide victims in California in 1971 were murdered by their husbands.[31]
- Nationwide in 1973, according to the FBI, one-fourth of all murders occurred within the family, and one-half of these were husband-wife killings. In assault cases wives are predominantly the victims, but in homicides husbands are the victims almost as often as wives (48 percent compared with 52 percent in 1973).[32] This phenomenon is partially explained by the fact that, according to a report made to a government commission on violence, women who commit murder are motivated by self-defense almost seven times as often as male offenders.[33]
- In 1974, 25 percent of all murders in San Francisco involved legally married or cohabiting mates.[34]
- Domestic violence not only endangers the lives of family members and marital partners, it accounts for a high percentage of the deaths of and injuries sustained by police officers who answer the calls. According to the FBI, 132 police officers were killed in the nation in 1974.[35] Twenty-nine of them died while responding to domestic disturbance calls—that is, one out of every five police officers killed in the line of duty in 1974 died while trying to break up a family fight.

It is worthwhile mentioning here that divorce statistics are not a reliable gauge of the frequency of wife-abuse, since mention of marital violence can be negotiated out of the record before the trial or because the wife was unable to produce medical and police records to prove it occurred. However, a survey conducted by George Levinger of 600 applicants for divorce in the Cleveland area revealed that 37 percent of the wives suing for divorce cited "physical abuse" as one of their complaints.[36] And a Wayne County (Michigan) judge stated that approximately 16,000 divorces are initiated in the county annually, and in 80 percent of those

15

coming before him, beating is alleged. Commenting on another aspect of the problem, this judge estimated that fifty to sixty hearings are held in the Third Judicial Circuit Court each month on wives' claims that their estranged husbands have violated injunctions restraining them from physically abusing the wives.[37]

Wife-Abuse: The Skeleton in the Closet

Common sense tells us that statistics relating to domestic violence reflect, to some extent, the incidence of wife-beating. "Wife-beating has been so prevalent that all of us must have been aware of its existence—if not in our own lives, at least in the lives of others, or when a wife-beating case that resulted in death was reported in the press," states Betsy Warrior.[38] But, although governmental agencies and social scientists have begun to concentrate on social violence in recent years, wife-battering has merited no special attention in those quarters. Nor has it aroused the shocked indignation it should have from the women's movement until very recently. The fact is, the issue has been buried so deeply that no real data exist on the incidence of wife-beating.

The news media have often treated wife-abuse as a bizarre and relatively rare phenomenon—as occasional fodder for sensationalistic reporting—but rarely as a social issue worthy of thorough investigation. *Time* magazine demonstrated the news media's head-in-the-sand attitude in 1974 when it ran an article on Erin Pizzey's Chiswick Center, but carried it only in the European edition. Apparently the *Time* editors thought that wife-battering would not interest Americans.

In *Violence and the Family,* Suzanne Steinmetz and Murray Straus surveyed various kinds of literature in an effort to discern trends in the treatment of wife-beating. In their review of four hundred items, they located little material on husband-wife violence other than murder, even in novels. They were particularly puzzled by the fact that anthropologists had not uncovered evidence of marital violence in their studies of other cultures. But Paul Bohannon suggested to one of their colleagues two possible reasons: (1) middle-class anthropologists share the middle-class horror of violence, and (2) people in cultures under anthropological investigation do not necessarily conduct their family quar-

16

rels in the presence of anthropologists; nor do they talk about the violent episodes that might characterize their private lives.[39]

Occasionally, psychiatrists admit to coming across cases of marital violence in their clinical practices, but therapy-prone professionals tend to treat such incidents as exceptions and to see them in terms of the individual's pathology. Psychological studies of family dynamics tend to overlook the physical conflicts between husband and wife; they usually concentrate on the causes of tension within families, not on the means by which it is expressed.

An example of how social scientists skirt the issue of wife-battering is in the otherwise well-researched book by Eleanor Emmons Maccoby and Carol Nagy Jacklin, *The Psychology of Sex Differences*. Commenting on an article on wife-beating that appeared in the *Manchester Guardian*, these writers state, "Although incidents of this kind exist as an ugly aspect of marital relations in an unknown number of cases . . . there can be little doubt that direct force is rare in modern marriages. Male behavior such as that described above would be considered pathological in any human (or animal!) society, and, if widespread, would endanger a species."[40]

The wishful thinking demonstrated in this passage—that "direct force is rare in modern marriages"—even in its mildest form has done its share to keep information on wife-beating from surfacing. The fact that such information is all but lost in the tangle of police statistics on domestic disturbances substantiates the suspicions of those who think—and would like to go on thinking—that wife-beating is not a significant problem and does not deserve attention. But Pizzey's experience at the Chiswick Center has proved these Pollyannas to be wrong. When she opened a refuge for women, many abused wives showed up. Their very existence raises the issue of wife-battering.

In *Scream Quietly or the Neighbors Will Hear*, Pizzey points out that people try to ignore violence inside the home and within the family. Many abused wives who came to Chiswick Center told Pizzey that their neighbors knew very well what was going on but went to great lengths to pretend ignorance. They would cross the street to avoid witnessing an incident of domestic violence. Some would even turn up the television to block out the shouts, screams, and sobs coming from next door.[41]

From one point of view, the battered wife in her secrecy conspires with the media, the police, the social scientists, the social reformers, and the social workers to keep the issue hushed up. We can picture a very thick door locked shut. On the inside is a woman trying hard not to cry out for help. On the other side are those who could and should be helping, but instead are going about their business as if she weren't there.

The Great American Family

The door behind which the battered wife is trapped is the door to the family home. The white-picket-fence stereotype of the American family home still persists from the days of Andy Hardy. The privacy of the home supposedly protects a comfortable space within which intimate and affectionate relationships among spouses, parents and children, and siblings become richer and deeper with each passing year. Loyalty, constancy, and protectiveness are demonstrated by the parents and learned by the children. If you modernize the picture by adding some self-deprecating humor gleaned from television's situation comedies, the image of the ideal American family will be complete.

In one sense, the family home is supposed to provide refuge from the stormy turbulence of the outside world. In another, it is a family factory, designed to perpetuate its own values and to produce two or three replicas of itself as the children in the family marry—whether or not they are ready for or suited for marriage. The nuclear family is the building block of American society, and the social, religious, educational, and economic institutions of society are designed to maintain, support, and strengthen family ties even if the people involved can't stand the sight of one another.

Until very recently, no acceptable alternatives to the family home existed in the United States. People who chose to live alone or to share their homes with non-relatives, those who chose to set up same-sex households, or who married but chose not to have children—all were seen as outcasts, failures, or deviants. This attitude is changing, albeit very slowly, possibly more as a result of overpopulation than of growing openmindedness and tolerance. But even now, the stereotype of the happy, harmonious family persists in American society. Compared with this ideal, most actual families composed of real people appear to be tragic failures, and in many cases they are.

In reality, the glowing image of the American family is a myth. The privacy that protects the family can also muffle the blows and stifle the yells of a violent home. People who would not otherwise consider striking anyone sometimes act as if establishing a household together gives them the right to abuse each other. "From our interviews," Richard Gelles says in *The Violent Home*, "we are still convinced that in most cases a marriage license also functions as a hitting license."[42] In his research, which admittedly was limited to eighty subjects who were legally married, Gelles found that numerous incidents of violence between married partners were considered by them to be normal, routine, and generally acceptable.[43] He also found a high incidence of violence in his control group and only one instance in which violence had occurred before the couple married. Furthermore, in the case of two couples in his sample who dated, married, divorced, dated again, and remarried, violence occurred *only* when these couples were *legally* married. These findings indicate to Gelles the possibility that violence between a couple is considered acceptable within, but not outside of, marriage.[44]

Unmarried women who have been beaten by their mates undoubtedly would take exception to Gelles's interpretation. It may well be that the shared home, not the marriage vow, is the key element here. Some men may feel that they have the right to exercise power over the women they live with whether or not they are legally married to them.

Our patriarchal system allows a man the right of ownership to some degree over the property *and* people that comprise his household. A feminist friend learned this lesson in an incident in Oakland, California. She witnessed a street fight in which a husband was hitting his pregnant wife in the stomach (a recurring theme in stories of wife-abuse). She saw the fight as she was driving by, stopped her car, and jumped out to help the woman. When she tried to intervene, the male bystanders who stood idly by watching the spectacle shouted at her, "You can't do that! She's his wife!" and "You shouldn't interfere; it's none of your business." Although the wife had begged the gathered crowd to call the police, no one did so until my friend was struck by the furious husband. (I have heard of a similar incident where a man interfered and *he* was the one who was arrested and charged with assault!)

Sociologist Howard Erlanger of the University of Wisconsin found that 25 percent of his sample of American adults actually approved of husband-wife battles. What is more surprising was that the greater the educational level, the greater was the acceptance of marital violence. Approval ranged from 17 percent of grade-school graduates to 32 percent of college postgraduate students, with a slightly lower 30 percent for those who had completed just four years of college. The study also showed that, contrary to popular belief, low-income respondents were no more prone to nor more readily accepting of violence in the home than were middle- or upper-income respondents.[45]

The popular assumption by the middle class that marital violence occurs more frequently in the ghetto and among lower-class families reflects the inability of middle-class investigators to face the universality of the problem. Evidence of wife-beating exists wherever one cares to look for it. Fairfax County, Virginia, for instance, is a suburb of the District of Columbia and considered to be one of the wealthiest counties in the United States. Police there received 4,073 family disturbance calls in 1974. They estimated that thirty assault warrants are sought by Fairfax County wives each week.[46]

Morton Bard's study of New York's 30th Precinct, a West Harlem community of about 85,000 people, is another example. This socially stable residential community consists mostly of working-class Blacks, with a sprinkling of Latin Americans (8 percent) and whites (2 percent).[47] Bard found that the number of wife-abuse cases reported in the 30th Precinct was roughly the same as that reported in another study conducted in Norwalk, Connecticut—a white, upper-middle-class area with approximately the same population.[48]

A survey conducted for the National Commission on the Causes and Prevention of Violence by Louis Harris and Associates bears out Erlanger's conclusions that a great many people approve of husband-wife battles. The Harris poll in October 1968, consisting of 1,176 interviews with a representative national sample of American adults, showed that one-fifth approved of slapping one's spouse on "appropriate" occasions. In this survey, 16 percent of those with eight years of schooling or less approved, and 25 percent of college-educated people approved of a husband slapping his wife.[49]

Rodney Stark and James McEvoy III further analyzed the Harris data and found that 25 percent of the Blacks, 20 percent of the whites, 25 percent of the males, and 16 percent of the females interviewed "could approve of a husband's slapping his wife's face." The percentage points rose in all of these categories (from 1 to 3 percent) when the question was reversed and subjects were asked if they "could approve of a wife's slapping her husband's face." Analyzed by regions of the country, persons from the West rated highest and the South lowest in approval of either action. Those with an income of $5,000 or less were considerably less approving than those in other income brackets. Persons under thirty years old were most approving, and those sixty-five years or older were least approving of husband-wife slappings.[50]

A slap in the face could be construed as a fairly innocent gesture compared with a full-fledged beating. But a friend of mine told me this story. Three months after her mother and stepfather were married, they had an argument and he gave her a sound "slapping." A few months later he "slapped" her again; this time the woman wound up in the hospital with her jaws wired together. When she came home from the hospital, her husband was contrite and conciliatory. He did his best to please her so that she wouldn't leave him. The woman stayed, though she never really forgave her husband. They still had their fights, but he never laid a hand on her again. However, two years later, when the couple got into a particularly heated argument in the kitchen, he grabbed a knife and killed her.

Later, my daughter was slapped by a friend's violent husband when she responded to the wife's call for help. He just slapped her on the cheek, but with such force that her head snapped back and pain shot through her head to the top of her skull. He struck her twice in this heavy-handed manner. Her face was sore for several days, though there were no bruises; she also suffered the effects of a minor whiplash. "I didn't think he would hit *me*. He was my friend," she said. "And I certainly didn't realize that a man could exert so much force with his open hand. It was just a short slap. He didn't need to take a long swing."

In the Harris poll cited above, if the word had been "hit" instead of "slap" would the results of the poll have been the same? Would 25 percent of the males and 16 percent of the females interviewed approve of a husband hitting his wife in the face? The answer to that question is anybody's guess. But there is a good chance that the interviewees would have considered the question an invasion of privacy had the word been "hit" rather than "slap." I cite this possibility to underscore the subtlety of the problem and the difficulty of interpreting the significance of the data.

Even agreeing on a definition of "violence" may be a problem for some people. Police, for instance, seem to think that few domestic disturbances are really violent. They tend to define violence in terms of its effect. Unless blood is drawn and injuries are visible, they are apt to discount the report of violence and call the incident merely a "family spat." To me, any physical attack by one person upon another is a violent act and an instance of illegal aggression, even if no visible injury results. Still, Gelles noted that after the bruises had healed, some of his subjects called even the most severe beatings they received "nonviolent."[51]

However the terms are defined, though, sufficient evidence of serious injury and homicide exists to show that domestic violence is a critical problem. In *The Violent Home*, Gelles determined where and when violence is most likely to occur. The "typical location of family violence was the kitchen. The bedroom and the living room are the next most likely scenes of violence. Some respondents are unable to pinpoint exact locations because their battles begin in one room and progress through the house. The *only* room in the house where there was *no violence* was the bathroom."[52]

Alex D. Pokorny says that murder seldom occurs in public places. The usual site is the home, though the car is the setting in a fair number of cases.[53] Other studies of homicides show that the bedroom is the deadliest room in the house and that the victims there are usually female.[54] The next most likely place for family murders is the kitchen; in those cases the women are more frequently the offenders.[55]

According to Gelles, couples get into violent fights most often after dinner, between 8 and 11:30 p.m. The second most frequent time is during dinner (5 to 8 p.m.), and the third is late evening to early morning.[56] The same timetable applies to those acts of violence that result in death.[57] Also, violence of either variety occurs most frequently on weekends.[58] Kansas City police cite Monday as another day of reckoning.[59]

22

The Children

If the American-family dream is a nightmare for spouses involved in domestic violence, it is even more so for their children. They suffer the consequences of their parents' battles simply because they exist. When violence becomes a pattern in the household it can take many forms. In her desperation, the battered wife may strike out at the children, scapegoating them as she has been scapegoated by a violent husband. And the man who beats his wife may also beat his children. In J. J. Gayford's survey of one hundred battered women in England, 37 percent of the women admitted taking their own frustrations out on the children, and 54 percent claimed their husbands committed acts of violence against the children.[60] The breaking point for many of these women came when the children were made into victims too. At that point many of the women resolved, or tried, to leave.[61]

Children who "merely" witness physical violence between their parents suffer emotional trauma. They react with shock, fear, and guilt. This fact was brought home to me when my eight-year-old grandson witnessed his friend's drunk father hit my daughter, who had rushed to the aid of the man's wife. The incident happened in front of the house. The husband jumped down from the roof to confront my daughter and grandson. Terrified, my grandson ran for the car and locked himself in. While he was in the car, he saw the man give his mother a couple of hard slaps. Later, when my daughter and the child arrived at my house, my grandson flung himself on the couch. He was emotionally devastated. He could only mumble, "It was horrible!" When he was able to talk about it, he blurted out that if his older sister had been there "she would have done something!" He had been scared; he hadn't known what to do and felt guilty about that. Not until we started discussing self-defense tactics did the little boy perk up. He wanted to form a plan of action so that he would know how to react in the future.

In Bard's study of the 30th Precinct in New York City, children were present in 41 percent of the domestic disturbance cases in which police intervened. "If this is typical, one can only speculate on the modeling effects of parental aggression on such children—not to speak of the effects of a variety of police behaviors on the perception of children in such situations," he said.[62] The behavior of police officers is bound to have a strong effect on children. If the police identify with the father and treat the incident lightly, they will be reinforcing the role models of violent male and female victim. But if police efficiently calm down the angry parents and effectively communicate the attitude that violent behavior is not to be excused or tolerated, the children will be receiving healthier signals.

Gelles's research shows that people who as children had observed their parents engaging in physical violence were more likely to engage in the same sort of activity with their own spouses than those who never saw their parents fight.[63] He found, too, that adults who were hit frequently as children were more likely to be violent with their mates than people who had never been hit as children. "Not only does the family expose individuals to violence and techniques of violence," Gelles concludes, "the family teaches approval for the use of violence."[64]

Pizzey agrees with Gelles on this point, basing her opinion on her impressions of violent husbands gleaned from interviews with women who had come to Chiswick Women's Aid. "A man who batters is a child who was battered that nobody helped," Pizzey says. "If we look at the histories of these men, they are either beaten children or actually watched it. . . . so the violence goes from one generation to the next. It becomes the norm."[65]

In an article for *Trans-action* on battered children, Serapio R. Zalba estimated (conservatively, he says) that between 200,000 and 250,000 children in the United States need protective services, and that 30,000 to 37,500 children may be badly hurt by their parents each year.[66] And according to Dr. C. Henry Kempe, who conducted the first national study on battered children for the U.S. Department of Health, Education and Welfare, more than one million children suffer abuse and neglect.[67] These figures are certainly horrifying in themselves, but in the light of Pizzey's and Gelles's conclusions as to the perpetuation of domestic violence, they are nothing short of mind-boggling.

Hidden behind the stereotyped image of the nuclear family, then, we find not only isolated instances of domestic violence, but also the potential for ever-increasing patterns of violence as, in literally millions of homes around the world, the children of battling parents establish their own families. If the building block of American society, the

24

modern nuclear family, is ever more frequently wracked by physical brutality, what hope can we have for society as a whole? Past president of the National Council on Family Relations Murray A. Straus declares, "I don't think we are going to understand violence in American society until we understand violence in the family. . . . The home is where violence primarily occurs."[68]

We must stop protecting our myths and lies, and stop teaching our children to strike out blindly with their fists. If there is battering to be done, let it be directed against that sacred front door to the family home.

3

WIFE-BEATING AND THE MARRIAGE CONTRACT

The Foundations of the Patriarchy

The historical roots of our patriarchal family models are ancient and deep. The task of tearing them up and establishing more equitable human relations is a formidable one. Still, new norms for marriage and family must be created, since the battering of wives grows naturally out of ancient, time-honored traditions.

In the beginning, human beings lived in a state of promiscuity, which by its very nature made all certainty regarding paternity impossible. Lineage in these early days could only be reckoned through the female line. Women, as mothers, were the only discernible parents and received a high degree of consideration and respect. According to Frederick Engels, all primitive societies passed through this initial stage of human relations; it was the precursor to all other stages of social development.[1]

Many anthropologists and historians conclude from their studies of primitive societies that women enjoyed more equality in ancient times than they do in the modern world. "That woman was the slave of man at the commencement of society is one of the most absurd notions that has come down to us from the period of Enlightenment of the eighteenth century," Engels stated.[2] "Women were not only free, but they held a highly respected position in the early stages of civilization and were the great power among the clans," he said.

In her study of three New Guinea peoples in the Pacific,

Margaret Mead described three distinct alternatives to the chiefly male-dominant mode of culture we have subsequently inherited. Men and women in the Arapesh culture, for example, *both* displayed personality traits which, from our present limited definitions, we would call maternal and feminine. Men as well as women were trained to be cooperative, unaggressive, and responsive to the needs of others.[3] Among the Mundgumor, on the other hand, Mead found that both women and men developed ruthless and aggressive personalities. Maternal traits were minimal in both sexes.[4]

Mead also found that in the third group, the Tchambuli, the sex roles displayed were the direct opposite of our own. The Tchambuli woman was the dominant, independent, managing partner; the man was less responsible and more dependent emotionally.[5] The strength and durability of our patriarchal culture rest on a belief in its own inevitability —the notion that men are by nature designed to take care of the business of civilization—but the existence of the Tchambuli proves otherwise.

Engels speculated that the transition from group marriage and the extended family to the pairing marriage—what we call the nuclear family—brought about the overthrow of the "mother right" and the enforcement of monogamy.[6] As a result of the growing density of the population, ever more complex economic conditions, and the prohibitions established against marriage between relatives, the pairing family gradually supplanted group marriage in the West. The accompanying change from polygamy to monogamy had nothing to do with "individual sex love," Engels says, and could only have occurred because women must "have longed for the right to chastity, to temporary or permanent marriage with one man only, as a deliverance" from the growing complexity of human life, even in those ancient times.[7] This trend could not have originated with men, Engels points out, because men have never—even to the present day—dreamed of renouncing the pleasures of polygamy.[8]

To Susan Brownmiller, in *Against Our Will*, "the growing complexity of life" had a more specific meaning: "Female fear of an open season on rape, and not a natural inclination toward monogamy, motherhood, and love, was probably the single causative factor in the original subjugation of woman by man, the most important key to her historic dependence, her domestication by protective mating."[9] If

Brownmiller is right, the female of the species paid a great price for protection. She sacrificed her power and, through monogamous loyalty to her husband, became the exclusive property of her protector. Polygamy and infidelity remained men's privileges, but the strictest fidelity was demanded of the woman in order to guarantee and authenticate the new "father right." Engels called this development in human relations (if it can be called a development) *"the world-historic defeat of the female sex"* (Engels's emphasis).[10]

Monogamy brought about the complete subjugation of one sex by the other, or, as Engels put it, "the proclamation of a conflict between the sexes entirely unknown hitherto in prehistoric times."[11] The practice of bride capture demonstrates the extent of the sexual inequality that resulted. To secure a bride, a man often abducted the woman forcibly and raped her, thereby staking claim to her body. According to Brownmiller, this practice was an acceptable form of mating in England as late as the fifteenth century.[12]

With the advent of the pairing marriage, the man seized the reins in the home and began viewing the people in it as units of property that comprised his wealth—in short, as chattel. The word "family" is derived from the Roman word *familia*, signifying the totality of slaves belonging to an individual.[13] The slave-owner had absolute power of life and death over the human beings who "belonged to him." Wives were bought and sold as if they were livestock. Prospective husbands (the buyers) paid fathers (the breeders) a "bride-price" for their daughters, and ownership was transferred. (This arrangement persists in many societies around the world to this day. In some cases the father pays the groom to take his daughter off his hands. Presumably the payment of the dowry is a necessary precaution, since nothing is more worthless in this system than an unmarried daughter past breeding age.)

Naturally, since marriage was a business agreement, often based on a carefully worked-out contract, the woman had no say either about the marriage itself or about how she was to live in the household of her husband/owner. If a woman showed any signs of having a will or a mind of her own, it seemed only natural that she be beaten as a strong-willed horse might be whipped and finally subdued.

The principle of monogamy had the power to dehumanize women in another way. Wives were inescapably slaves to their husbands' lust. Since there was only one woman per family in the monogamous culture, and since the sole pur-

28

pose of women was to breed children, the wife was kept pregnant as continuously as possible. Out of this tradition grew the horrible phenomenon, still prevalent throughout the world, of women dying, worn out and exhausted at forty, after having borne and cared for too many children.

The ideas of "purity" and "honor" are basic to the monogamous marriage, and so, therefore, is the double standard by which rightful behavior is determined. Spanish-speaking cultures, for example, insist that their women be pure and spotlessly virtuous, and the Catholic Church reinforces this insistence. But the men are under no such restrictions. In India a well-known proverb affirms that "men's honour is preserved through their womenfolk."[14] Among places where girls are married at an early age, often before puberty, the practice is meant to protect their purity —that is, to protect the well-used husband from the possibility of winding up with a second-hand wife. The Japanese, too, still adhere to a double standard by which the husband commutes back and forth between his wife and prostitutes, seeing the former as "holy motherhood" and the latter as a "poisonous flower."[15]

An Overview of Cruelty

Details of the mistreatment of women flow to us from every culture—monogamous and polygamous—and each one is an indication of how deeply entrenched sexual inequality is in human history. For example, women were often restricted to distinct parts of the house and guarded —in Asia by eunuchs and in Greece by hounds that were kept to frighten off would-be adulterers.[16] Athenian women were forbidden to leave the house unless accompanied by a female slave. Arab women, when allowed out, were forced to wear heavy veils and full-length skirts. Islamic religious police caned their legs if their skirts did not fully cover them.[17] In the sixteenth century, Russian women were considered honorable only when they lived at home and never went out. To be seen by strangers was shameful. Women were seldom permitted to go to church, and were rarely allowed to see friends except when they were elderly and less likely to attract suspicion.[18]

In India as well as Arab countries, it was and still is the custom for men to eat separately—and first. In times of famine, which are not uncommon in India, this practice means that many female children and women suffer from malnutrition and starvation.[19]

In Europe during the Middle Ages, squires and noblemen beat their wives as regularly as they beat their serfs.[20] The peasants faithfully followed their lords' examples. The church sanctioned the subjection of women to their husbands "in everything."[21] Priests advised abused wives to win their husbands' goodwill through increased devotion and obedience. A husband's displeasure was best dispelled by the woman's meek submissiveness. The habit of looking upon women as a species apart, without the same feelings and capacity for suffering that men have, became inbred during the Middle Ages. Many men today still feel that women can stand more pain and more humiliation than men. Such nonsense was reinforced in our time by Freud's theory that women are innately masochistic.

In her book *The First Sex*, Elizabeth Gould Davis recounts the many pretexts under which women were burned alive in medieval times: "for threatening their husbands, for talking back to or refusing a priest, for stealing, for prostitution, for adultery, for bearing a child out of wedlock, for permitting sodomy, even though the priest or husband who committed it was forgiven, for masturbating, for Lesbianism, for child neglect, for scolding and nagging, and even for *miscarrying*, even though the miscarriage was caused by a kick or a blow from the husband."[22] Thus, physical cruelty, and even murder, which has been institutionalized, can become a matter of habit. By incorporating their inhumane attitude into the dominant culture, men could avoid taking responsibility for their own behavior.

During medieval times, the law of the land was really the law of the church, and the civil courts were puppets of the ecclesiastical hierarchy. Judeo-Christian doctrine, which espoused the inferiority of women and the supremacy of men, gave its stamp of approval to domestic violence. For example, the Old Testament describes a "trial of jealousy" which a woman was forced to undergo if her husband became jealous but had no proof of her infidelity. The man would bring his wife to a priest with an offering of barley meal, called the "offering of jealousy." The priest would then take holy water from an earthen vessel, add some dust from the floor of the tabernacle, and place the offering in the woman's hands. If she had lain with a man other than her husband and had so defiled herself, she would be cursed by the bitter water: the water would go into her bowels, make her belly swell, and cause her thigh to rot. If the curse came to pass, the woman would be shunned by her people. If, however, she had not been defiled, she would be free and would "conceive seed." Thus whether from the curse or from pregnancy her belly would swell![23] All such cruel treatment was administered in the name of instructive discipline. In a medieval theological manual, now in the British Museum, a man is given permission to "castigate his wife and beat her for correction. . . ."[24]

Once in a while, a glimmer of relative sanity appeared; certain priests were moved to take pity and to protest on behalf of the wife/victims. Bernard of Siena in 1427 suggested to his male parishioners that they exercise a little restraint and treat their wives with as much mercy as they would their hens and pigs.[25] And, in the sixteenth century, the Abbé de Brantôme, though reluctant to argue against church dogma, nonetheless felt compelled to raise the question, "But however great the authority of the husband may be, what *sense* is there for him to be allowed to kill his wife?"[26] We can presume that the question was asked in all seriousness; it is thus a good measure of the extent to which inhumanity prevailed over reason.

In Russia during the reign of Ivan the Terrible in the sixteenth century, the state church sanctified the oppression of women by issuing a Household Ordinance that spelled out when and how a man might most effectively beat his wife.[27] A man was even allowed to kill a wife or a serf if he did so for disciplinary purposes. There being no restraints, such punishment meted out by Russian husbands often exceeded the bounds of reason. Dr. Samuel Collins, an Englishman who acted as physician to Tsar Alexei from 1660 to 1669, wrote about a merchant who beat his wife until he was exhausted, using a whip about two inches thick. Afterwards he forced the woman to put on a smock that had been dipped in brandy, which he then set on fire. She perished in the flames, and the man simply went on about his business scot free.[28]

Nearly half a century later, many Russian women rose up in desperation against such treatment. They fought back. They went on a rampage, murdering their husbands in revenge for all the injustices they had been forced to endure. Although there was no law against wife-killing, a law did exist to prohibit husband-killing. As punishment, the women were buried alive, standing upright with only their heads left above the earth. A guard was set to watch over them until they died. According to John Perry, an English engineer who lived and worked in Russia, it was "a common sight . . . and I have known them to live sometimes seven or eight days in this posture."[29]

The conditions of life for Russian women continued to be unremittingly harsh; not until the reign of Peter the Great in the late seventeenth century were some reforms instituted. Peter tried to bring women out of segregation by ordering that they be invited to public gatherings and entertained in the same room as men. He also introduced the idea of marriage by free choice instead of by the parents' arrangement. He issued an order that no young couple should be married without their individual consent, and that they must be allowed to visit and see each other at least six weeks before the marriage. He also gave married women the right to full ownership and control of their own property. Unfortunately, these reforms did not reach most people at all, and actually affected only the upper classes of St. Petersburg. Even so, the nature of the reforms made them notable developments.[30]

The Trend Toward Legal Reform

In America, early settlers held European attitudes towards women. Our law, based upon the old English common-law doctrines, explicitly permitted wife-beating for correctional purposes. However, certain restrictions did exist, and the general trend in the young states was toward declaring wife-beating illegal. For instance, the common-law doctrine had been modified to allow the husband "the right to whip his wife, provided that he used a switch no bigger than his thumb"—a rule of thumb, so to speak.[31] An 1824 decision in Mississippi allowed the husband to administer only "moderate chastisement in cases of emergency . . . ,"[32] but by 1894 even that right was overruled in Mississippi.[33]

In 1867, a North Carolina court acquitted a man who had given his wife three licks with a switch about the size of one of his fingers, but "smaller than his thumb." The reviewing appellate court upheld the acquittal on the ground that a court should "not interfere with family government in trifling cases."[34] But the "finger-switch" rule was disavowed in 1874, when the Supreme Court of North Carolina stated that "the husband has no right to chastise his wife under any circumstances."[35] This news sounded too good to be true, and so it was. The court went on to say, "If no permanent injury has been inflicted, nor malice, cruelty nor dangerous violence shown by the husband, it is better to draw the curtain, shut out the public gaze, and leave the parties to forget and forgive."[36] As a result of this ruling, a lower court in North Carolina twelve years later declared that a criminal indictment could not be brought against a husband unless the battery was so great as to result in permanent injury, endanger life and limb, or be malicious beyond all reasonable bounds. Short of these extremes the courts would not interfere.[37]

By 1890, the North Carolina Supreme Court ostensibly eliminated these last remaining restrictions on a husband's liability and prohibited a husband from committing even a slight assault upon his wife.[38] Evidently this prohibition still applies in North Carolina, though whether or not it is strictly enforced is another story.[39] A discouraging example is a 1972 North Carolina case where the defendant had shot at his wife with a gun and missed, in which an aggravated assault charge was lowered from a felony to a misdemeanor. Despite the fact that he had tried to murder his wife, the husband got off with a "simple" assault charge.[40] Although an old town ordinance is *still* on the books in Pennsylvania decreeing that no husband shall beat his wife after ten o'clock at night or on Sundays,[41] other state jurisdictions appear to have followed North Carolina's lead in outlawing wife-beating outright.

Legal reform was being instituted in England in the 1880s as well. There the law was changed to allow a wife who had been habitually beaten by her husband to the point of "endangering her life" to separate from him, though not to divorce him. Also, a law was passed in 1885 prohibiting a British husband from selling his wife or daughter into prostitution—but only if she was under sixteen years old. In 1891, special legislation was passed preventing a husband from keeping his wife under lock and key.[42] Since then the trend in England has been toward making wife-beating a crime. But though English and American courts rule that a man has no right to beat his wife, the application of the law is another matter.

In the United States in 1975, most states do permit wives to bring criminal action against a husband who inflicts injury upon her. But, as will be demonstrated in Chapter 6, the actual filing of these charges and bringing a case to trial is usually so difficult that the provisions may as well

33

not exist. In some states, in order that charges may be brought against a husband, the injury to the wife must be demonstrably more serious than injury inflicted in an ordinary case of assault and battery (that is, in a case not involving husband and wife). This shameless injustice smacks of the same kind of hypocrisy expressed in the century-old North Carolina decision that giveth with one hand and taketh away with the other: "The husband has no right to chastise his wife under any circumstances. However . . ."

Legal reforms in other parts of the world came much more slowly than in England and America. In France, for instance, the Napoleonic Code had embraced such quaint and feudal concepts as, "Women, like walnut trees, should be beaten every day."[43] But in 1924, a French court ruled that a husband did not have the right to beat his wife.[44] Several countries made wife-beating illegal in the early 1970s—among them Scotland and Iran.[45] In late 1975 a new penal code was proposed in Brazil to prohibit husbands from selling, renting, or gambling their wives away.[46] And, in May 1975, Queen Sibongile Winnifred of the Zulus was granted interim custody of her two children after alleging in affidavits to the Durban Supreme Court that her husband, the Zulu king, had whipped her while she was pregnant.[47] This ruling was surprisingly liberal for South Africa.

Sweeping reforms have been made in Italy in recent years. In the late 1960s, the killing of a wife, sister, or mother by a man upholding his "male honor" was made a serious offense in that country.[48] In 1974, an Italian court sentenced a man to two years in jail for raping his wife at gunpoint.[49] And in 1975, after seven long years of debate, a new family law went into effect in Italy. It touches on many aspects of Italian family life, and explicitly does away with the ancient Roman concept of *patris potestas,* which vested sole authority in the father. Included in the new legislation is the abolition of wife-beating, previously allowed by law as part of the husband's "correctional power" over his wife.[50]

With changes in the law regarding wife-beating gradually came other legal reforms changing the status of women. As early as 1845 Sweden passed an Inheritance Law giving women and men equal inheritance rights. But it was not until 1921, two years after Swedish women obtained the right to vote, that new marriage legislation gave wives legal independence and equal rights as parents. Laws were enacted in 1939 that prohibited dismissal of employees on account of engagement or marriage, and in 1946, the prohibition was extended to include pregnancy and childbirth. By 1960, 48 women were in the Swedish parliament, 34 having been elected to the Lower and 14 to the Upper Chamber.[51]

In 1945, French women won the right to vote and to be awarded equal pay for equal work. In 1966, the French wife also became entitled to take a job, spend or invest her earnings, and open a bank account without obtaining her husband's permission. The French National Assembly voted in 1970 to give mothers as much say as fathers in the upbringing of their children.[52]

After coming to power in 1917, the Bolsheviks accorded full political and legal rights to women and assured them access to all economic and cultural spheres of Russian society. Based on Engels's theory that equality for women was impossible "so long as the woman is shut out from social production labor and restricted to private domestic labor," the Soviet Union attempted to break down the family as a traditional economic enterprise. The petty housekeeping functions of the family were replaced by such progressive institutions of social welfare as crèches, social dining rooms, and social laundries. At the same time enlightened legislation dealt with the abolition of illegitimacy, the establishment of mother and child welfare centers, the creation of day nurseries, the liberalization of abortion laws, and the simplification of marriage and divorce procedures.

But these drastic reforms were short-lived in Russia. In 1936 the concept of marriage as a contract between two free and equal individuals was challenged and reversed. Divorce became more difficult and expensive, and abortions were once again illegal. By 1943 coeducation was abolished in the schools and replaced by separate education for boys and girls to prepare them for their different roles in marriage. In 1944, increased state aid was given to mothers and a tax was levied on single citizens or those with small families. In 1968 divorce was simplified for childless couples who agreed on the divorce. This complete turnabout of Russian policy revived the paternalistic concept of marriage and family. Beginning in the 30s and continuing to the present, the Communist Party has conducted a vigorous campaign to remind wives of their household responsibilities and to promote those definite masculine and

35

feminine characteristics expected in the father and the mother "as heads of the family with equal rights."[53]

In a paper on "How the Revolution Failed Women," Dale Ross Rubenstein blames the privileged bureaucracy that gained control of the Communist Party. Rubenstein says that the corruption of the bureaucracy in its attempt to retain power and its desire to discipline youth by the use of authority and power served as a "compelling motive for the restoration and support of the traditional family."[54] But the underlying fact really was that when there is a need for women in the work force, as there was right after the Russian Revolution, "then propaganda stressed the independence of women as workers, but when a population growth was needed women were shunted back to the home with clichés about the beauties of motherhood and the socialist principles of equality were forgotten."[55]

Rubenstein's point is reminiscent of what happened in the United States during and after World War II. "Rosie the Riveter" was a heroine during the war and a drag on the economy afterward when she was seen as a competitor for the traditionally masculine jobs. The propaganda of popular women's magazines exalting motherhood and housewifery eventually drove her back home. In the early 1960s President John Kennedy appointed a National Commission on the Status of Women headed by Eleanor Roosevelt. And in 1964 and 1965 Congress passed laws barring discrimination against women in employment and requiring equal pay for equal work. But for the most part the traditional marriage contract remains legally intact in America.

The Nature of the Marriage Contract

Though the tendency in the last century has been toward legal reform, wife-beating is still rampant in the United States and around the world. Though no longer legally condoned in this country, it is still all but ignored as a social problem. As is often true of legal reform, new laws may be on the books but the acts they prohibit are still committed with the force of habit behind them.

Often other factors influence the total situation even after the legal status of an act has been changed. In the case of wife-beating, the nature of the marriage contract has a tremendous effect on behavior. This contract has not changed appreciably in centuries; it reflects, perhaps more sharply than our laws, the male-dominant bias of our culture. To really comprehend the direct influence our culture and history have on our daily lives, we must look briefly at wife-beating in relation to the structure of the marriage contract. This perspective will be useful later in helping to explain the reluctance of the police and judicial system to interfere in marital disputes.

"The marriage contract is unlike most contracts," writes Lenore Weitzman in an article on the legal regulation of marriage. "Its provisions are unwritten, its penalties are unspecified, and the terms of the contract are typically unknown to the 'contracting' parties. Prospective spouses are neither informed of the terms of the contract nor are they allowed any options about these terms. In fact, one wonders how many men and women would agree to the marriage contract if they were given the opportunity to read it and to consider the rights and obligations to which they were committing themselves."[56]

Weitzman makes the point that the marriage contract and the restrictions it imposes on individual rights have been justified by the state's overriding interest in maintaining the traditional family structure. In other words, marriage is the mechanism by which the patriarchy is maintained. The definition of marriage in the early common law of England bears out this conclusion: "By marriage, the husband and wife are one person in law. . . . The very being or legal existence of the woman is suspended during the marriage, or at least is incorporated and consolidated into that of the husband, under whose wing, protection, and cover she performs everything."[57] It was under such provisions that husbands were given the legal right to beat their wives.

During the nineteenth century, various states adopted "Married Women's Property Acts." These acts were designed to correct some of the obvious injustices that existed with regard to married women's property rights. They allowed married women to retain control of property they may have possessed before marriage—instead of relinquishing ownership to the husband—and to seek employment and retain their earnings.[58] But present statutory and case law continue to uphold the old tradition. The husband is still head of the household and responsible for the support of the family; the wife is still responsible for housework and childcare.[59]

The married woman's loss of identity begins with the loss

37

of her name. She takes her husband's domicile; she becomes his legal dependent. In most states he has sole financial authority within the marriage. Although the law says the husband must support his wife, if he decides to give her no money or clothing, and provide her only with groceries for the table, she has no legal recourse. In a 1953 case in which a wife made such a complaint, the Nebraska court ruled: "The living standards of a family are a matter of concern to the household, and not for the courts to determine. . . . As long as the home is maintained and the parties are living as husband and wife, it may be said the husband is legally supporting his wife and the purpose of the marriage relation is being carried out."[60] For this kind of minimal support, which depends upon the husband's generosity or whim, the wife is obligated, according to a 1962 court decision in Connecticut, "to be his helpmeet, to love and care for him in such a role, to afford him her society and her person, to protect and care for him in sickness, and to labor faithfully to advance his interests." She must also perform "her household and domestic duties . . . without compensation therefore. A husband is entitled to benefit of his wife's industry and economy."[61]

Certain critical assumptions are built into the marriage contract, according to Weitzman, to which both parties subscribe whether they know it or not. These assumptions are that marriage represents a lifetime commitment, that monogamy should be enforced, that procreation is an essential element in the marriage relationship, and that a strict division of labor should exist within a family.[62] The exclusiveness and permanence of marriage mean that the wife is "permanently available" to the husband as a sex partner and is to be punished if she is unfaithful.

The terms of the marriage contract are changing, albeit very slowly. The most visible changes have occurred with respect to divorce. Until recently, divorces were granted only when the wife had committed adultery. Now it is possible for a woman to divorce her husband because of *his* adulterous acts. Moreover, in most states the wife can obtain a divorce on the grounds of mental or physical cruelty (see Chapter 8). And in 1969, California adopted a no-fault divorce law—by which either partner can request and obtain a divorce without the fear of being contested by the other—and other states have since followed this example.[63] Still, no comparable moves have been made to allow individuals to decide for themselves how to structure their marriages.

The state's expectations of any given marriage may differ very markedly from those of the couple involved, just as the wife's expectations may differ from those of the husband. Sociologist Hernán San Martín demonstrated this point very well in a study conducted in Chile between 1968 and 1970 on the reasons women and men give for wanting to get married. Most often a woman said that she wanted to get away from her parents' home and be free. Only five percent of the women surveyed said they wished to marry because they wanted children. Also low on the lists of womens' reasons were "to have and run her own home" and "because she needed support." Fairly evenly divided among the women were these additional reasons for desiring to marry: she was lonely; she feared becoming an old maid; her parents pressured her; she thought she was in love; and she really was in love. In contrast, the reason most often cited by men was "to affirm their masculinity." The next most frequent was the desire to father children. Love rated last. Other reasons men gave included: for domestic companionship; for the economic advantages and social prestige that marriage offered; and because of sexual attraction.[64]

Clearly, San Martín's results imply that even in a Catholic Latin culture, where one might expect strong adherence to traditional male-female roles, "two separate marriages" exist—his and hers.[65] Contrary to popular belief and to the assumptions inherent in the marriage contract, the women's prime reasons for marrying had nothing to do with an innate desire for motherhood, for running a home, or for being supported. The women's chief motives stemmed from what they saw as the consequences of not marrying and from their desire to be free from parental control. The men's answers were more in keeping with the interests of the state: that marriage should incorporate fatherhood and provide the man with a "companion" to do the housework, take care of his sexual needs, and look after the children.

The Economics of Marriage

For centuries men have railed against marriage as a trap set for them by women scheming to gain protection and security, but in reality the system seems to work in the opposite way. "Girls are reared to accept themselves as naturally dependent, entitled to lean on the greater strength of men; and they enter marriage fully confident that these expectations will be fulfilled. They are therefore shaken when they come to realize that their husbands are not really so strong, so protective, so superior," states Jessie Bernard in *The Future of Marriage.* "Like everyone else, they have been fooled by the stereotypes and by the structural imperatives."[66] Many women make a full-time career of protecting the self-image of their husbands. Most wives also provide their husbands with the security of a well-ordered home and a retreat from the cares of the outside world.

Bernard goes on to say of marriage, "Men have cursed it, aimed barbed witticisms at it, denigrated it, bemoaned it —and never ceased to want and need it or to profit from it."[67] The key word here is "profit." Research shows that marriage has positive effects on a man's mental health, his career and earning power, his longevity, his happiness, and his comfort. For example, the suicide rate for single men is almost twice as high as that for married men.[68] And once men have been married, research shows that they can't live without it: Most divorced and widowed men remarry;[69] widowers who don't often suffer psychological difficulties and have a high mortality rate.[70] Married men live longer than unmarried men.[71] And married men, compared with bachelors, are less likely to become criminals.[72]

Women do not fare as well. The bride who was catered to before marriage becomes the caterer after marriage. She is required to redefine her role, and often she must actively reshape her personality to conform to her husband's expectations. The husband's role proves to be the key to the marriage, and the wife finds she must accommodate, adapt, and adjust to keep the marriage intact. Research shows that, as a result of these pressures on the woman, wives express unhappiness, seek marriage counseling, and initiate divorce proceedings more often than husbands do.[73] More married women suffer poor mental and emotional health than single women do.[74] Married women commit more crimes than unmarried women do.[75] And, while women generally live longer than men, there is less difference in death rates between married and unmarried women than between married and unmarried men.[76]

Marriage takes its toll on women primarily through what Bernard calls the "housewife syndrome." She claims that, in terms of the numbers of people involved, housewife syndrome is the nation's number one public health problem.[77] The role of "housewife" is not a congenial one. Not all women have an interest in or an aptitude for the job. Housework is menial, degrading, isolating, no-future work. It offers no chance of promotion, no raise in pay, no opportunities to learn new skills—it is, in fact, never done.

"Obviously, woman's work is esteemed to be of no value at all to society other than that of her room and board; which is really just saying it's worth only enough to keep her alive and well so she can continue to do it," writes Lisa Leghorn in her article on women's work. "In this society, the common standard for recognition of work done is a wage; and for the worth of a product, its price. The more money one earns, the more highly regarded is that labor and that person; the higher the cost of a product, the more valuable it is considered."[78]

The wages earned by the husband are tangible, and they belong to *him*. The services the wife may provide are "natural" and expected. Whatever money the husband decides to give her is not hers but *his*. She merely acts as the buyer for the household; she is expected to watch for bargains and get the most she can for the money budgeted to her.

"The only mothers who do earn a standard wage for the labor of child-rearing are those on welfare," Jane Alpert points out, "and that pay is barely enough to sustain life. The job is without guarantees or security of any kind. Its work day is 24 hours, work week 7 days, no vacations and no holidays. Total dedication to the job is expected, and yet a woman who works 'only' in the house is regarded, with some contempt, as an unemployed housewife."[79]

If, however, a woman decides to go outside the home to look for a job—for money, self-esteem, self-expression, or just for something to do—she often finds herself having to fight against social pressures designed to push her back home. It is no accident that the old adage "a woman's place is in the home" is familiar to everyone. In a patriarchal society, a woman's place *is* in the home, and there are some very powerful economic reasons for this.

Capitalism benefits from the patriarchal family model. In one sense, if society succeeds in pressuring women to remain home, the labor market is cut in half, and competition for jobs, money, and power is thereby cut in half. Capitalism thrives on competition, but when too many qualified competitors go after the same goal, the system begins to get clogged up. Therefore, by barring certain groups from the running in the first place—the groups we call "oppressed," "disadvantaged," "perennially unemployed"—the people in power remain in power; when they die, their power devolves to their sons. Thus many married women who go to work simply have no hope of becoming authentic competing members of the work force, even if they work for decades. These women are often regarded as "temporary workers," and therefore dispensable. Not only are they kept out of the running for advancement, but they receive the minimum wage, for being non-specialized workers and therefore replaceable.

In the professions and job categories traditionally considered to be women's (usually the service professions, from domestic work through social work and nursing), fierce competition does exist. But the competition is on a lower scale than within the more powerful "male" professions and the stakes, in terms of wages and opportunities for promotions, are lower. Since men do not invade the female professions in significant numbers, even in times of severe unemployment, the stakes remain low. According to the Women's Bureau of the United States Department of Labor, the median income in 1973 for men working the year round was $11,186; for women it was $6,335, or about 57 percent of the men's median earnings.[80] Around the world, the trend is shown to be the same. Despite the United Nations' Declaration on Women's Rights, the pacts of the European Community and the Common Market, and the equal-pay-for-equal-work laws enacted in some countries, the gap between men's and women's wages is *increasing*.[81]

Federal laws do exist against job discrimination in the United States. These laws prohibit "women's work" classifications and sex-specific employment advertising. But violations of these laws are rampant, and complaints of discrimination become seriously backlogged. Five years can pass before a complaint is investigated.[82] There is no doubt, then, that many women who wish to work but don't become discouraged by the de facto discrimination they encounter, and allow themselves to be supported by their husbands in accordance with the traditional model of marriage. But what about women who *must* work to support their families?

There are more than 36 million working women in the United States, and among all families about 1 out of 8 is headed by a woman. Public childcare facilities are extremely limited relative to the need that exists. In 1974 there were 6.1 million children under 6 whose mothers worked, but the number of licensed day-care slots is estimated at only 1 million.[83] These are for the most part unavailable except to those who are classified as "poor." Need is based upon gross income, not take-home pay. A woman who has to hire private childcare help because she does not qualify as poor may find herself barely scraping by *because* she pays for the childcare. She may literally *have* to quit her job in order to qualify for childcare—in which case she will no longer need it! And, with regard to her other possible source of income, although the court may have ordered a woman's ex-husband to pay alimony and/or child support, forcing him to pay if he falls delinquent costs money in lawyers' fees and court costs.

Because of low wages, the unavailability or the high costs of childcare, and the difficulty in enforcing child support, a high percentage of head-of-family mothers in the United States go on welfare. They often find that welfare payments (which are tax free) exceed the amount they would take home after deductions and childcare costs in a regular job. But while welfare may be more profitable economically, the mother who depends upon it will find herself up against still another patriarchal authority. The woman on welfare has no real privacy. The welfare system demands that she report the most intimate details of her life in order that she may continue to qualify. In essence, she must remain celibate and divide all of her energies between caring for her children and reporting to the welfare office. In some ways, the welfare system attacks the self-esteem and self-respect of women recipients more directly than the traditional marriage model does.

The roles of "wife" and "husband," then, did not grow out of biological realities, but developed with the patriarchal nuclear family. The concepts of masculinity and femininity, which define these roles, create very powerful expectations as to how women and men "should" behave, and these expectations in turn reinforce the values upon which our culture is based. Men are seen as dominant (and thus strong, active, rational, authoritarian, aggressive, and stable), and women as dependent (and thus submissive, passive, and nonrational). But these role definitions are not natural to either sex. In modern society, particularly in areas where the traditional modes of life are changing, both men and women are having difficulty living up to these artificially determined roles. They blame and resent each other for expecting the traditional roles to be fulfilled. In this light, it is not difficult to see how serious conflict between social expectation and personal preference might tear a marriage apart. If that conflict expresses itself violently, as it very well may, the woman as the physically weaker partner is most apt to bear the physical brunt of the ordeal.

4

THE BATTERER— WHAT MAKES HIM A BRUTE?

Who Is the Batterer?

What kind of man beats up his wife? What are the underlying psychological and social causes of wife-beating, and what triggers this behavior? Are men naturally violent creatures? Or is aggressive behavior learned? These are key questions, but we can only really speculate as to the answers. Few wife-beaters admit to their own cruel and violent behavior, let alone discuss the reasoning behind it. They rarely see the problem *as* a problem and seek help for it. Therefore, few people outside the immediate family know when a man is a wife-beater. The police may know, but to them he is just a DD—a statistic and a nuisance. To unsuspecting friends he is probably a nice guy. But to his wife he is a dangerous, explosive man who can fly into a rage without warning.

Much of what is known about wife-batterers has been learned from their victims. A random sample of descriptions from battered women shows that the wife-beater can come from any walk of life. One wife described her husband as "a cultured man [who] had graduated, started his own business, and was rapidly becoming a successful businessman." But then he started coming home late, began stopping off for drinks on the way, became possessive and extremely abusive.[1] Another woman said her husband had the "male violence in him. He was *right*. He was *indisputable*."[2] A farm woman described her spouse as "a son-of-a-bitch. . . . He was one of those people, butter wouldn't melt in his mouth, and underneath he was as dirty and rotten as

45

they come . . . would work pretty hard for a week or so and then he'd go off on a drunk for a couple of weeks. . . . Worked hard when he worked, drunk as a pig when he drank."[3] A divorced woman described her battering ex-husband to me as "handsome, charming. . . . Everybody likes him." Another said that her husband was "a general practitioner and while at medical school was an amateur boxer, so he had plenty of brawn as well as brain, plus enough money to keep him well-supplied with as much whiskey as he wanted."[4]

One example, reported in the press, took a more ironic turn. Eisaku Sato, former prime minister of Japan, was awarded the Nobel Peace Prize in 1974.[5] Apparently the committee did not consider wife-beating a breach of the peace. Prior to his nomination for the award, Sato's wife had accused him publicly of beating her. In the tradition of the Japanese authoritarian and patriarchal culture, Sato's popularity skyrocketed after his wife revealed, "Yes, he's a good husband, he only beats me once a week."[6]

Battering husbands are described by their wives as angry, resentful, suspicious, moody, and tense. Though they may be terrifying, they often have about them an aura of helplessness, fear, inadequacy, and insecurity. The battering husband is likely to be a "loser" in some basic way. He is probably angry with himself and frustrated by his life. He may put up a good front in public, but in the privacy and intimacy of his home he may not be able to hide, either from himself or his wife, his feelings of inadequacy and low self-esteem. The man who is losing his grip on his job or his prospects may feel compelled to prove that he is at least the master of his home. Beating his wife is one way for him to appear a winner.

These general impressions have been gleaned from conversations with battered women. In the professional social-science literature, little concrete data on the batterer is to be found. Case histories exist on the wife/victims, but not on the husbands. Only when wife-beaters are charged with assault and battery and actually prosecuted in court—and this happens very rarely, as we shall see in Chapter 6—do batterers come under any sort of official scrutiny. Even then we learn little about these men except that they do indeed perform violent acts.

During the years 1957 through 1962, thirty-seven men charged by their wives with assault and battery were referred by the court and the police to the Framingham Court

Clinic in Massachusetts for psychiatric evaluation and possible treatment. Three doctors at the clinic—John E. Snell, Richard J. Rosenwald, and Ames Robey—routinely interviewed these men and their wives. The men, they soon learned, resisted the interviews and tended to deny that any problems warranting outside help existed in their marriages. The women, on the other hand, were much more willing to talk about their marriages and to seek counseling. The three doctors decided to take the easy way out. Though they had been charged with the responsibility of finding out more about wife-batterers, they ended up writing a paper on "The Wifebeater's Wife," which was published in the *Archives of General Psychiatry*. Needless to say, this paper did not contribute substantially to our understanding of wifebeaters.

In the one case history presented in that article, the husband was a shy-appearing man who for twenty-two years had worked with the railroad. Both he and his wife admitted to having recurring fights throughout their marriage, mostly when he was drunk. When not drinking the husband was apparently aloof and passive. He was very close to his elderly mother, who had lived with the couple during most of their married life. The husband complained bitterly about his wife's "coldness," but admitted that he rarely made sexual overtures (his wife called them "demands") except after drinking. The doctors concluded that this wife-beating husband was passive, indecisive, and sexually inadequate. Periods of violent behavior by the husband served to release him momentarily from his anxiety about his effectiveness as a man.[7]

In his article "The Wife Assaulter," Leroy Schultz describes a group of men who tried to kill their wives. Schultz concluded from his experience with these men that the batterer transfers his dependency needs from his mother to his wife. "The conflict is one between hostility toward the wife and dependency on her. The first was held in rigid control as long as the second was satisfactorily met." This childish dependency would account for aggressive outbursts when the husband no longer receives his wife's full attention, when some of it is diverted from him to a newborn baby, when the wife expresses interest in another man, or when she announces that she wants a divorce. "Such a threat of both physical and psychic withdrawal of love" is intolerable to the husband, Schultz contends, and his rigid hostility-control system breaks down.[8]

Like Snell and his colleagues, Richard Gelles had difficulty finding husbands who would consent to being interviewed. Of the eighty subjects in his study *The Violent Home*, sixty-six were wives while only fourteen were husbands. Gelles tried varying the times and the days of the interviews; even so, few husbands were available. At one point, in order to increase husband participation, he tried to conduct joint interviews involving both partners in a violent marriage. This plan was soon dropped, however, since altercations began to develop during the interviews.[9] Perhaps Gelles should have persisted—at least he could have collected first-hand data instead of having to rely on the subjects' recall. As it was, Gelles extracted a great deal of sound information about family violence in general, but he did not add much to our knowledge of the wife-batterer himself. Gelles's study concentrated on family interaction and social structure rather than on the personality variables that can be isolated in the wife-beater.

Another investigator, Tracy Johnston, tried contacting some of the violent husbands she had heard about, but to no avail. Most of the men were too embarrassed to talk to her about their violent behavior at any length. Deciding that she couldn't write about wife-beating without knowing something about the men who commit it, she ran an ad in the classified section of a San Francisco newspaper asking that men who had been repeatedly involved in marital violence provide information for a research project. She received one reply—from "Adam," who consented to an interview.[10]

Johnston describes Adam as a short, soft-spoken, delicate-looking man of thirty-one. He was a self-styled "genius" who made much of his IQ of 200. Although he came from a pleasant, happy family, Adam had developed an acid tongue at an early age to compensate for his size. Johnston saw in him a "combination of arrogance and helplessness."

Adam and his wife "Julia" met in college and married after a short courtship. From the beginning they had an unusual relationship. Adam saw himself as the genius in charge of the "long-range plans." Being a woman, Julia was to do the "immediate work" of earning the living, keeping house, and paying the bills. That Julia agreed to this arrangement says something about Adam's abilities. However, she failed to uphold her end of the bargain. Although she did support them during most of their marriage, she did not keep the house clean and she never managed to balance the budget. So Adam hit her. "I wanted her to take seriously the things I expected to be taken seriously," he explained. Adam also hit Julia when she said "something stupid." When he tried to control Julia's smoking and she defied him, he hit her because he was trying "to help her discipline herself." Her defiance put him into fits of rage and frustration.

Adam said he did not regret giving Julia one slap in a non-emotional way, but he did feel guilty about flying off in a rage. "I wanted to be more in control," he said. "One thing though, in all four years of our marriage, I never really damaged her." But Adam did admit that he caused Julia pain; often she had to rearrange her hair or tie a scarf around her forehead to cover the bruises. Toward the end, Julia started fighting back; she broke dishes, hit Adam with a poker, and threw things at him. They both threatened each other—with "murder, stuff like that." At one point Adam did try to stop beating Julia. But she had developed an acid tongue like his and knew how to get to him. When things were at their worst Adam hit Julia "maybe once a day." Finally Julia disappeared; she just walked out on him one day without a word. Adam has not seen her since. But even after five years, he does not altogether discount the possibility of their getting back together.

Adam is not at all the chest-beating bully we might expect him to be. His behavior is not beyond his control; he has reasons, however self-deluding, for his violence. Obviously, in talking to Johnston, Adam took the opportunity to justify his position one more time. Clearly he did not see the beatings he gave Julia as reason enough for her leaving him. Were we to collect more data of this kind, we would undoubtedly begin to see patterns in the rationalizations that wife-beaters offer for their violent behavior.

Erin Pizzey says that wife-beaters are alcoholics, psychotics, or plain and simple bullies. Most doctors, she says, will usually suggest that the husband who beats his wife has a "personality disorder," but few would use the term "psychopath." "No one likes the word 'psychopath'; everyone is afraid of it," Pizzey claims, "but this is exactly what he is—aggressive, dangerous, plausible, and deeply immature."[11] But Gelles disagrees on this point. He contends that an "irrational attack" within the home is the rare exception. Generally, he says, violence is a response to the stress of one's personal life, or to threat against one's identity.[12] Presumably because violent attacks can be explained by such variables they cannot, according to Gelles, be interpreted as "irrational."

What Triggers the Batterer?

In my own conversations with battered women, I have discovered that however a batterer may rationalize his actions to himself, those actions never seem warranted by the actual triggering event. For example, one woman told me she was beaten unmercifully for breaking the egg yolk while cooking her husband's breakfast. Another said her husband blew up because at their child's birthday party she instructed the youngster to give the first piece of cake to a guest, not to him. Another wife was battered because her *husband's* driver's license was suspended. Other women reported these reasons: she prepared a casserole instead of fresh meat for dinner; she wore her hair in a pony tail; she mentioned that she didn't like the pattern on the wallpaper. These incidents seem trivial in the extreme; in no way do they warrant a violent response. To my way of thinking, these are irrational attacks, even if they can be attributed, as Gelles argues, to the husband's stress and frustration.

Some women report that they just don't know what triggers their husbands' violent outbursts. Husbands have been known to come home and just start flailing away. Several women told me that their husbands started beating them as they lay asleep in bed. Ray Fowler, executive director of the American Association of Marriage and Family Counselors, describes the wife-abuser as "generally an obsessional person who has learned how to trigger himself emotionally." A man may interpret a reasonable comment by his wife as a nagging remark or a whining complaint. "Why is she treating me like this?" he might say to himself. "I deserve better than this." The man might allow this sort of inner conversation to escalate until it triggers his hostility. At the same time the interior monologue provides him with a justification for his violent acts.[13]

Battered wives report that when the husband erupts in a volcanic rage he generally uses his fists, not his open hand. And the practiced batterer knows how to aim his blows at the places that don't show, the women say. He goes for the breasts, the stomach (even during pregnancy), the base of the spine, and parts of the head where bumps and bruises will be covered by hair. Gelles says that slapping, scratching, or grabbing are most common when both parties actively participate in a fight, but that husbands predominate when it comes to pushing (down stairs, for instance), choking, shoving, punching, kicking—even throwing things.[14]

Threats of violence can be as frightening as an actual physical attack. Many husbands punch holes in the wall, break down doors, and fire guns to demonstrate their potential destructiveness. Gelles noted that "violent threats are typically used by the husband to intimidate or coerce deference from the wife," but he found no instances of a wife threatening a husband with violence.[15] But both Gelles and M. Komarovsky,[16] another investigator, found that wives threatened their husbands with other possibilities: that they would withhold sexual favors, call the police, or leave and take the children.

Verbal Arguments

In J. J. Gayford's study of British battered wives, 77 percent of the women surveyed reported that physical assaults were usually *not* preceded by verbal arguments.[17] Nevertheless, most professionals believe that physical battles grow out of arguments. Some theorists go to great lengths in support of this contention. In fights between intimates, they point out, each party knows the other well, is all too aware of the vulnerable spots in the mate's coat of armor, and can easily resort to below-the-belt comments that are deeply wounding to the other's self-esteem. When this happens, the quarrel becomes heated, and the potential for violence is unleashed.

"The conflict as it finally appears in the war of words is so sharp, the feeling of betrayal and loss so great, that redress must be physical and destructive. This impulse is the stronger because the person who wins the war of words— often the woman since she is perhaps ordinarily more facile verbally—is not necessarily the person with the greatest sense of outrage or even the better case to present. The person who is least fair may be the most competent in verbal attack," states William J. Goode in "Force and Violence in the Family."[18]

In his article on marital violence, Robert N. Whitehurst contends that middle-class wives probably feed into violence-prone situations in a less passive manner than lower-class wives. He assumes that middle-class wives have a more highly developed verbal capacity and are less willing to play the subservient role, thereby provoking their husbands' violent responses.[19]

Statements by both Goode and Whitehurst conjure up stereotyped images of the nagging wife whose husband has to hit her to shut her up, or the "strong, silent type" who shows forbearance, up to a point, in the face of "the little woman's bickering." There are men who see their wives' concerns as trivial and their complaints as provocation for a family quarrel, but for two articulate male writers to consider women to be verbally superior to men seems unaccountably female-chauvinistic. Furthermore, I disagree with the assumption that class determines verbal capacity.

Still, some marital disputes do undoubtedly grow out of verbal arguments. Men have been triggered to violence because their wives have raised their voices or talked "dirty." Goode gives new insight into why men so readily blame women for provoking aggression when he says, "Women are socialized to use less physical violence than men, but typically do not feel that the words they use justify violence against them. Men are trained differently and recognize far more clearly that certain degrees of verbal violence will have a probability of eliciting a physical counterattack, not only a verbal counterattack. With a different perspective women are more frequently surprised by a physical counterattack when they use stinging words."[20]

The male attitude about the power of "fighting words" is related to the ancient and very peculiar belief that when a man was insulted, he could retain his "honor" only by challenging his insulter to a duel to the death. Even in such instances, strict etiquette was observed with regard to the challenge and the duel itself. But when a husband feels insulted by his wife, no warning or rules apply. She is often treated as fair game.

Histories of Violence and Occupational Hazards

As noted in Chapter 2, people who engage in domestic violence often witnessed violence between their parents as young children. Battering husbands very often have been battered children. They are likely to have criminal records. Fifty-two percent of the husbands in Gayford's survey had prison records, thirty-three percent for violent offences.[21] In their study "The Assaulted Wife," Sue Eisenberg and

Patricia Micklow found that 8 out of 20 husband/assailants in their sample had previous criminal records. Half of them had been arrested or convicted for felonious assault, though none had been arrested or convicted for wife-assault.[22] And a study of 8 graduate students in social work at Western Michigan University, which was prompted by the Kalamazoo Area Chapter of the National Organization for Women, also showed that a significant number of wife-beaters had criminal records.[23] Many of these cases involved physical assault.

Eisenberg and Micklow also found that 90 percent of the twenty husbands in their study had been in the military service, and one-fourth of these had received dishonorable discharges. (They also noted that a number of wives specifically mentioned that their husbands had learned how to inflict nonvisible injuries while in the service.)[24] Other evidence seems to support the correlation between military experience and marital violence. In Gelles's study, for example, one-tenth of the husbands were in the military at the time.[25] Bill Peterson reported in the *Washington Post* two cases of wife-beating in Fairfax County, Virginia, involving retired, high-ranking Army officers. The victims contacted the *Post* after seeing an article on the hidden problem of battered wives.[26] And a chaplain at Oak Knoll Naval Hospital in Oakland, California, expressed concern about the number of wife/victims who have sought emergency care there.

An Army officer's widow, I am told, has opened up her home in Oceanside, California, as a refuge for battered wives. Most of the women who seek her help are wives of men stationed at Camp Pendleton. A large number are Asian women who married American soldiers overseas and returned to the United States with them. Asian women tend to be even more subservient wives than Americans, and G.I.'s have often cited this fact as a reason for marrying Asian women. That a majority of the women seeking shelter at a particular refuge are Asian leads me to wonder whether increased subservience might not add to a wife-batterer's contempt for his victim.

Though the correlation between wife-abuse and military service has not been studied or measured empirically, I strongly suspect that at least some instances of wife-battering are service-connected. The military is, after all, a school for violence. No matter how peaceful or sensitive a man may be before he enters the military, once in he is

53

processed by a totally male machine to become an agent of war. He is taught to idealize aggression and rugged masculinity. Under the tight control of an authoritarian, hierarchical, and highly disciplined system, he learns to maim and kill other human beings. He must become immune to the horror of what he is doing not only because it is done for a supposedly righteous cause, but also because he must live with it on a day to day basis. Violence becomes his daily bread; brutality is often his means of survival. When the war is over or his time is up, presto! he must instantly transform himself into a peaceful man and a gentle husband. But can a man who has been carefully trained to respond violently make the transition to civilian life so easily? Concern has been registered about how difficult it is to de-condition police dogs trained to violence. Is this situation analogous to the "debriefing" of a soldier trained for warfare? Is it far-fetched to think that there is a connection between military training or combat experience and wifebeating? I don't think so.

Among the cases at Chiswick Women's Aid cited by Pizzey is that of a woman who arrived on the doorstep with six broken ribs, burns on her thighs from boiling water, and bruises all over her face. She turned out to be a policeman's wife and a victim of his brutal temper.[27] The irony here is that, for want of a better alternative, the police are most likely to be called to help in a case of marital violence. Also, many police departments actively recruit from among those separated from the military, and veterans receive preference points in civil service ratings.

A former California Highway Patrol officer told me that when he first went on patrol and saw his fellow officers roughing up suspects, he would flinch. But after a while he became so calloused that the sight no longer bothered him. At that point he knew it was time to quit. It is my guess that he got out just in time. Someone who is immune to the pain of others is, in my estimation, most dangerous.

Class and Status Variables

Gelles believes that violence between husband and wife is the result of many socioeconomic-related variables. He sees social position, employment status, financial circumstances, self-concept, and personal and community values as contributing factors.[28] Many people would agree that domestic

54

violence is linked to class and social status. Some believe outright that it is a direct result of poverty and low social status. Prevailing stereotypes of ghetto life often incorporate images of women being beaten and thrown around as a matter of course.

But the available data does not necessarily bear out the contention that working-class families are more violent than middle-class families. In instances where the majority of wife-abuse reports do come from the working class (though, as noted in Chapter 2, this is not always the case), this statistical majority may be due to variations in reporting rather than in behavior. Lower-class families have fewer resources and less privacy, and are more apt to contact public social-control agencies, such as the police, which compile domestic-disturbance statistics. Middle-class families have greater access to private support services, such as marriage counselors and psychiatrists, who do not as a rule compile statistics. In the case of serious injury, lower-class victims are sent to emergency rooms in public hospitals; middle- or upper-class wives can afford to contact private doctors or hospitals. These differences make lower-class family violence more visible as police or emergency-room statistics, and therefore more available to researchers.

Suzanne K. Steinmetz and Murray A. Straus, editors of *Violence in the Family,* believe that violence-prone persons have a willingness and ability to use physical violence as a "resource," and that a "family member can use this resource to compensate for lack of other resources as money, knowledge, and respect."[29] Thus, when the husband is out of a job, does not make enough money, or is otherwise dissatisfied with his work, he will take out his frustration on his wife. The editors cite a report from Birmingham, England, which indicated that wife-beating rose sharply during the six-month period in which unemployment was also on the rise. The implication is that more lower- than middle-class families suffer from lack of resources and are therefore more violence-prone, but Steinmetz and Straus point out the obvious fact that unemployment is not limited to the lower classes. Engineers and accountants can lose their jobs, too— witness the many professional-class victims of the "recession" in the early 1970s.

Steinmetz and Straus do argue, however, that less educated people suffer a higher "frustration factor," that is, more dissatisfaction with their jobs.[30] But a college degree does not guarantee a prestigious job or a frustration-free career, as any secretary with a master's degree can tell you. More to the point, I found in discussion with wife/victims, husbands suffer less from a lack in their own education than they do when their wives are better educated than they are.

In "Violence in Husband-Wife Interaction," Whitehurst agrees that it is a vast oversimplification to characterize wife-battering as an essentially, lower-class phenomenon. He believes that nearly all families experience violence at one time or another, but that the middle-class male is more likely to strike out at his wife and then quickly regain control. Whitehurst thinks that the middle-class male will assess a violent situation almost immediately in terms of the total consequences of his behavior. He will probably perceive involvement with the law as a threat to his occupational standing, and intrusion of relatives, neighbors, or friends as a threat to his social position. Out of a sense of guilt and shame for his actions, the middle-class man will be apt to redefine, accommodate, and assimilate the violent incident within the family context. For these reasons, Whitehurst says, middle-class family violence is rarely reported, so no one has any real idea as to how frequently it occurs.[31]

Drunkenness and Alcoholism

The "Dr. Jekyll and Mr. Hyde" syndrome is a recurring theme in the stories that battered wives tell. When the husband is sober he is "pleasant" and "charming"; when drunk he is "a monster" or "a bully." Many wives say that they were beaten *only* when their husbands were drunk. One wife told Gelles, "He wouldn't ever slap me when he was sober, no matter how mad he got." Another who told the same story, however, added that "most of his life he was drunk."[32] These women and others Pizzey and I have talked with believe that if their husbands did not drink, they would not be violent.

Police and social scientists share widely in the view that many family disputes involving assaultive behavior can be traced to the use of alcohol by one or both participants. "Alcohol leads to violence, in many cases, because it sets off a primary conflict over drinking that can extend to arguments over spending money, cooking and sex," Gelles says.[33] Drinking thus serves as a trigger for long-standing marital quarrels.

But Morton Bard and Joseph Zacker, specialists in police

56

crisis-intervention, believe that the use of alcohol as an impetus to family violence is highly exaggerated. They studied the West Harlem police family-crisis program in which bi-racial pairs of officers specially trained in interpersonal skills responded to family disturbance calls. During a twenty-two-month period, these special officers visited 962 families on 1,388 separate calls. The complainant was observed by the officers to have used alcohol (though not necessarily to intoxication) in 26 percent of the cases, and the accused in only 30 percent of the cases—hardly the majority in either instance. It is also interesting to note that only 10 percent of the complainants alleged that the accused was drunk. Where a charge of drunkenness was made, the officers' impressions concurred in less than half the incidents (43 percent). The officers perceived alcohol to be primary in the origins of the disputes in only 14 percent of the total cases, although alcohol was noted to have been used by the accused in 21 percent of the cases.[34]

Bard and Zacker are therefore critical of the traditional police view, which emphasizes the role of alcohol in family disputes. These researchers found that alcohol was the primary cause in very few cases. When alcohol use *was* noted, it was by no means inevitably the cause of the dispute. The most that could be said was that alcohol use was one of a number of circumstances contributing to the dispute, most of which undoubtedly remained unknown to the police.

Bard and Zacker's study points up the possibility that regular training of police—which almost never includes specific instruction on handling domestic disturbance—predisposes officers to simplistic perceptions and self-fulfilling prophecies. If they *expect* involved parties to be intoxicated they may easily perceive and report them to be intoxicated. In this light, police data is of very little use in determining the significance of alcohol use as a variable in wife-beating.

Gelles agrees that to view alcohol use as a primary cause in interpersonal violence is to tread on very thin ice. He points out that alcohol is known to break down inhibitions, and often leads to "out-of-character" behavior. Therefore, a person who is potentially violent can drink with the sole purpose of providing himself with a "time out" in which he can lay the blame for his violent actions on the alcohol. "Thus, individuals who wish to carry out a violent act become intoxicated *in order to carry out the violent act*. Having become drunk and then violent the individual either

57

may deny what occurred ('I don't remember, I was drunk'), or plead for forgiveness ('I didn't know what I was doing'). In both cases he can shift the blame for violence from himself to the effects of alcohol"[35] (Gelles's emphasis).

Thus, by pleading drunkenness, wife-beaters and their families can deceive themselves as to what is really going on in their own homes. The aggressor, his victim, and other family members can admit that the violence occurred, but maintain also that the family is "normal," and that alcohol was responsible for the temporary lapse in "normality." Violent actions often seem to be more acceptable—or at least more comprehensible—in our society when they are performed by a person who is intoxicated. There is even a legal precedent, through the "diminished capacity doctrine," for reducing the degree of homicide to second degree murder or voluntary manslaughter when the offender is proved to have been intoxicated.[36] This legal qualification reflects the assumption that the intoxicated person is not fully responsible for his or her actions. Thus, even a battered wife can avoid seeing her husband as a wife-beater, thinking of him instead as a heavy drinker or an alcoholic. Notes Gelles, families that do interpret their domestic problems in this way and actually seek help usually wind up focusing on the husband's drinking problem rather than his uncontrollable aggression.[37]

Pizzey is more direct in this regard. She says, "Some of the men who batter are alcoholics, but stopping them from drinking doesn't stop the violence. Anything can release the trigger of violence in a batterer. It can be alcohol, a child crying, a bad day on the horses."[38] Alcohol is one of several factors that often contribute to the circumstances in which marital violence occurs. It may be used as an excuse for violence and it may trigger arguments that lead to violence. But, contrary to conventional beliefs, it is not necessarily a direct cause of violence and therefore does not help to explain the causes of wife-beating.

Jealousy

Under certain circumstances and for certain people, wife-beating has undertones of romance and drama. Throughout history, the wrathful husband has risen up in righteous indignation to strike his unfaithful wife—for her own good, for the good of their marriage, or simply because he feels he has the right to express his hurt and anger in this way. The romantic interpretation of the archetypal situation is that the trust of the loving man is betrayed by the unfaithful wife, and he is therefore unable to hide his pain and control his anger. A more mundane but to me realistic view is that not only has the trust of the husband been betrayed, but his territory (home) has been invaded and his possessions (wife) have been handled by an intruder.

To speak of "possessiveness" in sexual relations is not just to indulge in a figure of speech. As discussed in Chapter 3, in the early patriarchal system of marriage women were considered to be practically on a par with livestock. They were commodities with a price on their heads—either a brideprice or a dowry. Our family structure in the United States has evolved away from an out-and-out slave-market method of marriage, but the principle of ownership still operates. The male-dominated family system demands absolute fidelity from the woman; if she didn't agree to be controlled, the system would fall apart. Thus unfaithful women have been portrayed throughout history and literature as degraded (and degrading) seductresses—they have not been forgiven for daring to besmirch the holy marriage vows and humiliate the husband. Often in modern times the female is portrayed as oversexed for caring enough about sexual fulfillment to seek it outside her marriage.

The unfaithful man, on the other hand, has been portrayed as a player of the game. A husband is encouraged to develop his extramarital style to such a degree that, in our day and age, he is considered somewhat ridiculous for remaining faithful to his wife. It might even be said that in certain circles the only thing more ridiculous than a faithful husband is a cuckolded one—and therein lies the key to what has been referred to in the literature as "morbid jealousy."

When a woman is unfaithful to her husband, he realizes that he does not control his "possession." If he suspects that his wife has a will of her own without actually having proof of her infidelity, the husband may nevertheless suffer a profound insecurity at the *possibility* of her betrayal. If such insecurity invades the man's imagination, he might take pains to prevent *her* from living out *his* fantasies. Gay Search describes the case of a pregnant woman whose mate locked her and her small daughter in the bedroom every morning before he left for work. He took away their clothes, and just in case they might consider escaping naked into the street, he wired the door handle with electricity. When he returned at night he would beat the woman for "screwing the dozens of men" he was convinced had been in the room with her during the day.[39]

Examples of vicious behavior born of jealousy abound, but Jackson Toby's report of an interview with "Jimmy," a twenty-four-year-old prisoner, is a particularly illuminating example of the double standard in operation. Jimmy heard of the infidelity of another prisoner's wife; the husband was furious and wanted to kill the other man. "Why the other guy?" Jimmy asked. If it had been *his* wife, he would have "cut her face, cut her all open. . . . This is my *wife*. You know, this is not one of the bitches; this is my wife. This is the mother of my kids. I don't want her walking down the street, and every guy she says hello to, I would wonder if this is a guy that went to bed with her. I'd wind up killing her. . . . Let me tell you something. Me or you can go out with say fifteen different bitches, fuck every one of them. You can come down the street naked, cockeyed drunk, and fall flat on the ground. You get up. Let a woman do it, and she's finished. . . . If a man fools around some people will admire him. They'll say he knows how to bullshit a broad. Let a woman do it? She's a fuckin' whore."[40]

Another interview demonstrates the link between infidelity and wife-beating: "She was going out with other guys. I tried to discuss the problem and she denied the whole thing. After a while I got to her. . . . One night coming home from going out . . . something happened, she kept denying the thing. I just grabbed her and threw her on the lawn. I don't remember what happened then. I had a few drinks anyway."[41]

Sometimes the interrogations to which the wives are subjected take on the aura of a third-degree. One wife told Gelles that her husband kept "harping" on her supposed infidelity. He would just keep it up until out of desperation she would admit "anything in the world to get him to shut up. He would keep it up for five hours and not let me sleep. I would say, 'Yes! Yes! I did, are you glad?' . . . and then he would beat me."[42]

In their article on jealousy, Joan and Larry Constantine conclude that "sex is almost never the real issue, only the arena."[43] They see sex, like alcohol, as affording the husband a socially accepted excuse for venting his violent feelings, which erupt over the loss of control of his wife as property.

Pizzey mentions a bizarre aspect of this need to control: "Women who marry violent men are rarely *allowed* to use contraception, because along with the batterer's violent nature goes a tormented jealousy that can barely let his woman out of sight and which finds security in keeping her pregnant and thus captive."[44]

But, strange to say, some men beat their wives if they catch them taking the pill, and they beat them again when they inevitably become pregnant. Time and again, battered wives tell of being hit or kicked in the stomach while pregnant. Sometimes the beatings cause a miscarriage, premature birth, or a deformity in the unborn child. Eisenberg and Micklow describe a particularly gruesome attack by a husband on his six-month-pregnant wife: "Bitch," he screamed at her, "You are going to lose that baby!" And then he beat her repeatedly, concentrating his blows on her swollen belly, until she passed out. When she regained consciousness her husband was still beating her.[45]

This might sound like a scenario for a grade B movie, but the problem exists in reality, and it won't go away just because we consider it too horrible to think about. The question here is two-fold: Why do wife-beaters so often express their anger toward an unborn child or toward the woman for being pregnant? And why do the same men so often express ambivalence toward birth control?

A man who beats his pregnant wife may be expressing jealousy toward the newcomer and resentment against the change it will bring to his life. But in a larger sense, he may be reacting directly against the tremendous pressure our society places on men to marry and sire children. A man is expected by the society at large to accept his roles as husband and father; often his enthusiasm for these roles is a measure of his sense of responsibility. A gay male friend of mine inadvertently provided an example of how such social pressure works when he recounted his experience in applying for the management training program at the telephone company. He was turned down because (1) he was over thirty, (2) he wasn't married, (3) he didn't have any children to support, and (4) he wasn't head over heels in debt. To big corporations family responsibilities insure that a man will stay on the job.

Many men simply do not have the temperament or the inclination for marriage or fatherhood. They balk at the idea of being "tied down," and panic at each addition to the family, knowing that they must assume full responsibility for the added financial burden. Just because a man is a biological father, it does not automatically follow that he will show any particular aptitude for the care and treatment of children.

On the other side of this coin is the familiar attitude that a woman's sole function is to provide an heir for her husband's name and property. In this regard, a father once told me that he would have been devastated if his only daughter had had no children. In her he saw his only hope for what he called "immortality." If, as is very often the case, this lofty attitude is coupled with the fear of responsibility, some men's peculiar ambivalence toward birth control is understandable.

Gelles brought up a point in his article on violence and pregnancy that never occurred to me: Sometimes terminating a pregnancy by beating a wife is more acceptable (socially, morally, and even legally) than is abortion![46] "It is also much cheaper," Betsy Warrior adds, "if economics is a factor."[47]

Stereotyped Sex Roles

Jealous husbands and fathers fixate on the stereotyped sex roles that serve to maintain the double standard in our society: virginal, loyal wife; virile husband protecting his honor and property. It is as if these men swallow these ready-made roles whole and try to live them out without running them through their own imaginations. Jimmy, the prisoner whose friend's wife stepped out on him, is a striking example of someone who believes wholeheartedly in our culture's sexual myths. In commenting on the interview, Jackson Toby calls Jimmy's madonna/slut attitude an expression of "compulsive-masculinity."[48] Toby concludes that Jimmy's attitudes toward violence are subcultural: Jimmy has learned from the world around him that a man must protect his honor, show courage, and conceal fear, and that violence is an appropriate way to achieve these ideals.

To Steinmetz and Straus, the compulsive-masculinity syndrome results from "an anxiety over demonstrating one's masculinity," and is therefore "likely to be greatest in female-headed households. In these families there is no adequate male role model available." They further state, "(s)ince there are more female-headed households in the lowest strata of society than in other strata, one would also expect to find more compulsive masculinity and hence more husband-wife violence in lower class families."[49]

I contend that an "adequate male role model" may actually incorporate a good dose of "compulsive-masculinity." In fact, it may be safe to say that the standard male role model endorsed by our society is *synonymous* with compulsive-masculinity, and that only boys who *escape* that model will emerge as fair-minded human beings able to view women as equals and wives as partners. Those who are successfully socialized in schools, families, churches, and other institutions according to prevailing standards of masculinity may very well grow up to be dominating bullies. A boy who truly identifies with the role models reinforced by this society—for instance, the brutal cops or paternalistic, know-it-all doctors and lawyers on television—would grow up with a version of Jimmy's "compulsive-masculinity."

It is easy enough to discover what qualities are endorsed as masculine and feminine in our society. I had to go no further than the reference books on my desk. After consulting several dictionaries, *Roget's Thesaurus*, the Bible, and *The Psychology of Sex Differences* by Maccoby and Jacklin, I came up with this list of adjectives cited in definitions of the word "masculine":

aggressive	bold
assertive	noble
active	upright
brave	heroic
frank	rough-natured
resolute	intellectual
stout-hearted	rational
analytical	far-sighted
determined	profound
undaunted	authoritarian
virile	independent
hardy	paternal
daring	stable
courageous	self-sufficient
fearless	unwomanly
orderly	unfeminine

Tracking back through the same sources, I found the word "feminine" defined by these adjectives:

passive	delicate
tactful	sympathetic
motherly	maidenlike
artless	chaste
unsullied	sentimental
intuitive	lacking in
superficial	foresight
timid	docile
lacking in	prudent
self-confidence	envious
monogamous	masochistic
modest	tender
submissive	gentle
matronly	girlish
virginal	pure
mild	emotional
impulsive	frivolous
fragile	dependent
cautious	maternal
self-sacrificing	curious
home-loving	hysterical

The authors of the reference books from which these lists were compiled did not invent the definitions for "masculine" and "feminine." These books reflect commonly agreed upon definitions. One need only turn on the television or go to the movies to see how pervasive these qualities are in our culture.

In his study of masculine and feminine stereotypes, Hernán San Martín found that these same characteristics are considered "normal" and "natural" by people in Latin America.[50] He calls the stereotypes both real and mythical —real because they are, in varying degrees, a part of the daily existence of men and women; mythical because they are not innate, but rather a cultural acquisition. "Machismo," he says, referring to the almost fanatical belief in the masculine ideal, "has become an oppressive ideology expressed in many different attitudes and forms of behavior, especially in economic life, unemployment and sexual life."

In our own country, a strong-willed, independent woman or a passive, monogamous man need only think back to adolescence and recall the amount of energy—even defiance

—that was required to maintain one's integrity in the face of constant social pressure to become a "passive, dependent" girl or an "aggressive, rough-natured" boy. It is easy to understand how a man, caught in the spiral of today's over-competitiveness and rampant unemployment, must fight desperately and even resort to physical violence to prove himself to be "assertive," "independent," and "self-sufficient"—that is, masculine.

Socialization and Sex Roles

As noted in Chapter 3, the nuclear family has evolved into the basic social unit in our society. As such it is the most potent tool for socializing children. The mother and father, role-models closest to the child, are bound to have a powerful effect on the child's understanding of "masculinity" and "femininity." In his book *Fatherhood,* Leonard Benson explains that a small boy's relationship with his mother is usually one of warmth and loving acceptance. But at some point the boy perceives that he must identify with the father or another male figure if he is to achieve his manhood and the power that goes with it. He has to give up such feminine qualities as tenderness and loving-kindness, and take on aggressiveness as the symbol of his male identity.[51] A study by D. J. Hicks indicates that boys between the ages of five and eight imitate violent acts more often than girls do.[52] E. M. and Frankie G. Heatherington found, too, that among children four to six years old, boys imitated their fathers more than their mothers, and girls imitated their mothers more than their fathers.[53]

Letty Cottin Pogrebin suggests that at this stage in the socialization process it is often the *lack* of an admirable, humane, loving father that makes "masculinity" turn the corner toward brutality. That is, the father may encourage the boy to identify with the more aggressive elements in the masculine role, even to the point of suppressing his own natural gentleness. Pogrebin also cites other studies to demonstrate that mothers are usually less concerned about their children's "appropriate," or sex-typed behavior, than fathers are. She says that the father is usually determined that his children understand sex-role differences, while the mother tends to think of and treat children of both sexes simply as "children."[54]

Naturally, much of the socialization process derives from

how men behave toward women publicly within sight of the child. As an example of public behavior, Pogrebin cites an experiment created by three psychologists at Michigan State University in which a series of fights were staged on the sidewalk and the reactions of passersby recorded. The researchers found, much to their amazement, that passing men rushed to the aid of other men whether they were being assaulted by women or men. They also helped women who were being hit by other women. But *not one* male bystander interfered when a man was assaulting a woman.[55] (Recall my friend, cited in Chapter 2, who tried to help the pregnant woman being beaten in front of a group of onlookers. Needless to say, my friend was a woman.) During a symposium on violence broadcast on radio station WBAI in New York City a few years ago, a woman said that she had slapped a well-dressed businessman who was molesting her on the subway. The men in the crowd were outraged at *her* behavior![56]

Speculating on the public reactions of men toward violence, Susan Griffin writes, "Far from discouraging violence, the presence of other men may in fact encourage sadism, and even cause the behavior."[57] The implication here is that men in a public situation often feel the need to stick together. A man may suppress personal inclinations toward nonaggression in order to project a "masculine" image.

According to Whitehurst, most men, regardless of class, share the belief "that a woman will behave better and may even enjoy the feeling of being put in her 'rightful' (subservient) place by physical punishment. Part of the male folklore has it that women really enjoy a male domination-female submissive relationship."[58] Another factor in marital violence Whitehurst refers to is the "Sure Winner" syndrome, in which some men, low in the status hierarchy, engage in violence only when they are assured of victory. In other words, when all other sources of masculine identity fail to keep control, men can always rely on being "tough" —especially with a wife who cannot defend herself.

So far our discussion of roles and socialization has been limited to the dominant culture in our society, heterosexuals. But as Maccoby and Jacklin point out, "violent impositions of one person's will upon another can occur among members of the same sex" as well. They predict that "the potentialities for it are greater, however, between the sexes because of their unequal strength."[59] My own experience in the gay subculture indicates that violence does

66

indeed occur in some homosexual relationships. But the "equality of physical strength" does not appear to be the deterrent to violence that Maccoby and Jacklin expect. Rather, the degree to which the couple adheres to stereotypes of role-play seems to be the determining factor. Male homosexuals and Lesbians have been conditioned just as other men and women in our society have been. Everyone assumes they will be heterosexual. Gay people learn the same dominant and passive, "masculine" and "feminine" roles, which when practiced in their relationships are called "butch" and "femme." When they act out these roles (which are imitative of Mom and Dad, the only models they had as children), gays can fall heir to the same conflicts, the same power relationships, and the same potential for violence that can afflict heterosexual couples. On the other hand, I find that gay couples who have discarded butch-femme roles and struggle to relate on an egalitarian basis are less likely to engage in violence. This observation leads me to believe that the potential for disappointment and frustration that can result in violence is inherent in rigid male/female sex roles that foster the dominance of one sex or partner over the other.

Fathers who teach their sons to be tough, who pass along the notion that women *enjoy* being brutalized, and do not interfere when a man assaults a woman, are conditioning the next generation of aggressive males. It is inevitable that some of the boys trained by society to be "masculine" aggressors will grow up to be women-beaters. By the same processes those girls who are taught to be passive, submissive, docile, and dependent, are being set up as "feminine" victims.

Sexuality as Aggressiveness

The violent behavior of men toward women may be an understandable result of the socialization process, but I contend—against growing opposition—that violence is in no way inevitable. Because of the ever-increasing violence in our society, male theorists and doomsayers are trying to convince us that aggression is inherent in human nature, rather than the result of conditioning and reinforcement by a male-dominant society.

Anthony Storr is a classicist in this regard. Not only does he see aggression as innate and instinctive, but he believes aggression to be a normal component of sexuality. In his book *Human Aggression,* Storr states, "It is only when intense aggressiveness exists between two individuals that love can arise. Even sex itself does not seem to overcome aggression."[60] He builds part of his case on the Kinsey findings that anger and sexual arousal produce similar physiological changes and that it is not uncommon for one response suddenly to change into the other.[61] This is why quarrelling husbands and wives often end up in bed together and why some fights end in orgasm, he says.

Storr's theory gains support from the Freudian notions of the submissive, masochistic female and the dominant, sadistic male.[62] Dominance and "a touch of ruthlessness" in men are admired,[63] says Storr. The stability of the family and the sexual happiness of the couple depend on the dominance of the male. Aggression, he contends, is an important element of male sexuality because of the primitive necessity of pursuit and penetration. "The idea of being seized and borne off by a ruthless male who will wreak his sexual will upon his helpless victim has a universal appeal to the female sex,"[64] he declares. A little "fear of the more dominant male reinforces rather than inhibits erotic arousal in females."[65]

Storr criticizes the church for teaching men to conceive of love in terms of self-sacrifice and gentleness, making them too restricted to enjoy "the full splendor of sexuality."[66] If their aggressiveness is inhibited, he says, "their wives cannot fully respond to them, and they themselves fail to gain complete sexual satisfaction." Insecure men who are unable to achieve complete sexual satisfaction often have sado-masochistic sexual fantasies of which they are ashamed. But Storr adds, "(t)here is generally a wide gap between fantasy and reality, in that men who find themselves the prey of sadist imaginations seldom actually hurt their partners, whom they wish to enjoy the role of helpless victims."[67]

Like Storr, many men view sexual intercourse as an act of aggression and conquest. To such men lovemaking is not the physical expression of affection and pleasure-giving. To them, sex means battle—they can act out their fantasies of aggressor and vanquisher. A little violence adds to their sexual excitement. Men who experience sexuality in this way often anticipate with pleasure the increased intensity of intercourse after a fight.

With the emphasis on "conquest," sexual intercourse is

considered to be a vital source of a man's self-esteem, and rejection by a lover can therefore have extremely grave effects. Storr warns that rejection can result in extreme rage from a husband who feels insecure about his masculinity.[68] He goes on to say that a man who is not masterful and who fears women may become impotent.[69] J. C. Rheingold, in *The Fear of Being a Woman,* concurs: "A woman can, under certain circumstances, make a man impotent. Expression of reproach, derogatory remarks, indications of disinterest, or expressions of exaggerated anxiety may have a castrative effect on a sensitive man and lead to lasting disturbance."[70] The implication here is that a woman who causes impotency in a man by threatening his self-esteem should *expect* the rage that accompanies a beating. In this roundabout way, she can be held responsible for the physical punishment she receives.

Wolfgang Lederer, in his scholarly and comprehensive book *The Fear of Women,* points out another possible link between sexual insecurity and male violence. He says that some "wifebeaters . . . are potent only with a woman defective or somehow inferior."[71] If their wives do not assume that they are inferior and consider themselves equal to their husbands, apparently these men feel they have to beat them down to size. If his wife is attractive, the batterer, in order to maintain his potency (that is, his male supremacy), has to disfigure her. Perhaps another hidden motive exists—to make her less attractive to other men.

These theories all reflect a general assumption that *male* sexuality and insecurity are the stakes being played for. They concern themselves with the grave effects of sexual dissatisfaction in the male. But what of the woman and *her* sexual fulfillment? Phyllis Lyon, co-director of the National Sex Forum in San Francisco, is explicit with regard to this bias in our culture at large: "Historically, in our culture women have been seen as nonsexual, existing only as receptacles for the pleasure of their husbands. Prior to World War I it was not ladylike for a woman to gain pleasure from sex, and more than one woman went to the doctor for relief of her unseemly feelings. Consequently most women were raised to be sexy, not sexual." Thus, women learned to repress their sexual feelings before they went too far.

"Historically, too, men were told that they must be masterful in the bedroom," Lyon adds. "Husbands were supposed to be skilled lovers who take total initiative in all sexual relations." Young men were encouraged to have sex before marriage in order to gain experience and to learn technique. The partners they used for their education were "loose" women or prostitutes—beneath contempt as compared with the virginal maidens they expected to marry.

Thus, with the historical emphasis on the man as the master sexually, and the traditional association between sexual intercourse and the conquest of the weaker sex by the stronger, it is no wonder that sexual pleasure becomes confused in some men's minds with physical strength and, by extension, with physical pain. Some people may even be tempted to see wife-beating as an expression of the kind of sadism associated with sexual pleasure. Indeed, the literature is full of references to the masochism inherent in the female of the species. Chief among the adherents to this theory was Sigmund Freud, whose effect upon the thinking of the twentieth century, particularly with respect to the concepts of pleasure and pain, is beyond measure.

We have no way of determining whether a correlation exists between wife-beating and sadism, but sadism may be relevant to our understanding of wife-beating from an entirely different point of view—with respect to domination rather than sexual pleasure. Erich Fromm's discussion of sadism could very well be a description of the dynamics of a male-dominated marriage—or in fact, any situation where one person aggresses against another: "I see the passion to control another being, that is, to completely control, to have in my power, to do with him what I will, to be, so to speak, his god, to be almighty. This situation is realized in the form of injuring someone else, to humble him physically, so that he cannot defend himself. With sadism, it must be that the other person is helpless and weak. Sadism never has a strong person as an object."[72] Fromm goes on to speculate on the desperation the aggressor could be expressing: "The more powerless a person is, the more likely he is to compensate for his weakness by sadism. He may even risk his life for a moment of absolute power."[73]

Fromm's insight penetrates to the heart of the sad problem of wife-battering, and it is perhaps the premise which all the literature attempts to substantiate. If a wife-beater does not risk his life when he beats his wife, at least he sacrifices his sense of right and wrong for the feeling of power he derives from harming someone weaker than him-

70

self. Can the wife-beater come to understand that he risks his very humanness for a moment of false power?

Aggression: Prevent It or Vent It?

In considering how aggression and violent behavior could be prevented, we jump into an on-going controversy. Theorists are divided into two camps: those who encourage learning how to control or redirect anger, and those who see it as both desirable and necessary that pent-up anger (or accumulating aggressive drives) be expressed in one way or another. The latter are called "ventilationists."

Leonard Berkowitz is leery of the ventilationist theory. In his article "The Case for Bottling Up Rage," he says that therapists or group-therapy members usually approve and therefore reward a subject's display of aggression, thereby heightening the likelihood of future aggression. He points to several experiments in the behavior of young boys. R. H. Walters and Murray Brown gave seven-year-olds intermittent rewards for punching a Bobo doll. When the boys competed against their peers several days later, they proved to be more aggressive than their control group. Berkowitz feels that the occasional rewards had done more than strengthen their "playful" approach, that it had also strengthened the boys' aggressive responses.[74]

Other experiments cited by Berkowitz were conducted by Feshback, Mallick, and Candless. Here young boys who were initially low in aggressive behavior were given aggressive toys to play with. Their overt hostility increased significantly after the free-play experience. Instead of "draining" their pent-up anger, the aggressive make-believe evidently lowered the boys' restraints against aggression.

Berkowitz expresses his concern that violence on television and in the movies promotes aggressive behavior. In his own research, he found that a person who watches violence is more apt to become aggressive himself, whether he is angry at the time or not. The viewer is not purged of angry impulses as some argue, but is stimulated to violence. In another study children who witnessed a victim's defeat and submission were found to be likely to act aggressively themselves. These conclusions, coupled with the frequency-of-TV-violence studies cited in Chapter 2, are horrifying indeed.

George R. Bach and Peter Wyden have devised a sort of modified ventilationist technique to cope with marital disputes. They believe that if married disputants could overcome inhibitions and express their emotions directly, it would eliminate disturbing tensions and promote deeper and more meaningful relationships. Bach and Wyden encourage couples to fight, but train them in what they call "constructive aggression." In their book *The Intimate Enemy—How to Fight Fair in Love and Marriage*,[75] the authors describe a technique of verbal conflict in which the couple talk about their feelings and describe their emotional reactions.

Bach and Wyden's technique presupposes that the husband regards the wife as a person in her own right. Negotiations and compromises are impossible if a husband regards his wife as chattel. But most battering husbands believe they have the right to make all the decisions for the family and to mete out punishment if their demands are not met. The wife has to accept her husband's authority or expect to take her lumps.

Whitehurst reminds us that "men are not programmed to be other than aggressive" and that "much of the aggressive hostility vented on wives must be seen as a product of our sexually schizoid culture." He concludes, "Our culture teaches men to be tough and ready to fight if necessary. To expect men to also become tender lovers and responsive husbands seems to be asking more than logic can allow."[76] I agree with Whitehurst; we expect too much if we think these changes will come about by themselves. It is an enormous task, involving nothing less than a cultural revolution of attitudes and values.

5

THE VICTIM—
WHY DOES SHE STAY?

A London Survey

The British survey of battered wives cited in Chapter 4 was conducted by J. J. Gayford, senior registrar in the Department of Psychiatry of Westminster Hospital in London. The results were published in the *British Medical Journal* on January 25, 1975.[1] For the purposes of the survey, a battered wife was defined as a woman who had received deliberate, severe, and repeated beatings at the hands of her husband or lover and had suffered severe physical injury as a result.

Gayford does not presume that the results of his survey apply to all battered wives. Most of the one hundred women surveyed had sought refuge at Chiswick Women's Aid. The sample was heavily weighted with women whose husbands drank, gambled heavily, or were unemployed, probably because Women's Aid, by the nature of its services, attracts women who are without financial resources. Still, the survey was a first step in using social-science methodology to describe the plight of battered wives. Keeping in mind the limitations of the sample, we can use Gayford's findings to help us view the predicament of these battered women with some objectivity.

Of the one hundred women surveyed, 85 were married and 15 were living out of wedlock with their mates. The ages of these battered women ranged from 19 to 59. Both the length of their relationships and the period during which they were subjected to continuous beatings ranged from 1 to 25 years. All subjects had suffered the minimal injury of severe bruising. All had been hit with a clenched fist, the blows being more damaging when the husband/assailant wore heavy rings on his fingers. Forty-four women suffered lacerations, and in 17 cases husbands used sharp instruments to inflict wounds on the women. Nine women had at some time been taken to the hospital after being found unconscious. Eighteen of the women were suffering from chronic physical ailments other than trauma from beatings, and 71 were taking anti-depressants or tranquilizers at the time of the survey.

Suicide attempts among the battered women had been frequent: 34 tried taking poisonous drugs, and 10 repeated the attempt; 7 tried self-mutilation (3 repeats); and 9 used various other methods (2 repeats in this category). Sixteen of the women claimed they had really wanted to die, but 21 admitted that they had only wanted to draw attention to their plight or to get away from the situation.

Suicidal "gestures," as Gayford calls them, were usually treated in the hospital without the true facts being disclosed to the doctors. Severe injuries, whether resulting from beatings or suicide attempts, were often passed off as accidents to medical personnel. Occasionally the husbands prevented their injured wives from seeking medical attention; in other cases they removed the women from the hospital prematurely.

Eight women fought back when their husbands beat them, while 19, seeing what was coming, tried to get out of the way. Only 6 found it possible to call for help, and 42 wives claimed they could see no possible way, however ineffective, of avoiding the assault or lessening its severity.

All but 19 of the women had left their husbands on one or more occasions; as many as 36 had left home more than 4 times. In 54 cases the violence had extended to the children, and this was one of the reasons the women cited for leaving. When they left, 51 women stayed with relatives. Most of the others stayed with friends, in a hotel, or in a hostel. Eleven went to the hospital. Unaware of any emergency housing that might have existed in their areas, nine women wandered about with no roof over their heads.

The wives who left gave these reasons for returning to their husbands: he pleaded and promised to reform (27); he threatened and/or performed further acts of violence (17); she had nowhere else to go (14); the children were still in the marital home (13); she felt love or sorrow for

74

the husband (8). Inevitably, when the wives returned home, further assaults occurred, sometimes within a few hours, and the cycle began all over again.

Help had been sought from the police by one-third of the wives, and from social agencies by about three-fifths of them. Almost nine-tenths of the sample had sought refuge or help from Chiswick Women's Aid. Of the latter, one-quarter needed protection from their husbands, over one-third needed legal assistance, and one-fifth saw housing as their major need. Over one-half of this same group were looking for a new start in life, and more than one-tenth wanted to live in a protected community.

As for the backgrounds of these battered wives, only 65 had been reared by both parents to the age of 15. In 53 cases the relationship between the parents had been good. Violence had occurred in 23 of the families; the father had been drunk often in 24 and unemployed in 7. Twenty-seven of the women had only a grade school education, 32 had received a high school diploma, and 30 had been to college or had received some higher education.

Surprisingly, half the women expressed satisfaction with their marital sex life, though 68 said their feelings for their husbands had deteriorated to the point of indifference or hatred. But few of these battered women were vindictive towards their mates: only 10 really wanted him to suffer or die, 33 just wanted to get away or out from under his oppression and abuse, 37 thought he needed help, and 10 felt long-term custodial care was essential for him.

The women tended to come from large families and to have lots of children. The 100 wives had a total of 315 children, though some of them were childless. Prior to marriage, 85 had engaged in sexual intercourse without contraception. Forty-five were pregnant by the husband before living with him, and 15 were pregnant by another man. Fifty-eight of the couples had been married with no period of engagement, and 23 of the wives had been married before. In 37 cases, the man was known to have been married or living with another woman previously. After marriage, 8 women had suspicions and 45 women knew that their husbands were having extramarital affairs. Seventeen of the women admitted to having had extramarital affairs. In 25 cases, battering had occurred before marriage.

Gayford sums up his findings by stating that all the women he interviewed had "made disastrous marriages, often undertaken by a desire to leave home and attracted by the protective image of their man" (the same reasons for marrying cited by the Latin American women in San Martín's study of sex roles and machismo). The women in this survey left school between the ages of 7 and 18; the median age was 15. The age at which they married was between 16 and 29, but the mean age was 20. Thus a great many of these women married very young and started having babies immediately. They wanted to get out from under parental control, but had little education or training for a job that could buy them time and economic independence. They knew that marriage and having children was expected of them anyway and, having no alternatives, they rushed headlong into "disastrous marriages." Once caught in the trap of a violent marriage, they had no way out.

The fact that all these women made "disastrous marriages" and had great difficulty in extricating themselves alerts us to another kind of skewing in this data: Gayford's sample represents women who, for whatever reason, remained at home or returned to their homes after they had been beaten the first time. But, though we have no way of estimating the number, we know there are a great many women in the world who walked out the door, never to return, the first time their husbands raised a hand to them. The subjects in Gayford's survey, and in all other studies on battered wives, are self-reported; that is, the subjects identified themselves as battered wives whose histories were relevant to the study. A woman who has been beaten but who manages to end the violent relationship and start a new phase of life cannot be expected to respond to an investigation on the problem of wife-battering. It must be remembered, then, that all available data on the subject have been gathered from women who, at least at the time of the studies, saw themselves as trapped, not from women who managed to get out and stay out.

Many women have said to me, "If my husband gave me just one beating, that would be it. I'd leave." Consistently most people ask, "Why do these wives stay? Why don't they pack up their bags and walk out?" These are fair questions. Even the woman whose letter appeared in Chapter 1 admitted that her story would have been incomprehensible to her had she not lived through it. Probably the most understandable explanation, and paradoxically the one most commonly disregarded, is fear.

Trapped by Fear

Battered wives give many reasons or rationalizations for staying, but fear is the common denominator. Fear immobilizes them, ruling their actions, their decisions, their very lives.

"It's fear," one woman told a reporter. "Your belly's full of it. It usually happens at night when there is no place to go. I used to take the baby carriage out at night and walk the streets to get away."[2]

"When he hit me, of course I was afraid. Anybody would be if somebody larger than you decided to take out their anger on you," a woman in the Eisenberg-Micklow study declared. "I really couldn't do anything about it. I felt as if I was completely helpless." Another subject recalled, "I would cover my head with my arms and crouch in the corner. I was too afraid to fight back." So shocked and frightened by their husbands' violence were these women that they were unable to respond to the situation. They cowered in terror.[3]

"The police don't seem able to differentiate between a woman in danger and a woman just trying to put a scare into her spouse," Marjory Fields told *Newsweek*.[4] An Army officer's wife said it took her eleven years to get up enough nerve to go to the police, and when she did "they were insulting and sarcastic."[5] A call to the police is generally an act of desperation in an emergency. By the time the police arrive, however, the wife may be so terror-stricken—so threatened and intimidated by her husband—that she may be unable to articulate the facts about the incident and may even turn the officers away. Police, who are all too aware of the danger to themselves in responding to a domestic disturbance call, seem to be almost oblivious to the danger to the wife/victim. Once the police leave the scene, the woman and her attacker are face to face again —this time with the knowledge between them that she called the police *on her own husband in his own home!* Doubtless many women have called the police, discovered that they had inadvertently worsened their plight, and chosen to endure silently their violent husband's outbursts from that time forward.

Fear of reprisal also prevents the battered wife from running to her neighbors for help during an attack. The woman may be less concerned with protecting her secret at the moment than she is with protecting her neighbors. Her husband may be so thoroughly possessed by his anger that he would strike out at anyone who got involved. Thus, out of fear of endangering others, her children as well, the woman may choose to sacrifice herself.

If the wife does manage to escape, her husband often stalks her like a hunted animal. He scours the neighborhood, contacts friends and relatives, goes to all the likely places where she may have sought refuge, and checks with public agencies to track her down. If she works, the battered wife is afraid her husband will show up on the job, make a scene and cause her to be fired. If she has taken an apartment of her own, she lives in constant dread that he will find her. With every car idling on the street, each footstep in the hall, every noise outside her door, she freezes in sheer terror. Pizzey tells of the wife who obtained temporary welfare accommodations, but her husband found her, broke in and threatened her. She returned home, explaining it was better to be where she knew he was than to sit night after night in fear waiting for him to catch her.[6]

Unless she can afford to leave town and effectively disappear, a woman is never quite safe from a stalking husband. Sometimes the harassment, the threats, and the beatings continue for years after a wife has left. One woman who had been divorced for three years wrote to a woman's group for help:

"In every place where I have lived, my house has been watched so closely by my ex-husband that I have been virtually a prisoner. I have been endlessly followed and relentlessly pursued. My life has been threatened many times, and I have occasionally been severely beaten. My friends and all those who have ever exhibited sympathy or who have attempted to aid me have likewise been harassed and threatened. This had the effect of driving away what little support I had, leaving me more susceptible than ever to my ex-husband's bullying, intimidation and reign of domestic terror. Two weeks ago he cornered me in the drugstore. He repeatedly and very forcefully threatened my life in front of a dozen witnesses. When I finally escaped his grasp, I ran home. I called the police, but they didn't come. I am afraid to leave the house. I have been unable to go to work; I can't send my children to school. I am running out of food, and my landlord has asked me to move. Yesterday my husband parked his car in front of my home for six hours. I don't know what to do. My life is in jeopardy; my resources are nearly depleted. And my husband is circling my house like a buzzard."[7]

The man, after all, has a lot to lose if he lets his wife walk out on him. He loses the stability of married life that is so significant to his mental health, as was noted in Chapter 3. He loses "his" woman, the scapegoat that is living proof of his superiority. A husband's desperate need to hold on to these symbols often makes divorce meaningless to him. Some men would rather kill "their" women than see them make a new life.

A woman from a small city in Oklahoma told me she had left church one night after a class to find that the tires of her car had been slashed. She froze; she knew that her alcoholic ex-husband had found her and was watching her from somewhere in the shadows of the parking lot. She was right. He suddenly jumped out of the darkness and held a knife on her, forcing her to take the wheel of his car. She drove him to her home. Later, when she called the police, they asked her why she had taken the violent man home where the children were. She said she had been afraid not to, that she would have been at a disadvantage in a strange place, even if she had been able to think of somewhere to go. At home at least she had the advantage of knowing the layout and size of the rooms, where the telephone was, where the doors led, and how they locked—strategically important information. She was sure he would not harm the children; he had never done so in the past. She also knew the pattern of her ex-husband's behavior, that his violent energy would soon be spent and he would pass out. When he did, she called the police; because she was divorced and intruded upon in her own home they removed the man with no delay. (She may not have been as lucky if she had still been married.) Soon afterward, she went out and bought herself a gun and announced to her ex-husband that if he ever came near her again, she would not hesitate to use it. She meant it, and he knew it. She never saw him again.

This woman was lucky. She knew how to frighten her husband off and she took measures to do so. But other women may be terrified or repelled by the idea of owning a gun and issuing threats with it—and with good reason. What should they do? Fear may be the main motivation in such women's lives. "Very few people understand this kind of fear," says Pizzey. "It is the fear of knowing someone is searching for you and will beat you when he finds you. In the mind of someone who has been badly beaten, this fear blots out all reason. The man seems to be omnipotent."[8]

Thus a woman who is in physical fear for life and limb may find herself with no alternatives at all. Some people may criticize such a woman for too passively accepting her fate, but in *The Psychology of Sex Differences,* Maccoby and Jacklin have this to say about the relation between fear and passivity: "Fear is an arousal state, and although it may be confusing to link it with passivity, the possibility exists that females show immobilization and other 'passive' behavior primarily when they are afraid."[9] As we have seen, a battered woman may have good reason to become "immobilized" in the face of threat.

Aside from cold fear, women give other, more subtle reasons to explain why they stay with a violent man. These reasons are related to the social and cultural expectations we acquire concerning marriage.

Socially Determined Reasons

After fear, the answers women give to "Why stay?" range from "It's part of marriage" to "It's better than trying to raise the kids alone." The reason cited most often in the Gayford study was that the husband promised to reform. In most cases, such reasons do not even begin to explain why women risk continual physical danger in their own homes.

In *Woman's Fate,* a young woman in a consciousness-raising group speaks of her early childhood: "When I was eight, my father remarried. My new mother was decent, good, hardworking—an utterly standard person. She always meant extremely well with me and shielded me from some of my father's most brutal outbursts. . . . Anyone who challenged his macho-power was to be beaten." One day the young girl asked her stepmother why she put up with the father's violence. The older woman sighed and replied, "Claudia, that's the way men are. You just have to take it."[10] In this way, many women, along with many professional theorists and therapists, are brainwashed into believing that male aggression is innate and therefore inevitable. "You just have to take it."

A recently divorced mother of five spoke of the violence

she endured during her eighteen-year marriage: "Well-educated, well-to-do people don't discuss such things. I became a super cover-up artist. Shielding five children from the fact their father took swipes at their mother was easy compared to the elaborate excuses designed for friends." With exceptional candor this woman recalled her own reaction when a friend confided that *she* was a battered wife. Instead of empathizing, she was "appalled" and felt "pity" and "disgust" that her friend would continue to live with this man. "I couldn't allow myself the solace of confiding to her that I was a fellow sufferer. Perhaps pride stood in the way. My reaction to her disclosure merely reinforced my vow never to discuss my own situation with anyone."[11]

This woman evidently believed that anyone, including herself, who stuck around for such treatment was not deserving of sympathy. Therefore, instead of comforting her friend, she took the opportunity to strengthen her own resolve never to leave herself open to judgment by another. In this way a battered woman may spend more energy in keeping her secret and trying to salvage some self-respect than in trying to extricate herself from the trap.

Another woman, a mother of four, told me her rationale for staying: "Sometimes I would talk about leaving him, but I never really meant it. I knew I had to keep the family together. It wasn't as if there weren't any good times—there were lots of them too. And it wasn't as if he pounded on me all the time—just occasionally when things got to be too much for him. Besides, I listened to some of my married women friends. They weren't being beaten, but the things they went through—what happened to them—seemed even worse to me. In spite of our occasional fights, believe it or not, I had it a lot better than they did." This response is a common one and sounds eminently sane until one realizes that a woman may be risking permanent harm or even death in her "occasional fights" with her husband. In this context, the reasonable, soft-spoken rationale sounds like raving lunacy.

William Goode found that two human traits emerge during marital conflict which are at odds with the behavior of most animals: the unwillingness to submit and the unwillingness to escape.[12] When it is about to lose a battle, a wild animal either demonstrates submissive behavior which acts to inhibit the other's aggression or allows itself to be driven from the scene. Both alternatives serve the same function: they save the weaker animal's life. But, though she may be

81

temporarily intimidated by a demonstration of her husband's strength, a woman will not necessarily submit entirely to his will; nor will she necessarily run away, never to be seen again.

Thus, as Maccoby and Jacklin noted, the woman may respond to a threatening situation with passivity and, often with very good reason, do nothing at all. In suppressing her flee-or-submit instinct, however, she puts herself in a state of suspended animation in which no element of the situation can change. A woman who finds herself stalemated in this way is in great danger of losing all self-respect. To me this is one of the saddest, if not the most dangerous, consequences of the battered woman's plight. For only a woman with great inner strength and hope for the future will see her way clear once she finds herself trapped this badly. Self-respect is the source of inner strength; without it the woman is lost.

Sex-role conditioning by our society, as discussed in Chapter 4, is by no means limited to men. According to current cultural values, though a woman may have other interests and pursuits, her primary source of satisfaction is her marriage. If a woman accepts this premise, she will take great pride in a good marriage, and often take full responsibility for a bad one. Her sense of responsibility will lead her to feel ashamed if her marriage "fails," and she will try above all else to save face.

"I didn't think I had the right to talk about it," one battered woman told me. "You just didn't let anyone else know about anything like that. There had never been a divorce in our family. No one ever admitted that there was anything wrong in their marriage." This woman felt compelled to add another perfect marriage to the line—her family expected it of her, and she expected it of herself. It is no wonder that she not only suffered her beatings in silence, but also tried to convince herself that everything was all right. Against great odds, a woman in this situation will excuse her husband's violence, calling it a momentary outburst. Or, if she cannot escape the fact that he has been repeatedly violent, she will try hard to believe that he will change.

Women in our culture are encouraged to believe that the failure of a marriage represents their failure as women. Many believe that marriage gives their lives meaning, that they have no value as individuals apart from their men. A woman who believes that she has no value will not have the will to take responsibility for herself. She will be paralyzed when it comes to making a radical change for her own sake, rather than for the sake of the marriage, even though that marriage is a living hell. From time to time she may have a friendly exchange with her husband. At these times she might convince herself that hope exists and that her husband will see the light and change his behavior. Many wives live from one of these good moments to the next, doing their best in between to suppress the knowledge of their husband's cruelty and their own crippling passivity.

Another common rationalization for staying that results from the conventional understanding of marriage is the "oh-but-he-needs-me" syndrome. A woman who takes her role as nurturer very seriously will probably believe—as she has been conditioned to believe—that she is not "complete" unless she is caring for another person. She may easily conclude that the more violent her husband is, the sicker he really is and thus the more he needs her. She has been taught that her role in life is to care for her man; she has promised to stick by him in sickness and in health. She can try to convince him to see a doctor or to seek counseling. If he refuses and continues to express his sickness by beating her to a pulp, her sense of responsibility for his well-being is only increased. This rationalization forms its own tight little circle of logic: The more he beats me the sicker he is; the sicker he is the more he needs me. In some cases, alas, the circle is closed with "the more he needs me the more I love him"—a peculiar but very common permutation of marital affection.

In each of these rationalizations, the key factor is guilt. Feelings of guilt are the monitors of behavior in our culture; they act as abstract forms of punishment. Rather than having our hands slapped or being thrown in jail, we are taught to feel unworthy, inadequate, even worthless for misbehaving or failing to meet the expectations of family and society.

Since the role of wife is central in a society built around the nuclear family, the dos and don'ts, shoulds and shouldn'ts defining the wifely role are very explicit. Schools, churches, clubs, parent organizations, books, magazines, movies, television, newspapers—are all sources of conditioning that reinforce our attitudes as to how a "good wife" should behave. A woman has plenty of opportunity to feel guilty if she does not conform to the socially approved version of "wife." If things go wrong, well-trained wives feel ashamed for having failed their husbands in some way. They may even believe they deserve their beatings. Attempting to improve, but failing to end the beatings, they sink further and further into despair and misery. When such women do seek outside help and, as is usually the case, do not receive it, their circumstances begin to seem utterly hopeless. They feel trapped and regard attempts at freeing themselves as futile.

As a sidenote to this situation of ever-increasing futility, Fowler reports that a woman will rarely seek help after the first incident of violence in her marriage. She is more liable to express her anger and hurt to her husband after the episode and let it go at that. But trying to reach the husband at that point is useless and may even be counterproductive, Fowler contends. The wife tells him how hurt she is at a time when he too is feeling guilty and is already full of remorse. "Her husband is psychologically groveling. He's not on a rational level where a discussion of the event will have positive effects in the future. He may, in fact, hold his wife's display of emotion against her after the remorse period is over."[13] Thus, even a wife who is psychologically prepared to discuss the problem and perhaps work out some solution may face a partner whose understanding of his own behavior is clouded by remorse. From this point of view, the marriage becomes a prison for both partners—each trapped by their own private feelings of guilt.

The Facts of Life

If a battered woman does manage to hold on to her self-respect, other factors may be keeping her home. Very often the battered wife's sense of futility is related to the state of her pocketbook. More than likely it is empty, or nearly so. Even if she has a place to go (a separate problem, to be discussed in Chapter 7), she may not have the money to get there. Housework, after all, pays in room and board only; and a man who beats his wife is not likely to provide her with spending money. I have found that violent husbands generally handle all the money; sometimes they even do the grocery shopping themselves. Wives of affluent husbands may have access to charge accounts, but seldom to checking accounts. And Eisenberg and Micklow report that in some cases the husband takes the car keys and money whenever he leaves the house.[14]

Abigail Van Buren, who writes the syndicated newspaper column "Dear Abby," has printed a number of letters which describe that "trapped" feeling. One woman wrote: "My husband doesn't think I need to leave the house. He doesn't even let me go to church because he doesn't care to go. I can't belong to any clubs or organizations because my husband thinks a woman's place is in the home and no place else. He wouldn't even let me join the PTA, and our two oldest boys are so ashamed because their teacher has never met me. We don't socialize with anybody because my husband says we don't need friends. The only time I get out of the house is when we go marketing together once a week. He handles all the money. We get into quarrels every time I say I want to go somewhere. Both our families are far away. When I ask him to please sit down and talk things over, he says there is nothing to talk about. If I talk back to him, I end up with a busted mouth, a black eye, and bruises. I mentioned divorce once and he beat me up so bad I could hardly get out of bed for two days. Abby, I can't take the boys and leave because I don't drive, and I don't have five dollars to my name."[15]

One woman in the Eisenberg-Micklow study managed to save $1.75 over a two-year period! Adding that to the five dollars her grandmother sent her for Christmas, she had just enough money to buy bus tickets for herself and her young daughter.[16]

Another woman summarized the situation when she told a newspaper reporter why she continued to live with her violent husband: "Where would I go? My college education was interrupted to marry and have a large family. I was a suburban housewife, a wife of a successful businessman and well versed in entertaining and dressing to fit the right occasion. None of these qualities are particularly sought on the job market. In Texas child support is the only thing offered the divorcée. At age thirty-six one does not run home to Mother and Dad, especially with five children in tow. So the trap is built—stay in the marriage, make the best of it and gradually lose not only your identity but your self-respect."[17] Wives of wealthy husbands may live in luxurious homes, but they are usually no better off financially than women whose husbands earn less. These women do not necessarily have access to ready cash, and they may be totally unprepared to live alone and support their children.

But not all wives are wholly dependent upon their husbands. Some work to augment the family income, and in some cases the wife may actually be the primary breadwinner in the household. Why would a woman who has a source of income put up with beatings from the man she supports? A friend told me of such a case: A woman in Iowa had seven children and was the breadwinner in her family. On pay day her husband would be right there to collect her check, a good portion of which he spent on booze and other women. He beat her up habitually. She would often show up at her factory job with her eyes blackened and her mouth cut. She had married right out of high school, and at thirty she looked like a woman in her late fifties—her hair was gray and she had deep dark circles under her eyes. My friend, a co-worker, asked her why she stayed with a husband who treated her so badly, particularly since she was the wage earner. She answered, "I wouldn't know what to do with seven children all by myself; the kids need him, and so do I."

To me this woman's answer is a particularly poignant expression of the lack of self-confidence and imagination common to women who have resigned themselves to living out their failed marriages. Admittedly, a woman with no money needs great determination, even great courage, to leave a marriage and make a new life for herself. But a woman with her *own* money! What can she be thinking when she says she *needs* a man who takes her money and her will? What can she be thinking when she says her children need a father who not only exploits but beats his wife?

The fact is, she may not be thinking for herself at all. Such a woman is probably operating within the confining stereotypes reinforced by our culture; she may be unable to imagine herself in another role. The few approved roles that women are allowed to play in this society are for the most part limiting and narrow. A woman's value is almost always judged with reference to her marriage, and as discussed earlier, she learns to judge herself in this way.

Granted, women's roles are changing. In cosmopolitan areas of the country where the women's movement finds its fullest expression, single women, gay women, divorced women, and single mothers are establishing new values for living on their own. The idea that remaining single or divorcing represents failure is fading. Society is slowly beginning to acknowledge that these women have great potential for living full and satisfying lives. Still, the change is not happening quickly enough or penetrating the nation deeply enough to help women who have long ago given up hope. Only by bringing the buried problems of wife-beating and financial exploitation into the open can we begin to inspire the imaginations of those women who silently wait out their time as scapegoats in violent marriages.

6

THE FAILURE OF THE LEGAL SYSTEM

The Laws a Wife-Beater Breaks

When people suffer pain at the hands of others, when their right to the pursuit of happiness is interfered with by others, society at large is responsible for meeting the needs of the oppressed group. These responsibilities are implied by the Bill of Rights. Ostensibly, our society does offer protection against bodily harm and deprivation of freedom, but in reality, the law, or its application, becomes very ambiguous when the parties involved are husband and wife. The sanctity of the family home pervades the world of law enforcement. A man's home is his castle, and police, district attorneys, and judges hesitate to interfere with what goes on behind that tightly closed door.

Citizens rarely understand the subtleties of the laws that affect them. They generally know that assault and battery are crimes against persons, and that laws do exist to protect people from these crimes. Most people expect that should they be victimized by another's violent behavior, the law will be enforced on their behalf. It is true that laws exist for defining what constitutes bodily harm, establishing legal defense against charges of causing bodily harm, and meting out fair punishment to someone convicted of inflicting bodily harm on another. These laws are invoked almost automatically when one person beats up another—provided the two are not bound together by a marriage contract. In this chapter I will speculate as to the reasons why the laws are *not* automatically invoked in cases of wife-beating. First, though, it will be useful to consider the crimes a wife-beater most often commits when he abuses his wife. They include assault and/or battery, aggravated assault, intent to assault or to commit murder, and, in cases where the woman is coerced sexually, rape. Laws specifically against wife-abuse, and the relevance of civil law to wife-beating are discussed in later sections of this chapter.

The sources of laws as well as their application differ from state to state. In California, among other states, assault and battery are defined by the penal code: "An assault is an unlawful attempt, coupled with a present ability, to commit a violent injury on the person of another." [whereas] "A battery is any willful and unlawful use of force or violence upon the person of another." [and] "Every person who commits an assault upon the person of another with a deadly weapon or instrument or by any means of force likely to produce great bodily injury is punishable by imprisonment in the state prison for six months to life, or in a county jail not exceeding one year, or by a fine not exceeding five thousand dollars ($5,000), or by both such fine and imprisonment."[1]

Some states do not specifically define assault and battery, but merely fix the punishment. In this situation, case law actually defines the crimes. By case law, in Michigan, for instance, an act is deemed an assault when any injury whatsoever, no matter how slight, is actually inflicted on another person in "an angry, revengeful, rude or insolent manner." If no injury occurs, the act is a simple assault; if physical injury results, the offense is assault and battery. The only recognized legal defense against assault in Michigan is self-defense—the contention that the defendant was in imminent danger and that this danger was the motive for the act. Voluntary intoxication is not an admissible defense against the charge of assault and battery. Nor can obscene or insulting language justify an assault.[2]

Self-defense is the most common legal defense to assault (and battery), but other states do allow a defendant to plead insanity or voluntary intoxication. The latter, in many jurisdictions, serves as a partial defense to any crime where *intent* must be established. The theory is that intoxication negates the necessary intent, a factor which Gelles disputes, if you recall in Chapter 4, when he says that many batterers drink to give themselves an alibi for their violent actions.

Laws prohibiting assault and battery, whether defined in

the penal code or by court decisions, exist in every jurisdiction in the nation. These crimes are always misdemeanors punishable by incarceration in the county jail. "Aggravated assault" is assault that results in great or grievous bodily harm. It is more serious than simple assault, and by virtue of the punishment involved, it is always a felony. Conviction of a felony usually calls for a sentence to the state penitentiary. Other laws applicable to wife-beating involve possession of a deadly weapon with intent to assault, whether or not actual harm is sustained. These laws are invoked in cases involving threatening behavior. Intent to commit murder, a felony, is obviously a more difficult charge to prove.

American law does not recognize the crime of rape within marriage. As a matter of fact, many rape statutes explicitly exclude rape within marriage. Therefore, married women who have been attacked both sexually and physically by their husbands can only bring assault and battery charges against them. A case in New Jersey currently pending trial may reverse this situation, however.[3] At the behest of Prosecutor Joseph P. Lordi, the Essex County Grand Jury recently indicted a man for raping his estranged wife. If this man is found guilty, a precedent could be established for acknowledging that rape can occur within marriage, and that a husband can be prosecuted on the charge of raping his wife.

The defendant in this case was charged with rape, assault, illegal entry (having been previously ordered to stay away from his wife), and impairing the morals of his children (having allegedly forced the young children to watch as he beat and raped their mother). When the original charges were brought, the judge refused to refer the matter to the Grand Jury. He based his decision on the common law tradition that a husband has an absolute right to have sexual relations with his wife.

Prosecutor Lordi opposed the judge's decision. He took the position that a "wife is an independent spirit, not the chattel of her husband," and that a husband "should be held responsible for his criminal acts whether they involve a wife or a third person." Lordi said he was attempting "to get a definitive court ruling as to whether or not such an act as charged here will be regarded as a violation of the rape statute." This case offers hope, but the system of appealing existing laws and legal precedents is slow and cumbersome. A definitive ruling in this case could take years. In the meantime, women are not protected by rape statutes when they are married to their assailants.

Arrest Procedures

Conditions for arrest are also determined by law or legal precedent. Usually, in misdemeanor cases a police officer can only make an arrest on the spot if the act is committed in his presence or if a warrant has been issued. As to the first condition, police rarely witness acts of marital violence; they are usually called to the scene after the fact. And in order for a warrant to be issued, the victim must make a trip to the district attorney's office to file a written complaint. This procedure, fraught with its own complications, will be discussed separately under the heading "The District Attorney's Office."

When a felony has been committed, an officer is authorized to make an arrest on "reasonable belief" or "probable cause"; that is, if he has sufficient reason to believe that a felony has been committed and that the person identified by the victim or witnesses committed the crime. But this provision, being the most subjective and also the easiest to ignore, is rarely invoked in wife-abuse cases. Alix Foster, an attorney with the Seattle Legal Services Center, cites the right of police in Washington state to arrest on "probable cause" for certain misdemeanors. She wrote, "My experience with this statute is that, while it exists on the books, the police either do not know about it or refuse to exercise this power."[4]

The wife/victim who wants her husband taken into custody does have one other option. She can make the arrest herself—that is, she can make a citizen's arrest. With this procedure, she is responsible in the event of a later charge of false arrest. Unfortunately, police are not always in the habit of informing battered women of their right to make a citizen's arrest. If a woman is aware of this right and chooses to exercise it, police will often try to discourage her from doing so. (For this reason, Daly City Legal Services in California supply potential or previous victims of marital violence with the form to be completed for a citizen's arrest. This enlightened practice insures that at the very least the victim will know of her right to make such an arrest.[5])

Citizen's arrest is further complicated in some states by

the requirement that the accuser take *physical* custody of
the accused and deliver him or her over to the police. Considering the obvious fact that men generally outweigh wom-
en and are usually stronger as well, expecting the woman
to take her attacker into physical custody is tantamount to
preventing the arrest. If she could handle him, she probably would not need to call the police in the first place.

Susan Jackson dealt with the problems of citizen's liability and physical custody in citizen's arrest situations in a
report on marital violence to the Women's Litigation Unit
of the San Francisco Neighborhood Legal Assistance Foundation. She cited *People* v. *Campbell* in which a citizen observed an attack, pulled the attacker off the victim, and
then merely pointed the attacker out to the police who
then took physical custody. The court held that these actions constituted a legitimate citizen's arrest, even though
the citizen neither physically delivered the accused to the
police, nor told the accused that he was under arrest. Jackson concluded, therefore, that a wife/victim should only be
required to verify the offense, point out her attacker to the
police, and say she wants to make an arrest. The police
should then take him into custody.[6]

At a public hearing in San Francisco, Jackson referred to
a California statute that makes a patrol officer's failure to
act upon a citizen's arrest a crime. She suggested that "discouraging" citizen's arrest would be covered under this
statute, and that police officers could and should be prosecuted under it. And in a statement before the city's Police
Commission, Jackson insisted that police should be required
to inform all victims of their right to make a citizen's arrest.

Elizabeth Truninger suggests that if a woman is reluctant
to make a citizen's arrest, she might make the charge of
"disturbing the peace." Disturbing the peace applies to
conduct such as threatening, quarreling, fighting, or even
using "vulgar, profane, or indecent language within the
presence or hearing of women or children, in a loud and
boisterous manner."[7] Since this crime occurs in the presence
of police officers more frequently than instances of wife-
abuse do, arrest on this charge is, theoretically at least,
more likely.

Police action is often designed to protect the department
rather than the victim. For example, attorney Alix Foster
told me that the Seattle police do encourage women to
make citizen's arrests, but not necessarily for the purpose

of bringing the man to justice. "In that way," Foster explained, "if ever an action for false arrest is brought, the police are immune from liability. The man would have to sue the woman." But Susan Jackson claims, with reference to this possibility, that "[p]olice arguments that wives can be liable for a false citizen's arrest are disingenuous, since it is highly unlikely that the wife will be mistaken as to her attacker's identity or as to the crime which has been committed against her."[8] If her arrest is made in bad faith, however, then Jackson agrees that the husband would have the right to sue her and not the police. In such a case the wife would certainly deserve to be sued.

Police Policy and Practice

"Crisis is the domain of the police. . . . Immediate response is the *mode* of the police. Instant communication and highly mobile response capability are technologically more sophisticated than in any other existing human service system."[9] This self-congratulating statement is made in a police training guide, *The Function of the Police in Crisis Intervention and Conflict Management,* prepared for the United States Department of Justice's Law Enforcement Assistance Administration.

The police department is the only public agency readily accessible on a twenty-four-hour basis in times of crisis. When a battered woman calls the police, she expects an immediate response. But many police departments give domestic disturbance calls low priority, taking anywhere from twenty minutes to several hours to respond, and sometimes not showing up at all. Furthermore, the most common complaint heard from wife/victims is that if and when police arrive on the scene, they rarely do anything at all. One explanation for this hands-off policy is to be found in the legal conditions for arrest already discussed. But, as might be expected by now, other more complex factors contribute to the problem.

The actions and attitudes of the police are major factors in wife-beating as a social problem. Those concerned with the battered woman's plight often assume that once the police are called, the matter is as good as settled. Rarely do they imagine that the police will be reluctant to act, often as a matter of policy. Such a case was described by Marjory Fields, an attorney who handles divorce matters for the South Brooklyn Legal Services Corporation.[10]

The first time Maria called the police, she had been left bruised and bleeding merely because she had asked her husband, who had just come home from work, what time he would like to have dinner. The police arrived and told Maria that she should try to settle her differences with her husband amicably. After they left, her husband beat her again. He also made it clear that if she ever called the police again he would strangle her. The next day Maria met Fields—a great stroke of luck for Maria—and started divorce proceedings. Because of the threat to her life, Fields gave Maria's case an emergency priority. With the help of the welfare department, she managed to move Maria and her three children into a new apartment and obtained the divorce as quickly as possible. It took five months, during which time the husband entered Maria's new home forcibly five times, on each occasion beating her up in front of the children. The police were called each time; on the *fifth* call they finally arrested the husband.

The procedure for handling domestic calls as detailed in the Police Training Academy in Michigan illustrates very well police reluctance to take any action in such cases:

a. Avoid arrest if possible. Appeal to their vanity.
b. Explain the procedure of obtaining a warrant.
   (1) Complainant must sign complaint.
   (2) Must appear in court.
   (3) Consider loss of time.
   (4) Cost of court.
c. State that your only interest is to prevent a breach of the peace.
d. Explain that attitudes usually change by court time.
e. Recommend a postponement.
   (1) Court not in session.
   (2) No judge available.
f. *Don't* be too harsh or critical.[11]

The non-arrest policy of the Oakland, California, Police Department is stated explicitly in its *Training Bulletin on Techniques of Dispute Intervention:* "The police role in a dispute situation is more often that of a mediator and peacemaker than enforcer of the law. In dispute situations, officers are often caught between an obligation to enforce the law on one hand and, on the other, the possibility that police action such as arrest will only aggravate the dispute or create a serious danger for the arresting officers due to possible efforts to resist arrest. Such a possibility is most likely when a husband or father is arrested in his home; he is upset in the first place, and if he is taken into custody in front of his family, desperate resistance can result to prevent loss of face. There are some situations when there is no reasonable alternative but to arrest, such as when a serious assault has been committed. Normally, officers should adhere to the policy that arrests shall be avoided except as necessary to (1) protect life and property and (2) preserve the peace. [Later the manual states,] . . . when no serious crime has been committed but one of the parties demands arrest, you should attempt to explain the ramifications of such action (e.g., loss of wages, bail procedures, court appearances) and encourage the parties to reason with each other."[12] It is hard to imagine another situation in which police would be officially advised to encourage a victim to "reason" with an attacker.

Encouraging people to refrain from exercising their rights could be interpreted as denying them their rights, but the usual rationale police give for discouraging arrest is that they prefer not to interfere in "domestic squabbles." They gain their point by declaring that the husband, if arrested, could be out on bail or on his own recognizance (allowed in some jurisdictions in lieu of bail) in a matter of hours and return to take vengeance on his wife. And, they argue, generally the wife drops the charges anyway, and refuses to follow through with the prosecution. These developments may occur at times, though Carol Murray, former director of the San Francisco Neighborhood Legal Assistance Foundation's Domestic Relations Unit, claims she has never seen any "statistics to indicate that women prosecuting their husbands for violence fail to proceed in greater numbers than do any other variety of prosecuting witness." Murray continues, "I would suggest that a failure or reluctance to give evidence is present in any case where only one party is available to offer incriminating testimony."[13] In any event, it is in no way the function of the police department to give legal advice or make decisions based on what might happen.

In their article "Wife-Beating: Crime and No Punishment," *Seattle Times* reporters Susan Schwartz and Dale Douglas Mills suggest that the police make their own unwritten law by misinterpretation and misrepresentation. One

Seattle patrolman told them of stopping a woman when she started to pull up her blouse to show him her bruises.[14] Her action would have provided evidence for arrest on probable cause; he preferred to try to calm both the husband and wife down and get them to "make peace."

The legal advice police give frightened victims is sometimes wrong and can be downright harmful, Schwartz and Mills contend. They tell of a woman who had fled through a window with her baby and taken refuge in a nearby restaurant because the man she had lived with had been throwing rocks through the windows and threatening to kill her. This woman was told by a patrolman that he could not take a report on the incident because it was Sunday. She would have to go downtown on Monday to file a complaint—an outright lie, presumably designed to discourage the woman from taking action.

Eisenberg and Micklow cite an example from Wayne County, Michigan, in which a wife called the police because her husband was breaking up the furniture. "Well," replied an officer, "it's his house, his furniture, it's his community property. He can do whatever he wants to it. If he wants to, he can burn it; it's his just as well as yours." The police then left the scene, but they were called back a short while later to find a huge bonfire on the front lawn. The husband had evidently taken the officer at his word![15]

A woman in London told me a story on the same theme. Her estranged husband, ostensibly on a visit with the children, went on a rampage, slashing her clothes and furniture and breaking all her dishes. Police told her that they could do nothing, the reason being that because their divorce was not final and no property settlement had been made, all the woman's belongings really belonged to her husband, who had a right to destroy them if he wished to. This woman was working at two jobs in order to make ends meet and provide for her children. Replacing the necessities her husband destroyed was a hardship for her. It was particularly disheartening knowing she had no recourse should he decide to destroy her things again.

"Police often refuse to make an official report of a complaint made on account of abuse. 'Oh, ma'am, it won't be so bad; your husband isn't such a raving maniac. Come on, I'll take you home.' Or: 'Look, if we got involved with this kind of thing, we wouldn't be able to handle all the cases we'd get. This is a marital argument and in such cases the police are powerless.' An obviously injured woman was sent home: 'He's asleep now anyway, and by tomorrow he'll have calmed down again.' Police often advise a woman not to file a complaint: 'Ma'am, if you do that, you'll never survive it.' Abuse is punishable. On paper."[16]

These reactions are typical of American police, but this quote was taken from an article published in Holland and refers to the Amsterdam police. The reluctance of police to interfere in "family spats" is not a purely American phenomenon. Women from all over the world complain of police inaction, except perhaps where refuges have been established for battered wives.

Spokespersons for shelters are consistent in reporting that police are generally cooperative when accompanying a woman to the refuge. Officers stand by while she gathers her personal belongings together, transport her to the refuge, and provide protection for the facility itself. Police are evidently more certain of their role once the woman has made a decision to leave home. Emphasis shifts from criminal action, which police refuse to recognize as viable, to protection of the woman and children—a more passive function involving less risk.

The preference for non-action no doubt takes many forms and appears in many guises. In a case described to me by a female San Francisco probation officer, it took the form of fraternal loyalty. She had a man jailed for violating the terms of his probation—he had beaten his wife. The man, an ex-taxi driver, was known to the police, and some officers were outraged when he was incarcerated. The probation officer actually received several phone calls from police officers who asked, "Why are you doing this?" and exclaiming, "You are the only one doing this!"

Presumably, the non-action policy protects police against the risks of liability for false arrest and physical danger to interfering officers. But battered women and their attorneys tend to believe that the reluctance to arrest can be attributed to subtle personal reasons. Alix Foster expressed a common suspicion when she summed up for me her experience in marital violence cases: "It seems as if they never arrest the man, that they never exercise the power given to them when the woman is the complainant. It seems to bolster the view that women are hysterical and not to be trusted!"

Police officers are usually male; therefore, they identify more readily with the husband than with the female victim. The officer is apt to consider a battered wife "hysterical" and give more credence to the husband's "reasonable" account of what happened. Police almost never have sufficient training to fully comprehend the plight of the abused woman. They are not encouraged to perceive the trauma she suffers, the probability that she will be threatened and injured again, and her inability to escape on her own due to financial dependency. The officer may truly believe that the disputants can and should patch things up, but the stress on non-arrest mediation is thoroughly unsatisfactory for the victim. "Not only does it minimize the seriousness of the husband's actions and misstate the law, but also it effectively traps the wife with children in the home," states Elizabeth Truninger.[17] Considering the number of domestic disturbance calls the police receive, one might conclude that though the police cannot avoid perceiving the gravity of the problem, they simply do not know what to do.

Commander James D. Bannon has been a member of the Detroit Police Department since 1949; he is currently working for his doctorate in sociology at Wayne State University. Bannon has begun to speak out publicly against non-action policies.[18] He not only believes that police have problems with "intra-family violence," but also declares forthrightly that police contribute to the violence. "Those of us in law enforcement, who are the first official representatives of government to respond to violence in the home, are socialized in precisely the same manner as the citizens we are expected to protect," Bannon says. "Policemen, as are most males, are taught self-reliance and the 'fight your own battles' philosophy from the cradle. Similarly, we are socialized into the conscious perceptions of masculine-feminine roles. In our society this translates into dominance-submission terms. The man is the boss, the owner; the female the subordinate."

The attitudes Bannon describes develop naturally into a laissez-faire policy. Women can hardly expect protection from men who consider domestic violence to be a personal matter. "In Detroit, as in many other cities," Bannon asserts, "the treatment of female victims of assault of the domestic variety could charitably be termed cavalier. Not so charitable, but perhaps more accurate, would be an allegation of misfeasance."

Bannon cites Detroit's police-call screening procedure as an example of police attitudes influencing policy. Some years ago, calls for police service exceeded the department's ability to respond. The decision was made not to bother with certain types of calls, and the first calls to be screened out were those on family troubles. Battered women actually had to resort to saying that their assailants had guns, even though they did not, in order to get police to respond. Eventually this tactic lost its effectiveness because of overuse. It had limited value anyway since the responding officer, on discovering the ruse, often left after an angry outburst and didn't even make a report. "His display of non-interest could be expected to instill in the aggressor a feeling of permissible, though limited, violence," says Bannon. "It seems that police agencies are inept in their efforts to successfully intervene in social conflict situations —they are adept, however, at homicide investigations. If our present attitudes continue, we will become increasingly good at homicide resolution."

Schwartz and Mills claim that in Seattle at least "there is a way for a woman to file criminal charges against an assailant without ever trying to convince police of her case, or without waiting for the prosecutor's decision." Three days a week between 10 and 11 A.M., a battered woman can go to a Seattle Municipal Court and describe her case to a judge who will decide then and there whether it is worth pursuing. The hitch is that wife/victims rarely find out about this method. In fact, the writers' own phone call to the police to check it out drew a blank. The clerk who took the phone call knew nothing about the court proceeding at all. Also, if the city prosecutor decides to drop a case, he rarely tells the complainant that she has this option.[19]

In the District of Columbia, as in some other jurisdictions, police have the authority to make a valid warrantless arrest on probable cause if they believe a person has committed an assault and may cause injury to others. Even so they adhere to the non-arrest policy in domestic cases, almost always referring battered women to the Citizen's Complaint Center, which is open from 9 A.M. to 10 P.M. Monday through Friday. Most wife-assaults occur in the middle of the night or on weekends, however, when the police are the only resource available for immediate protection.

In her unpublished paper on the situation in the District of Columbia, Lois Yankowski tells of a woman who spent the night in the bus station because she was afraid to go home. "Another refused to leave the police station and would not leave until the police threatened to arrest *her* for an unlawful entry. She had just filed a complaint against a man, her lover, who had broken down her door and threatened to kill her with a butcher knife, while a friend witnessed the incident. Previously he had kicked her and broken her back. The police went back to her apartment and found the man there but refused to arrest him. They referred her to the Citizen's Complaint Center."[20]

One final example illustrates the fact that the police have no real binding obligation to protect citizens in need. In 1972, a suit was pressed against the San Jose Police Department on behalf of the estate of Ruth L. Bunnell for wrongful death due to police negligence.[21] On September 4, 1972, Ruth Bunnell telephoned the police to report that her estranged husband had called her, saying that he was coming to her residence to kill her. She requested immediate police aid, and was refused; she was told to call the department again when Bunnell actually arrived. Approximately forty-five minutes later, Bunnell entered the woman's home and stabbed her. When police finally did arrive, in response to a neighbor's call, Ruth Bunnell was dead.

During the year prior to her death, this woman had called the police at least twenty times to complain that her ex-husband was committing violent acts against her and her two daughters, and on one occasion Bunnell was arrested for assault. John Hartzell, the executor for Mrs. Bunnell's estate, filed suit against the San Jose Police Department—despite the fact that the California Tort Claims Act specifically bars claims "for failure to provide sufficient police protection service." Hartzell claimed that the police should have been able to assess the very real danger to Mrs. Bunnell based on their knowledge of her past history, and that their failure to make that assessment constituted negligence. The lower court dismissed the case. The California Court of Appeals affirmed the dismissal stating that there was no indication that "the police had induced decedent's reliance on a promise, express or implied, that they would provide her with protection. . . ." Mrs. Bunnell found out the hard way that the police had no obligation to protect her and that her reliance on them was in no way based on a promise to protect.

Wife-Abuse Laws

Buried in a mountain of dusty legal machinery are laws which specifically prohibit child- and wife-abuse. In her article "Marital Violence: The Legal Solutions," Truninger cites the 1945 California statute: "Any husband who will-fully inflicts upon his wife corporal injury resulting in a traumatic condition, and any person who willfully inflicts upon any child any cruel and inhuman corporal punishment or injury resulting in a traumatic condition, is guilty of a felony, and upon conviction thereof shall be punished by imprisonment in the state prison for not more than 10 years or in the county jail for not more than one year."[22] Since the offense specified in this law is a felony, the police may make an arrest even if the violence is not committed in their presence.

In order for a defendant to be convicted on this law, the degree of violence must conform to legal definitions of "corporal injury" and "traumatic condition." According to Truninger, "corporal injury" is the "touching of the person of another against his [her] will with physical force in an intentional, hostile and aggravated manner, or projecting of such force against his [her] person." A "traumatic condition" is an "abnormal condition of the living body produced by violence as distinguished from that produced by poisons, zymotic infection, bad habits, and other less evident causes . . . the word generally implying physical force." In short, harm to the victim must be greater than simple assault, but less than aggravated assault.

Because California's wife-abuse law describes a felony, and because it requires proof of corporal injury resulting from a traumatic condition, application of the law on behalf of battered wives is very difficult. Police and district attorneys are usually unwilling to charge an assailant with a felony because of the higher bail and longer jail sentence involved. The husband is more likely to contest a felony because of the heavy penalties, and there is a greater chance all around that the charge will be dropped. But even if the case does go to trial, the wife may have great difficulty producing witnesses and the necessary medical proof of injury.

San Jose Superior Court Judge Eugene Premo dismissed a charge made under this law against a husband in 1975 because, he charged, the California wife-abuse law discriminates on the basis of sex and is therefore unconstitutional. In his memorandum, Premo noted that the statute makes conviction a felony; a husband found guilty of break-ing this law would be subject to a term in the state prison. "A wife, however, inflicting the same injury and trauma can be subjected to no more than misdemeanor prosecution under assault and battery sections." In other words, no equivalent law exists making husband-beating a felony.[23]

I fully support the concept of equal rights and equal penalties under the law, but Judge Premo's decision is in itself a blatant demonstration of discrimination based on sex. It takes advantage of the existing male bias within the criminal justice system and denies the value of laws created to correct existing imbalances. Even more galling is that sexism—the underlying *cause* of marital violence—was cited as the means by which this assailant/husband escaped prosecution. At the present time, hundreds, if not thousands, of laws exist that clearly discriminate against women, but in countless cases the courts have not seen fit to declare them unconstitutional under the provisions of the Fourteenth Amendment to the United States Constitution. For this reason women fought for almost fifty years to get Congress to pass the Equal Rights Amendment, which simply states, "Equality of rights under the law shall not be denied or abridged by the United States or by any State on account of sex." As of this writing the Equal Rights Amendment still needs ratification by four more states before it becomes the law of the land.

Civil Law

Although assault is a crime, practically speaking most of the remedies open to the wife/victim fall under the civil law. All branches of the criminal justice system are influenced by the "family" nature of wife-abuse. Generally, therefore, district attorneys and judges prefer not to press criminal charges. In the state of New York for instance, even though a battered wife has the right to file a complaint in Criminal Court, obtain a warrant, and have her husband arrested, her case will almost certainly be transferred to Family Court, which has exclusive jurisdiction over such cases. In Family Court, the most a woman can hope for is that an injunction or an "order of protection" will be issued against her husband. Rarely will a Family Court judge decide that a case before him should be tried in Criminal Court.

Most states, whether the case is heard in Family Court or not, have provisions for court injunctions or orders of protection. A restraining order, the most common type of protection order, is issued by the judge who decides there is cause after hearing evidence of the husband's threatened or repeated acts of violence. The order, which is good for a specified period of time, "theoretically requires the husband to stay away from his wife or simply to abstain from the offensive conduct," says Emily Jane Goodman, New York attorney.[24] The order may also instruct him to remove himself completely from the family home. Usually a restraining order is issued only after a divorce suit has been filed. When a husband disobeys the judge's order he can be cited for contempt of court, a misdemeanor.

Another type of protection order is the peace bond. After hearing the evidence a judge may issue a warrant, and if the information is substantiated at a court hearing, order the husband to post not more than $5,000 as "security to keep the peace." If the husband fails to post an ordered bond, he is committed to prison and the judge may make payment of the security a condition for release. Also, the undertaking is considered broken and the money is forfeited if the husband is convicted of a breach of the peace.[25]

Peace bonds are the means used most frequently to control domestic violence in Illinois and New York. Nevertheless, many attorneys agree that peace bonds violate constitutional rights, though as yet no appeals challenging the legality of the peace bond have been filed. Truninger explains that several objections obtain but the most serious is that the conditions of the peace bond can violate the right to equal protection under the law. An indigent who is unable to provide the bond will go to jail, even though inability to pay a peace bond is not a crime, whereas the person who can provide a peace bond is not subject to such imprisonment. Clearly, the poor man's right to equal protection is denied.[26] Also, Susan Jackson points out that placing a person in prison for failure to pay a debt is a violation of the Thirteenth Amendment to the Constitution, which expressly prohibits states and individuals from practicing involuntary servitude.[27] Furthermore, the peace bond subjects a person to double jeopardy, since conviction for breach of the peace is regarded as conclusive evidence of a violation of the security provision.[28] In such case the offender forfeits the bond *and* is also imprisoned. Another civil remedy, open to wives in some states at least, lies in the woman's right to sue her husband for damages. This right to tort action is sometimes denied because of the common law doctrine that recognizes husband and wife as a single legal entity, thus affording them "interspousal immunity." But Eisenberg and Micklow say that at present eight states allow husband and wife to sue each other and only six states actually prohibit interspousal suits by statute.[29]

In California, the State Supreme Court denied the legality of interspousal immunity and opened the way to tort action between spouses by reversing a lower court's decision that tort action "would destroy the peace and harmony of the home." Justice Peters, who wrote the opinion, wondered how "peace and harmony" could be maintained if the only legal action to which a wife had recourse was to bring criminal charges against her husband.[30] I would make the additional point that after a man has beaten his wife little peace and harmony remain to be disturbed!

I bring up tort action as a possible avenue of redress here not primarily as a means of obtaining justice, but on the outside chance that the court might grant a wife monetary damages for the physical injury and emotional distress she suffers at the hands of a violent husband. Since many women claim they cannot leave their brutal husbands because they have no money, such an award might provide the means by which such women could begin life on their own.

On the surface, civil procedures may seem well-suited to the needs of battered women, but as the following sections will show, these remedies do not really address the problem and usually work against the woman's interests. The main goal of Family Court, for instance, is that old familiar refrain, reconciliation. And although protection orders are commonly issued against violent husbands, enforcement is practically nonexistent. Conflicts also arise over arrest procedures when court orders are violated, and questions of "equal protection" come into play as well. Taken together, these factors spell delay or inaction. They either discourage a woman from proceeding with her case or nullify the protective function of the procedures she is forced to rely on.

Family Court

In 1962, wife-abuse cases in New York were transferred from the jurisdiction of Criminal Court to that of Family Court by an act of the state legislature. When a case comes before Family Court civil procedures apply. On the wife's complaint a protection order might be issued. The husband never faces the harsh penalties he would suffer if found guilty in Criminal Court for assaulting a stranger. "The

Family Court Act is not geared with punishment as a primary objective," says Justice Joseph B. Williams, administrative judge of New York City's Family Court. "We're trying to stabilize the family."[31] Clearly the aims of the Criminal and Family Courts differ sharply. In New York, a woman seeking protection or trying to escape from her violent husband is forced to rely on a system intent upon "stabilizing" her family.

According to attorney Emily Jane Goodman, "Family Court cannot remand the husband to jail for the 'original misbehavior,' but only for willful violation of its own order." She deplores the fact that the legislature, police, and judges do not deal with wife-beating as a crime, but as a problem encountered in a "troubled marriage."[32] This view of the matter is confirmed by Judge Liston F. Coon, who has served in both the County Court and the Family Court. In his opinion, "the procedure in Family Court is entirely inappropriate for the handling of felony assaults. In fact, the lack of adequate penal sanctions make many simple assault cases more appropriate for prosecution in criminal courts."[33]

In a paper on wife-beating and the law in New York, E. Lehman states: "It would appear that Family Court is designed to protect the family assailant rather than the family victim. The female petitioner's treatment in court is not equal to the treatment received by the male respondent." Whereas the husband may have the benefit of legal counsel, the wife is on her own. In practice, the probation department, rather than someone trained in the law, has the power to decide whether jurisdiction exists, Lehman says. "The petitioner has probably waited between three and six months to receive the court's last word on her problem. She has had to fulfill evidentiary requirements without benefit of counsel. She has had to listen to court clerks and probation officers try to convince her to file a support petition rather than a family offense petition. Throughout this experience she has had to rely solely on her own resources and has probably reached the same conclusion that everyone else reaches about Family Court: it doesn't work."[34]

Protection Orders

The police often advise an abused wife to apply for a restraining order to be served on the violent husband. The procedure for obtaining the order is complex and expensive, and once the order is obtained its value is questionable, to say the least. A restraining order can be acquired only after the victim has retained an attorney and paid costs for filing, unless she qualifies for Legal Aid. Filling out questionnaires, filing petitions, and anticipating court hearings are nerve-wracking ordeals in themselves. The woman may decide to abandon the whole thing once she finds out what is involved.

The prepared petitions must be filed with the court. If the order for the husband to appear in court is granted, and if the woman does not qualify for Legal Aid, she must pay for the personal service of this order on her husband. The order must be served at least ten days before the date set for the hearing. The woman must then testify at the hearing to show cause—that is, to explain why the restraining order should be granted. These steps must be taken while the husband is still under no restraint and may be living under the same roof with the complainant.

Once the restraining order is granted, what can the woman do with it? "So she waves a piece of paper in his face and he thumps on her anyway," a Legal Services attorney said to Schwartz and Mills.[35] If the husband threatens her again and she calls the police, they will tell her they can do nothing until he actually hurts her. If he does injure her, the police are likely to tell her that because the husband is under the restraining order, the matter is now civil, not criminal, and thus out of their jurisdiction. She will be advised to see her attorney and institute contempt proceedings.

Since instituting contempt proceedings is also a civil procedure, the wife must file *another* petition with the court to obtain *another* order for her husband to appear in court. And again, if granted the order must be served on the man (and paid for by the woman). At least another ten days will lapse before the court hearing, since the order to appear must be served ten days before, but court calendars being as congested as they are, even more delay is probable. If the husband is found to be in contempt, and if it is his first violation, he will probaby be warned but not sentenced. If he does not appear at all, a body warrant may be issued and another court date set. And round and round it goes.

Whether or not the restraining order really transforms a wife-abuse case into a civil case is a matter of controversy. Some argue that since the restraining order restrains conduct which is probably illegal anyway, police should be expected and required to enforce the law irrespective of the court order. Susan Jackson says one advantage is that the restraining order "partially nullifies California community property law and theoretically, at least, allows a police officer to arrest a husband for simply entering the family home." But if police did arrest when cause existed in the first place, restraining orders would not be necessary. Again we come up against the original problem—the reluctance of police to arrest a husband for an offense against his wife.

A public debate on the civil-criminal aspects of the issue and the role of police in enforcing restraining orders took place in Sacramento in 1972. Legal Aid attorney Robert Shuman had protested the fact that police did not arrest for violations of court orders, and Sigrid Peck, legal affairs writer for the *Sacramento Bee,* interviewed those in authority and recorded their various positions.[36]

Police Chief William Kinney's response to Shuman's charge was that violators of restraining orders may only be held in contempt of court, and he issued a general order to his department: "It is neither the duty nor within the legal jurisdiction of peace officers to enforce the provisions of a restraining order." His position was supported by Sacramento County District Attorney Vincent Reagor and Judge Charles Johnson of the County Superior Court, who argued that a restraining order itself is not the "determining factor" for arrest in a domestic dispute. "The determining factor is whether or not a crime has been committed and whether or not the wife or husband is willing to sign a complaint for arrest of the other party." The remedy for violation of a restraining order, Judge Johnson added, echoing Chief Kinney, is a contempt proceeding.

Sheriff Duane Low seemed to be the man caught in the middle in the Sacramento dispute. He agreed with Shuman that restraining orders were practically worthless. He granted that "it is a difficult problem. I really feel empathy for the female who is threatened." But, he added, "there is a void in the law. There is not a thing I can do to enforce the guarantees of a restraining order." As a possible solution, he said, the courts "should recognize the gravity of the situation and order arrest under 166." Section 166.4 of the California Penal Code states that "willful disobedience of any process or order lawfully issued by the court" is a misdemeanor. And back we are at square one, since police usually cannot or will not arrest for a misdemeanor that is not committed in their presence.

Some argue that a patrol officer on the spot may have difficulty determining whether an order has actually been violated. The wording of these orders is often so complex that it is even difficult to tell if it has expired or been superseded by a later order. In answer to this objection, Alix Foster told me that police in the state of Washington at least can make arrests for violation of a restraining order *if* the judge includes certain language in the order authorizing them to do so. And Mary Vail suggested that police keep restraining orders on file at police headquarters the way they keep outstanding traffic tickets so that an officer could call in and check the wording and date of an order. If the real object of the legal game were enforcement of court orders, these sensible procedures would probably be in operation already. But as far as I can determine, restraining orders are really delaying tactics, designed to discourage the wife rather than protect her.

A Sacramento Legal Aid worker told a reporter of a case in which the police department itself proposed a bizarre alternative to arrest when an order was violated. A client who had a restraining order against her ex-husband called the police fifteen to twenty times to no avail. The woman claimed that the police told her "to kill him if he busted in again." The department, of course, denied this claim, but the woman was equally emphatic. She said that her husband had threatened to kill her and her children, and that he had already broken her jaw. The husband had come to the house three times with guns, but the police merely took the guns away and let him go.[37] If the police will not offer her protection, and if the courts will not act, what is a woman whose life is in jeopardy to do—take the advice and kill her husband? According to the National Commission on the Cause and Prevention of Violence, "although women exhibit a much lower homicide rate than men, when they do kill they are more likely to kill their husbands than any other category of person."[38] Is it any wonder?

In another case, also in 1972 in Sacramento, Joyce N. Ruiz filed suit in Superior Court against the police, charging that they had refused to enforce a court order against her estranged husband. She had called the police on seven separate occasions when she had been beaten and threatened by Ruiz. In addition, he had threatened to burn her employer's house down, had illegally taken one of the couple's six children with him to New York, and had refused to pay child support. Mrs. Ruiz's attorney, Jerry C. Graham, stated plainly that "police departments throughout the state, and perhaps in other states too, simply are not enforcing the law."[39] The suit was designed to require the police to enforce the law. The case went to court and was unfortunately—but predictably—dismissed. Perhaps Ruiz would have stood a better chance if she had sued Police Chief Kinney personally. After all, he had issued the general order to police personnel restraining them from enforcing the provisions of court orders. She might also have brought a personal suit against District Attorney Reagor for supporting Kinney's position.

Obviously, a woman who goes to the considerable trouble of applying to the court for a restraining order has little hope of receiving true protection. The great danger, though, is that a woman might believe in the value of a restraining order to the point of letting down her defenses and feeling that she is out of danger. Schwartz and Mills cite the example of Alice, a Seattle saleswoman in her forties, who was threatened and harassed continuously by a man she had broken off with. She filed for a restraining order and he was ordered by the court to stay away from her for six months or face jail. When the time was up, he started in on her again. Back to court they went, but sentence was deferred again, this time on condition that he have no contact with Alice for a year. Five days after the trial he began to follow her again. "No one's going to do anything. My luck is going to run out," Alice complained. Alice is afraid for her job. She is also afraid for her life. She took the alternative legally open to her and is no better off for having gone to the trouble.[40]

Carol Murray maintains a healthy contempt for the restraining order as a course of action open to battered wives. With the help of the law students interning in her office, she assisted 2,500 poor clients a year when she was director of the San Francisco Neighborhood Legal Assistance Foundation's Domestic Relations Unit. "We do not have the resources to perform meaningless acts," Murray stated in a letter to the director of San Francisco's Bureau of Family Relations. "We feel it is useless to obtain restraining orders which the police fail to enforce. To raise the hopes of a woman by obtaining a meaningless piece of paper is cruel and shows a lack of respect for the intelligence of our clients."[41] Many legal aid attorneys take this position; they simply refuse to apply to the court for restraining orders, considering them a futile waste of time and energy.

The District Attorney's Office

The victim of domestic violence has another alternative—she may file a criminal complaint with the district attorney. If the district attorney authorizes the complaint, he or she then goes before a judge to ask that an arrest warrant be issued against the husband. As with the other courses of action open to battered women, what sounds like a routine procedure is really a can of worms. The first difficulty is persuading the prosecutor that the case is worth pursuing. Again, resistance is often encountered. With the crime rate rising steadily all over the nation, district attorneys' offices are without exception overloaded with work. Therefore, though the complainant's purpose in filing the complaint is to bring the assailant to justice, the prosecutor's main concern may be to clear away all cases in which a conviction is not guaranteed. Local district attorney's offices use various ways of sorting through complaints and deciding which ones should go to court.

The San Francisco District Attorney's Office, for example, has a Bureau of Family Relations. For years the Bureau served as a screening agency to decrease the large volume of caseloads and to investigate complaints of an alleged criminal nature arising among members of a family or a quasi family. A spokesperson for the Bureau listed the "fundamentals" that must exist in a case before the district attorney will authorize a complaint and seek an arrest warrant before a judge: *a crime,* as defined by the penal code; identification of *a specific defendant; proof,* such as *witnesses* and *documents* (if children are the only witnesses, the district attorney will not accept the case); *severe injuries; willingness of the victim to testify* (some deputy district attorneys require the victim to sign a statement promising to testify in court before they will authorize her complaint). Another investigator in the Bureau added that in the old days "we could just say 'he hit her' and get a warrant, but now we need as much evidence as we can get." She added a few more "fundamentals" to the list: that *two* witnesses are usually required, that a police report must exist, and that there must be a history of previous attacks. Significantly, only eight of the several thousand cases processed by the Bureau during the fiscal year

1973–74 led to a formal complaint and prosecution. All eight were felony wife-beating cases.[42]

The Family Bureau is proud of its "reconciliation record," though the staff really has no way of knowing what that record is. All that the investigators know with certainty is that they accomplished their main purpose: dispensing with a large number of complaints on behalf of their boss, the district attorney. Bureau personnel do not follow up on these cases, so they do not know whether the couple took advantage of their referrals to other agencies for long-term counseling. It is generally true that batterers will not seek counseling voluntarily, and there are many reasons why the wife will not return with a new complaint, not the least of which is disillusionment. She may have been beaten into submission, or become fed up with pounding on closed doors; she may have given up hope of finding anyone who will understand the danger she is in. She may even be dead, but her case will still show up as a "favorable" statistic in the Bureau's "Annual Report to the Mayor" come budget time.

Standards set by prosecutors for accepting a case for trial are so restrictive that wife-abuse cases rarely qualify. A woman would be lucky to produce one witness other than her children, let alone the two often required, even if her injuries were serious enough to require hospitalization. Neighbors and friends, if they do appear, usually do so after the fact and are not present to see the actual blows being struck. They might be able to testify that the injuries existed (often having healed by the time of the trial), which is merely hearsay, but the prosecutor wants witnesses who can testify that the injuries were really sustained from the beating.

The San Francisco assistant district attorney, who headed the assault team that handles serious injury cases, denied that his office has set such stringent standards. He claimed that the decision to proceed with a case depends mainly on the emotional control of the complainant and whether she will be a credible witness. Such mixed messages revealed that obvious communication problems existed within the district attorney's office. It was also apparent that too much authority had been delegated to the Family Bureau—composed of four "investigators" who are caseworkers and not lawyers—to determine whether a case qualified for prosecution. Complainants who failed the prosecution tests were granted a "citation" hearing, which is an informal meeting with the husband, the wife, and a representative from the Bureau. Here the parties discuss their marital situation, are informed of the law and referred to community agencies for counseling and other related social services. The husband was usually told no more than "don't do it again."

A change of policy was made in 1976 when the new district attorney, Joseph Freitas, took office. He assured an ad hoc committee of feminists concerned with the disposition of marital violence cases that an attorney would review each complaint. A wife/victim can now bypass the Bureau of Family Relations. If the charge is a felony, her case will be assigned to the assault team; misdemeanors are referred to the general works division.

In Oakland, California, all cases of marital violence go to a citation hearing, and few to trial. Charges are brought only if a verdict is likely, if the injuries are serious, or if a man is "belligerent," according to a deputy district attorney. The deputy's attitude is typical: Conviction is difficult because juries know there are elements of "provocation" in domestic disputes, making it hard to determine who is at fault. Few women who file complaints really want to go through with it; mostly they want someone else to tell their husbands to stop beating them and do not want to see their husbands arrested. The deputy D.A. believed that the citation hearings are generally successful, although he admitted that one woman was killed the year before shortly after a hearing.

In wife-beating cases, as with rape, the burden of proof is on the victim, who must overcome centuries of male bias to convince a prosecutor of the seriousness of her charge. Eisenberg and Micklow take pains to emphasize in their study that prosecuting attorneys in general "are rarely exposed to the true pattern of these cases. They treat the problem in isolation, as an exceptional event, when it is much more likely that the victimized wife has suffered a series of repetitive attacks throughout her marriage." Police and prosecutors frequently assume these attacks are "one-punch" fights, but when the twenty victims of Eisenberg and Micklow's study were hit, it was invariably more than once. Usually they received a beating that lasted anywhere from five to ten minutes to over an hour. Once the beatings took place, they were usually repeated on a fairly regular basis. Wives in the study sustained such physical injuries as ripped ears, bald spots where hair had been pulled out, choke marks, concussions, miscarriages, fractured jaws, dis-

112

located shoulders, broken arms, cracked ribs, and burns on the breasts and arms from lighted cigarettes or hot irons.[43] A woman who finally works up the courage to file a criminal complaint against her husband for treating her to such abuse can hardly be expected to feel grateful for an investigator's gestures at mediation.

Schwartz and Mills describe a cruel refinement to the basic procedure followed in the prosecutor's office. The Seattle prosecutor usually decides within a few days whether a case is worth taking to court. If he decides against pursuing a case, the victim is not notified; she can only learn of the decision by calling and asking. If the prosecutor decides to take a case, the woman is sent a form letter telling her that if she wants to prosecute, she must contact the court unit within seven days. "We tell her it's seven days, but there's no law on it. She can come anytime. We like to get these cases cleared up," said one official who handles the paperwork. Court employees do no follow-up work on these cases. They say they have no idea how many women do not answer the letter because it never arrived or was intercepted by the husband. One woman was in the hospital when it arrived, and by the time she got out the seven days were up. She thought it was too late to press charges and did not bother to respond, thereby becoming another "no-show" statistic.[44]

Columbus, Ohio, has a Night Prosecutor Program, a pilot project funded by the Law Enforcement Assistance Administration (LEAA). The program offers twenty-four-hour service and the focus is on pre-arrest diversion tactics. Domestic disputants are brought before trained hearing officers for mediation. During the first year, only two percent of 3,626 direct complaints resulted in criminal charges. The stated purpose of the project is to avoid the prospect of a costly and often unsatisfactory solution through arrest and formal prosecution of the respondent.[45] The only advantage I can see in this much-touted project is the round-the-clock service, since most wife-battering takes place at night or on weekends. The emphasis on mediation is an old, discouraging story.

The lesson demonstrated in this section is depressingly familiar. Clearly, prosecutors resist trying cases of marital violence unless they cannot avoid doing so. Citation hearings are cruel hoaxes, designed to distract a complainant from her original purpose and to make her believe something is being done while the district attorney disposes of his caseload. The future safety of the woman is not considered in the citation hearing. Neither prosecutors nor their investigators are necessarily trained to deal with complex family issues, and they may not recognize potentially dangerous situations. Warnings and threats are useless unless the district attorney is prepared to follow through if the husband calls his bluff.

Another common impediment to prosecution has to do with "discovery" or the "rule of disclosure," requiring the complainant to disclose her present address to the defense. By law "the defense has a right to know" the present circumstances as well as the background of the complaining witness, and to obtain her pre-trial statement. But a battered wife often prefers to keep her whereabouts secret, fearing that her assailant might seek her out and harm her, order or no order. Furthermore, in order to protect their residents, most refuges for battered wives try to keep their addresses secret. A victim who avails herself of such a shelter would break a house rule and jeopardize other residents as well as herself to comply with this legal procedure. Obviously, the police or the district attorney need to know how to reach the complainant to proceed with the case, but forcing her to divulge that information to the defense is another matter.

At a meeting with representatives of interested women's groups, San Francisco District Attorney Joseph Freitas claimed that his office did not have the power to waive the rule of disclosure.[46] He said the matter would have to be argued before a judge; an attorney would have to prove that the complainant was in danger. An assistant district attorney said that if the husband did in fact harass, molest, or threaten the complainant after the case was filed, a judge might be convinced. In other words, the original act of violence would not be sufficient to prove present danger and warrant waiving the rule of disclosure. Whether they mean to or not, then, district attorneys and judges continue to expose the wife/victim to danger. Judges have the final say in the matter, but district attorneys (who are presumably the advocates for the complainant) rarely understand the danger involved and seldom make strong enough arguments on their client's behalf. Therefore, a complainant who persists in seeking prosecution risks the possibility of another attack. No wonder wife/victims often drop the charges!

James Bannon, the Detroit police commander quoted

earlier, rightly sees the attrition rate of marital violence cases as a measure of the danger to the women involved: "The attrition rate in domestic violence cases is unbelievable. In 1972, for instance, there were 4,900 assaults of this kind which had survived the screening process long enough to at least have a warrant prepared and the complainant referred to the assault and battery squad. Through the process of conciliation, complainant harassment and prosecutor discretion fewer than 300 of these cases were ultimately tried by a court of law. And in most of these the court used the judicial process to attempt to conciliate rather than adjudicate." These cases, Bannon noted, had been culled over several times so that only where the injury was extreme or the offense repeated would a warrant be issued. "You can readily understand," he continued, "why the women ultimately take the law into their own hands or despair of finding relief at all. Or why the male feels protected by the system in his use of violence."[47]

The Judge

Once a complaint has been authorized by the district attorney, a warrant issued, and the case brought to trial, the struggle is by no means over. The woman/victim is often forced to undergo an unofficial trial herself to determine whether she will actually testify against her husband when the time comes. Judge R. Patrick Corbett, presiding judge of Seattle's Municipal Court, was quoted by Schwartz and Mills: "Every time an assaulted wife gets on the stand, she says it didn't happen, it wasn't that bad, we've made up now, the children need him. I've had very few cases where she went ahead and testified when the trial comes up. It's human nature. I've long since given up trying to diagnose it."[48]

The woman who actually manages to have an arrest made and withstands the conciliation attempts of the prosecutor's office must expect cynicism regarding her intentions at every stage, even inside the courtroom itself. The fact is, since she may well have had to continue living with her husband or at least with the danger that he may seek her out and repeat the attack, she may have reconciled with him or forgiven him in self-defense by the time of the trial. But the business of the prosecutor is to prosecute when a criminal act has been alleged; the business of the judge is to hear the case impartially. Predicting the outcome of a case based on past experience is decidedly *not* among the duties of the prosecutor's office or the judge.

Another common problem at this stage is the desire, this time on the part of the judge, to see the couple reconciled. A Recorder Court judge in Michigan demonstrates this point of view very well: "I am very sympathetic toward people involved in that situation because obviously that person doesn't like to be hit or abused. What they need is marital counseling. . . . And I don't say that I necessarily, or that the prosecutor necessarily, conducts the hearing as a genuine criminal proceeding. Essentially what all of us want to hear is what the history of the situation is, what they think is best in terms of reconciliation."[49] This judge ordinarily places the man on probation, and assigns both husband and wife to someone in the probation department for help in reconciling their differences.

A judge has the option to issue an order to get a violent husband out of the house during the pre-trial period. But Justice Yorka C. Linakis, of Queens Family Court, takes issue with this position. In doing so she expresses an even more emotional plea than the Michigan judge: "All the havoc that can be created by the absence of the father from the home can be tremendous, and Family Court judges are most reluctant to order spouses from the house." Is the presence of a violent father psychologically more healthy than no father at all? Justice Linakis implies that her opinion on this question is the basis for her decisions in family-dispute cases. And her opinion on the question is based on shaky emotional grounds at best, as demonstrated in her statement to a conference on the abused wife held in New York in 1975: "There is nothing more pathetic than to see a husband going to his home—usually in the company of a policeman—to collect his meager belongings."[50] Is a woman who trembles in anticipation of her husband's next attack any less pathetic?

Many authorities who recognize the seriousness of wife-beating still assume the solution lies in marital counseling. "Reform is channeled again to rely on the wife as problem-solver," say Eisenberg and Micklow. "She must initiate the change in the marriage relationship and must often tolerate the abuse for a longer period of time to effectuate the goal of preserving the marriage. Certainly, mediation and reconciliation techniques should be available alternatives. However, these options should not preclude the choice of demanding immediate and effective law enforcement protection and support. If a woman chooses to file a criminal complaint or to seek a divorce, or both, she should not be denied on the basis of arbitrary and discriminatory responses."[51]

The argument here is not merely based on intellectual ideas of fair play. The consequences of a judge's lenient attitude—whether it results from a belief in the husband's right or a belief in reconciliation—can be as terrible and irreversible as in Adolph W. Hart's satire for *The New York Times* that was based on a true story.[52] Hart describes "Loretta's" vain efforts to break through the resistance of New York City's judicial system. Loretta brought charges against her former common-law husband *five times* for beating her savagely—*five times within a year and a half*. Each time she pressed charges, she followed through and testified in court, with the backing of the police and the assistant district attorney. On each occasion the Criminal Court judge released Thomas, telling him to stay away from Loretta in the future. During the third incident of violence, Thomas broke into Loretta's apartment and beat her on the head and face with a broom handle until she was unconscious. Her face was a bloody mess; in the city hospital her right eye was removed. But each time Thomas appeared in court, the judge, having been apprised by the police and district attorney of the previous assaults, released Thomas on the promise that he would stay away from Loretta in the future. The ironic title of the article was "Thomas Promised That He Would."

One might very well wonder what on earth the judges who heard Loretta's case were thinking. Was it not enough that the police and district attorney verified her statement? Was the loss of her eye insufficient proof that harm was sustained? Were her tireless efforts to exact protection through the legal alternatives open to her completely beside the point? Will the criminal justice system continually refuse to treat wife-abuse as a crime no matter what the wife does? Examples of actual cases are not encouraging.

District Justice Patsy F. Spadafora in Reading, Pennsylvania, says, "If the woman files a harassment charge, I can issue a warrant and send the man to jail for four or five days. Usually after four or five days, things cool off and the husband and wife are ready to get back together. But this is the case with first offenders. The more serious cases must have the district attorney's approval."[53]

But, as already indicated, prosecutors are not always inclined to bother with wife-beating cases. They can also mislead the judge as to the seriousness of the case. According to Cynthia Krolik of the *Michigan Free Press*, Judge Su Borman had a "simple" wife-assault case her first week on the bench, in which the male prosecutor suggested that charges be dropped. "Whether concerned about physical or economic survival, or defeated by the many official obstructions, the victim agreed," Krolik says. But two weeks later Judge Borman discovered that the "simple assault" she had dismissed consisted of the husband's tying his wife to the bed and slashing her genitals with a knife.[54]

A Michigan Circuit Court judge told Eisenberg and Micklow that many assaults are not unilateral by any means, but are provoked by the wife and the tense situation in which the couple lives. "I try to work out what I think is a possible, practical solution for solving the problem between these two people. And the most practical one that I can come up with is to put the husband out of the house, if possible." With that I can agree. But another of this judge's solutions is outrageous: he has been known to decide that the violence was provoked, to cite the wife for contempt on that basis, and to sentence *both* husband and wife to jail.[55]

Another example of misplaced levity appeared in a 1975 Reuters report from Kinghorn, Scotland: Magistrate George MacKay fined a husband $11.50 for hitting his wife in the face. But, the report added, "he could have smacked her bottom with impunity." The magistrate told the guilty husband, "It is a well known fact that you can strike your wife's bottom if you wish, but you must not strike her on the face." MacKay also expressed his belief in the ancient principle "that reasonable chastisement should be the duty of every husband if his wife misbehaves."[56]

On the other hand, men are put in jail for cruelty to animals. According to a summer 1975 KCBS radio news report, a man in California wanted to get even with his ex-wife. He took a bow and arrow and shot at her horse. Luckily for the horse his arrows were dull and his aim was poor. The court ruled that the man should pay $100 in veterinarian fees and gave him ninety days in the county jail. Suppose the wife had been the victim? He would probably have gotten off with a warning.

If judges would get tough and act like judges, rather than counselors or even practical jokers, perhaps battered women could obtain relief through the judicial process. Lieutenant George Rosko of the San Francisco Police Department suggests that a first-time wife-batterer should be remanded to a counseling center in the same way traffic violators are sent to traffic school. The offender would be warned explicitly that if he "ever lays a hand on his wife again" he will be sent to jail. If judges took that position and made it stick, Rosko believes, we might be on our way to solving the problem of wife-battering. As a police officer himself, Rosko sees the judge as the only representative of the system who has the authority to follow through on his warnings.[57]

The intimate nature of a husband-wife dispute adds one more depressing dimension to an already disastrous situation. If a woman does succeed in bucking the system and actually pushes her complaint through to trial, and if the husband/assailant is convicted of a crime, *she* may wind up suffering the punishment imposed on *him* by *her* complaint. In Gayford's words, "A fine causes hardship to the whole family, probation and a suspended sentence may result in violence, and further violence to deter the wife from taking court action again. Short prison sentences release a man in under a year, who has changed little and has grounds for an increased grudge against his wife."[58]

7

SOCIAL SERVICES—
THE BIG RUNAROUND

It is one thing to try to push a case through the criminal justice system, and another to keep a roof over your head while you are doing it. Many women stay with their violent husbands for the simple reason that they have nowhere else to go and no means of supporting themselves, even for a night, if they do leave. If the husband controls the bank account, the wife's hands are completely tied. But even if she does have some money of her own, taking a hotel room for an indefinite period or paying holding and security deposits on an apartment are expensive commitments. One must be either very lucky or extremely well-prepared to afford them at a moment's notice. I am assuming, while considering these contingencies, that the woman is not physically debilitated by the beatings that drove her away.

If the woman has taken her children with her, the urgency of the situation is greatly increased. A woman alone might miss a meal or two without suffering much. She might dare to impose herself on a friend in the middle of the night. But a mother could be reluctant to impose herself *and* several frightened children on an unsuspecting friend or relative who may be in little better financial circumstances than she. Few households can provide space, bedding, clothing, and food for a second family. Temporary arrangements are often made willingly by concerned friends. But a woman who has left home in the middle of the night probably has no idea how long she will need to intrude or accept a friend's hospitality, nor when her outraged husband might show up to cause more trouble. Generous friends may be putting themselves in danger just by offering to help.

This kind of anxiety and discomfort is bad enough for one or two nights, but imagine the prospect of such a makeshift life stretching indefinitely before the woman who has never been on her own before. Imagine her wondering how she will support herself and her children, especially if she has no work experience. Imagine her trying to make decisions—whether to stay away, whether to give up and go home—in a situation where she has neither time, nor space, nor quiet to consider what has happened to her and what she must do now. These circumstances alone—and they are common to women who leave home for whatever reason—are, understandably, enough to drive a battered woman back to the quasi security of a violent but familiar home that provides food and shelter.

Coordinating Information

Of course, there is always the social agency. Almost without exception social agencies are subdivisions of monolithic institutions such as state governments or charitable organizations. As such they usually offer specific services to certain kinds of people. Agencies spend a lot of time determining whether an applicant fits the agency's target population and whether her needs are suitable to the agency's stated purposes. Since wife-beating has not up to now been considered a social problem in our country, very few —if any—of the existing social agencies cater specifically to the needs of battered women with nowhere to go. A woman who has patience, mobility, and an understanding of the system *can* get help, but these qualities are not necessarily to be expected in a woman who has just left her home out of desperation and fear for her life.

Suzanne Schilz, in *Majority Report*, recounted the story of "Frances," who testified before the Special Issues Committee of the Seattle Women's Commission.[1] One night, a few days after Frances and her husband had separated, she heard a knock on the door. It became louder and more insistent by the minute. Since it was after midnight, Frances assumed that it was her husband, probably drunk and angry and ready to beat her up again. She became frightened, woke her children, and fled with them out the back door. They ran for several blocks before stopping for breath. Not knowing what else to do, Frances went to the police for protection and legal advice. They simply told her there was nothing they could do. It was three o'clock in the morning, and Frances didn't know where to turn. She and the children stayed at the police station for awhile, hoping someone would help them. But a man just released from custody started to harass her, so she phoned a friend and left.

Frances had left home without clothes and without her medicine, so she called the police the next day explaining that she was afraid to go back home alone. "They said I should wait two blocks from the house and someone would pick me up. I waited two and a half hours and called the police three more times, but they did not come." Finally she asked a neighbor to go home with her.

That afternoon Frances called a local crisis clinic to find out how to get a restraining order issued against her husband. They referred her to the public defender, who told her to call her own attorney. Since she didn't have one, they gave her a reference, who then told her she would have to see a judge. She went immediately to Municipal Court, but it was Saturday and the court was closed. On Monday Frances finally got a lawyer to draw up a divorce action and apply for a restraining order.

Her legal problems out of the way, the next stop was the welfare office. Frances filed an application for immediate emergency assistance. She had no food or money. She was given an appointment to see a caseworker in nine days. When she insisted that her case was an emergency, the intake worker retorted, "People like you come in every day!"

Frances then called the mental health clinic to ask for help. The caseworker replied that nothing could be done unless Frances and her husband wanted to come in for counseling. By chance, this caseworker advised Frances to go to the Salvation Army for emergency funds. There she was given $12.50 for food and $2.00 for gas. On Wednesday, Frances's husband was served with the divorce papers and the restraining order, and she finally went back home.

Luckily, Frances had a place to stay during the five nights and four days she was away from home. Even so, she had to expend a tremendous amount of energy to come up with the most basic information. Each person in the chain gave Frances a little bit of information, but not enough. She happened to catch some attorneys in the office on a Saturday, but no one took the time to explain the legal procedure or to mention that she would have to wait until Monday to go to court. The mental health clinic, not the welfare office, informed her about emergency funds—and that by chance.

Frances's story demonstrates the great need in our cities for the coordination of information about available services. The publication *Off the Beaten Track*, a compilation of services in Philadelphia prepared by Women Against Abuse, is just that sort of useful tool. It lists resources for women and comments on the services provided by each agency, noting the hours and days the agency is open, the cost of the service, and whether or not an appointment is necessary. Three women spent more than one hundred hours on the phone to compile this list of services. "In the process of telephoning," they write, "we could not help but wonder how a woman who is physically abused by her husband can know where to call or go for help. She certainly doesn't have a hundred hours to find out."[2]

Off the Beaten Track is meant for victims who do not know enough about the helping game to ask the right questions. For instance, most people know that hospitals have emergency rooms, but not everyone knows that most hospitals have a social service department or that public health nurses can visit the home if further treatment is necessary. In this regard, Pizzey says that English health visitors, analogous to our public health nurses, are "always treated as the Cinderella of the social services," and are really the backbone of any help families can hope to receive.[3] The fact that the very existence of public health nurses is relatively unknown in this country demonstrates our great need for a coordination of information.

There is also a need for *geographical* coordination. Social services are not necessarily set up to be easily accessible. A person in need of several different services may have to spend a lot of time on the bus traveling from one agency to another. Many women who require such services may use up their bus tokens before finding help.

Joanne Richter, of the Fort Lauderdale Police Department's Victim Advocate Office, is frequently confronted with women who have been assaulted by their husbands and who feel they have no alternative to staying home and enduring their trouble. "Personally," she wrote to me, "I would like to see a central facility provided where women who find themselves in this situation can learn employable job skills, have their self-confidence restored and receive the legal and social service counseling necessary to make them independent, self-supporting members of the community."[4] Fort Lauderdale presently has the legal, psychiatric, and social services necessary to assist female assault victims. However, these services are not centrally located and, as a result, are unable to coordinate with and complement each other effectively.

In a Minneapolis workshop on battered women held in February 1975 and instigated by Women's Advocates, social-worker participants decided to form a consortium to address the problem of coordinating social services.[5] They realized that different people and professions perceive the problem of battered women differently, and that each view, while it may have some validity, is incomplete by itself. The stated purpose of the consortium is to encourage various agencies and professions to interrelate and coordinate their approaches to the complex problems of battered wives. One of the first projects was the design of a card to be handed out by police to female assault victims. One side of the card stresses the importance of getting medical help, gives the address and phone numbers of the county hospital emergency facility, and lists numbers of crisis lines. On the reverse side, the procedure for bringing legal charges for assault is explained. The consortium is currently at work on an in-service training program to enable social-service professionals to deal more adequately with battered women as clients. This group is also developing remedial legislation to strengthen protective services and setting up more emergency housing.

Emergency Housing

The most pressing need is for emergency housing. How is a woman to get through her first day or her first week on her own without a roof over her head? Task forces across the country are presently grappling with this desperately urgent problem. In some cases women's refuges similar to Chiswick Women's Aid are beginning to take shape. A very few shelters already exist. Accounts of efforts to establish these refuges are to be found in Chapter 10. I will limit myself here to an overview of the more conventional kinds of emergency housing, which up to now have been the *only* kinds of shelters in the country:

- San Francisco, California: In 1975 Maxine Brown, chief of the Urbanization and Development Division of the Association of Bay Area Governments, made a survey of emergency housing available in San Francisco. She told me there were twelve shelters in all. But only three of these accepted women, and only one would take children. The maximum stay allowed is usually three nights. One place requires residents to vacate the premises during daytime hours. Other refuges open to women cater to ex-prisoners or formerly institutionalized mental patients exclusively. The Salvation Army in this city has no facilities for women and only limited finances to provide food and lodging in cases of dire emergency. In a desperate situation the Salvation Army will rent rooms in an inexpensive downtown hotel.
- Los Angeles, California: A 1973 survey by the San Pedro Chapter of the National Organization for Women revealed that Los Angeles County had 4,000 beds for men, only 30 for women and children, and none for mothers with sons over four years old. Trude Fisher, with Marion P. Winston, checked out some of these facilities for an article in the *Los Angeles Times*. The Hollywood YWCA has rooms, but they are for rent and no children are allowed. The Salvation Army Women's Emergency Lodge in downtown Los Angeles had to be sold; the other facilities of this agency are for men only. The Bibleway Mission, too, serves only men. Sometimes Travelers' Aid helps, but only if the woman is from out of town; then they send her back where she came from. The Sunlight Mission in Santa Monica, which does take women and children, is generally fully occupied.[6]
- Santa Clara County, California: Brandon House is the only emergency shelter for women and children in all of Santa Clara County. This crisis shelter has a capacity of 40 beds.[7]
- Washington, D.C.: Telephone calls made on March 31, 1975 by women of Spectra Feminist Video to numerous shelters on the Women's Center resource list revealed that only two facilities offer assistance

to displaced wives in the District of Columbia—the Salvation Army and the D.H.R. Emergency Family Shelter. Both prefer *not* to deal with abused women and their children, and discourage them from asking for help. The Salvation Army does not want to "break up homes," and actually encourages the wives to stay with their husbands. If a woman perseveres and persuades the Salvation Army to let her stay, she is limited to a maximum of three days. The D.H.R. Shelter's primary function is to provide emergency housing for families that have been evicted. A D.H.R. spokesperson told the caller that if a battered wife showed up there she might receive accommodation, but the shelter did not consider these cases a priority and preferred not to be listed as a referral.[8]

- Fort Lauderdale, Florida: Women in Distress takes women only (over eighteen—no children). The Salvation Army is open seven days a week from 8:00 A.M. to 10:30 P.M.; women and children are accepted on a one-night-only basis. On a more encouraging note, Emergency Housing is an agency which receives referrals from the city's Community Affairs and Housing Department, and women with children are eligible. Also, after 5:00 P.M. and on weekends women can get help through the Fort Lauderdale Police Department's Community Relations Unit or its Victim Advocate Office.[9]

- Philadelphia, Pennsylvania: Women Against Abuse say in *Off the Beaten Track* that the Philadelphia Housing Authority can handle some emergencies, *but* people who go there are usually put on a waiting list. The Authority serves low-income people only, and rent receipts and children's birth certificates are required. Appointments are not necessary, *but* interviews are held only between 9:00 A.M. and 5:00 P.M. on weekdays (the usual intake hours for all social agencies). The Mid City YWCA has three rooms available to women without income, *but* all clients must be referred by a social agency. The Southeast Philadelphia Neighborhood Health Center helps to relocate women and children, *but* no emergency housing is available in the meantime. The Neighborhood Action Bureau will help a woman find housing, *but* she must have a court order, be

126

on public assistance, or have a job. Ludlow Social Service provides immediate help for emergencies, including temporary housing, *but* preference is given to women in the Ludlow area. The Kensington Women's Resource Center does provide housing for women in need at the Kensington "Y."[10]

The wife who grabs her children and flees her violent husband in the middle of the night is lucky if she has time to gather the necessary clothes, let alone the "vital statistics" many agencies require for determining eligibility. A woman in this predicament cannot wait until an agency opens its doors in the morning. She cannot wait to be referred by one agency to another. Her needs are immediate, but few public agencies offer nighttime and weekend services or are prepared to handle on-the-spot emergencies.

The huge discrepancy between the number of shelters open to men and the number open to women is a disgrace. Even worse, so few places across the nation accept women *and* children that they may as well not be counted. This imbalance not only reflects discriminatory attitudes, but also shows how outdated the public assistance agency system is. It is still based on the assumption that only men will be transient or caught without means and a place to stay. Women are supposed to stay at home with their parents or their husbands. They are not expected to need overnight accommodations, particularly if they have their children along.

Unfortunately, the projects springing up across the country to correct this inequity are coming into being at a time when money is scarce. Federal, state, and city budgets are currently being pared to the bone, and private foundations are cutting back on the number and size of their grants. Therefore, though they continue to write proposals and lobby for government funds, many concerned people are taking battered wives into their own homes if necessary. Barbara Pavey, of Serve Our Sisters, has established an SOS crisis line in Seattle, where she tries to place wife/victims and their children in private homes. And through the efforts of Cameron Weeks, the downtown Seattle YWCA has begun to take in battered women overnight.

Still, the long-term activity continues and in some cases has already shown results (see also Chapter 10). For example, Kathleen M. Fojtik, president of the NOW chapter in Ann Arbor, Michigan, has published a booklet called

"Wife Beating: How to Develop a Wife Assault Task Force and Project."[11] The Ann Arbor NOW Wife Assault Task Force, which was formed in April 1975, has developed a step-by-step "how to" program. Using their own materials and experience as a model, they demonstrate how women's groups can be organized in other cities. They focus on methods of challenging the community to offer needed service for battered women. And in New York City, Abused Women's Aid in Crisis (AWAIC) was formed after a conference on battered women held in January 1975. AWAIC, under the direction of Maria Roy, offers a referral service and group-counseling sessions to wives who need support in breaking out of the victim syndrome.[12]

Admittedly, establishing a shelter and keeping it in operation is an expensive proposition. But certain stop-gap measures can be taken to provide accommodations where a full-scale shelter is either economically infeasible or a long way from being realized. These steps could be taken by local task forces while they await funding and need not cost a lot of money or even a lot of energy. For example, where existing facilities are lopsidedly reserved for men, agencies should be persuaded to change their policies so that emergency housing can be more evenly distributed between the sexes. Also some existing facilities were originally set up for specific purposes that have become outdated; they are now underutilized. Surely at least a portion of such buildings could be turned over to battered women and their children. In San Francisco, for example, the Mary Elizabeth Inn was established to provide a low-cost residence for young working women and female students. The Inn was opened in 1914 when such a facility was necessary, but it is not used very much any more. Recently, in fact, the Inn's administrators, the Board of Global Ministries of the United Methodist Church, sent a bulletin to all San Francisco Methodist parishes reminding them of the existence of the facility and encouraging them to use it.[13] Surely some rooms in this residence could be reserved for battered wives who are presently dependent, but wish to acquire skills that will qualify them for work. The same applies to the Florence Crittenton Homes for unwed mothers. And it seems only logical that the YWCA Hotel should make one floor available to battered women in need of temporary shelters. Why couldn't facilities like these open their doors to the women who currently need them?

Existing facilities are going to waste. Even where refuges

for battered wives are in operation, these older facilities could handle the overflow, which, according to the experience of operating shelters, is bound to occur. One other possibility is the utilization of hosptial facilities. If a hospital happens to have some empty beds, couldn't an injured woman seeking emergency medical aid be allowed to stay overnight and check with the hospital's social service department in the morning?

As a matter of fact, during the course of their study on assaulted wives, Eisenberg and Micklow made a similar suggestion to hospital directors in Detroit. The responses were ominously familiar. The directors answered that the problem of battered women was out of the realm of their professional concern. Eisenberg and Micklow explained that physicians and hospital personnel, along with police, comprise an important point of contact between the battered wife and the "service community." Even if they could not offer refuge, surely emergency-room personnel could make an effort to identify battered women and refer them to helping organizations that might exist. No, the doctors insisted; they had to maintain a non-judgmental approach to their patients, and they had neither the time nor the inclination to determine *how* a woman had sustained her injuries.

The doctor in charge of the Emergency Room at a large hospital in Detroit took the position that the woman's story is none of his business even if her explanation of her injuries rings false. Eisenberg and Micklow quote him: "I do not ask her or delve any further . . . It's a personal problem between a man and wife, and if she doesn't want to prefer charges, that's her privilege and her right . . . She was the one that was beaten, not I."[14] It is hard to imagine a more disinterested attitude or a less compassionate one. The fact that a woman is in the hospital in the first place should cause a doctor to understand her reasons for not preferring charges—fear, ignorance as to how to go about it, and shock due to injury. A doctor who treats a battered woman's wounds and hands her back to her assailant may be exercising a kind of professional detachment. But he is also passing up what may be society's only contact with a lonely woman who needs help.

. One doctor, an administrator of the emergency service at another Detroit hospital who was in a perfect position to help battered women, chillingly explained his attitude on the subject: "There is a certain masochism to a woman who gets beaten up more than once that you can't deny. That I can't deny. I go back to the same place and I get beaten up more than once, then there is something in me that is making me do that. I don't have to get the shit beat out of me, do I? I mean, you don't have to have very much intelligence to know that you can leave."[15] Nor do you have to know much to realize that a woman who is injured, or has no money, or has nowhere to go will probably go home. There she will stay until by some miracle she discovers a refuge, gets a job, or works up the courage it takes to walk away from home with no money, no prospects, and the terrible fear that she is being pursued.

Public Financial Assistance

A spokesperson for the San Francisco District Attorney's office told the Women's Litigation Unit of San Francisco Neighborhood Legal Assistance Foundation that battered women are not really trapped, that they can always leave, take the children, and go on welfare. Or the woman can escape to another county, apply for funds through the Aid for Dependent Children program (AFDC), and probably get money for food and housing immediately.[16]

These suggestions were probably made in all sincerity, and they do sound logical. But common sense does not always prevail; sometimes one branch of the government bureaucracy really does not know what the other is doing. In this realm in particular, theory and practice very often have little to do with each other. Erin Pizzey writes of seeing a letter from Edward Heath, then Prime Minister, to Jack Ashley, a member of Parliament who had taken up the cause of battered wives. In the letter Heath stated that any woman who asked for help from social security in order to escape from a brutal husband would be given funds for housing and food. Pizzey's comment was: "This statement was either a barefaced lie or a reminder that politicians and the civil servants who advise them are too often the last people to know and understand the real situation."[17]

In 1975, the California Senate Subcommittee on Nutrition and Human Needs held hearings on marital violence. Sue Millhollon, of the Salvation Army's Social Service Bureau, testified at the hearings as to the frustration her agency experienced in helping fleeing women deal with the public social services.[18] In one case she cited, a battered woman and her children were told that the husband's income made the family ineligible for welfare. The wife and her children had been subject to continued beatings, and were trying to make a break from this unbearable situation though they had no money of their own. But the intake worker was not moved. The woman was classified ineligible and forced to go back to her violent husband.

The reasoning behind this social worker's decision was typical: as long as a woman has a home to go to and a husband to support her and the children, no matter what the circumstances she cannot qualify for public assistance. Technically she is not destitute or homeless, the only conditions that qualify an applicant for public aid. Once again we are faced with the assumption that a married woman is not an individual in her own right, but is only an adjunct to her husband. As far as the government bureaucracy is concerned, she has no needs of her own, separate and distinct from the needs of her husband. Millhollon in San Francisco, and Pizzey, half-way around the world in London, come to the same conclusion: a woman cannot get help unless she has filed for divorce and established herself in a home of her own, but she cannot move out and establish that home without financial assistance. Therefore, she is stuck right where she is.

The suggestion that a woman can escape a brutal husband by moving to another county and applying for aid once again presupposes that she has some money for bus fare or a car with plenty of fuel. She must arrive at the welfare office before five on a weekday. She must apply for emergency food and accommodations to see her through until her first check arrives. But suppose she did not bring the legal documents required (birth certificates and so forth). Suppose she finds herself at the bottom of a long waiting list. What then? All across the country, applicants for welfare often wait as long as ten days for the first interview to determine eligibility and, if they qualify, another two weeks or so for the first check. The idea of a woman dropping in on the welfare office after she has left home simply does not hold up.

Millhollon raised another problem when she told of a woman who fled her own apartment with her child to escape the beatings of an ex-boyfriend. The woman left on a Friday; and her lawyer told her he could not file for an arrest warrant with the district attorney's office until Monday. The woman was afraid to return to her apartment where the man was holding out, so she sought emergency help—food and accommodations for herself and child for the weekend—until the legal process could be set in motion. The Department of Social Services refused her any aid because she had already received her welfare check for the month.

It should come as no surprise that the government social services are no more prepared to meet emergencies than the legal system is. Rules, regulations, and procedures are rigid and do not allow social workers any flexibility in responding to crises. But the social services are designed to serve people with problems and those problems are likely to include crises and various kinds of emergencies. Why should victims of situations that occur outside of business hours be denied aid? Contingency funds should be made available for unusual emergencies, and some provision should be made for crisis situations that happen at night or on weekends when offices are closed.

Victim Aid

On the positive side of the picture, battered women may begin to receive both monetary and physical benefits from the relatively new victim-aid programs developed by the police or the state around the country. They reflect an attitude of official concern. Since the authorities have not yet acknowledged wife-beating to be a true social problem, battered women are not specified as aid recipients in these programs. Still, the very existence of victim-aid programs is encouraging. If the concerned community can bring battered wives out of their isolation and loneliness so they can be identified, perhaps these new victim-aid programs can respond to their needs.

The battered wife may already claim compensation legally for her injuries in some states. California, for example, has established a program to indemnify and assist in the rehabilitation of victims of violent crimes.[19] This program, effective since July 1, 1974, pays out-of-pocket wages lost and medical and/or burial expenses incurred as the result of violent crime. It also pays for job retraining or similar employment-oriented rehabilitation services. Police are required by law to notify victims of violent crimes that this program exists. In San Francisco, for instance, police distribute notices printed in English, Spanish, and Chinese.

Claims in the California program are paid to the victim or the victim's dependents in cases of serious financial hardship *if* the claimant cooperated with "a law enforcement agency in the apprehension and conviction of the criminal committing the crime" and did not substantially contribute to his/her own injuries by "the nature of his [her] involvement in the events leading to the crime." These conditions for eligibility represent the fly in the ointment as far as the battered woman is concerned. From what we know of the legal system's treatment of female victims, "cooperating with a law enforcement agency" could mean reconciling and going quietly home. But, in true Catch-22 fashion, if a woman goes home quietly, she may have great difficulty proving she did not contribute to her own injuries—that is, that she did not provoke the beatings. Also, if the woman brings charges against her husband and cooperates with the police but the prosecutor later decides not to take her case, that decision may influence whether or not she will be granted aid. If she is unable to produce the witnesses other than her children that are often required by prosecutors, the board might also decide she has no case and disqualify her claim. And if she does not file for a divorce, but remains under the same roof with her assailant because she has nowhere to go and is financially dependent, will the validity of her claim to aid be clouded? To my knowledge no battered woman has filed a claim under this program, so these questions remain unanswered.

Pizzey writes that battered wives are *not* eligible for a similar compensation program in England. Victims of crime legislation in some United States jurisdictions expressly exclude victims who are "related" to the offender. But several police officers and attorneys have expressed their belief to me that battered women have the same right as any other victim of a violent crime to state-given compensation in California. At least the California law does not expressly exclude these victims. Perhaps if enough injured wives put this act to the test, the state would begin to comprehend the gravity and extent of the wife-beating problem. And as an incentive for women who could claim, the provision for rehabilitative job training in this program should be emphasized; it may represent a wife/victim's chance for economic independence.

New York City's Crime Victims Service Center is designed to assist victims of violent crime who live in the Bronx. Circulars describing the very important services of the Center are written in Spanish as well as English. The services include assisting victims in completing forms, counseling, dealing with specific problems the victim may have, and referring victims to appropriate agencies: the Crime Victims Compensation Board (for compensation similar to California's), outpatient clinics or hospitals, rehabilitation programs for physical disabilities, legal services, and emergency funds. When referrals are made, Center counselors do follow-up interviews to be sure the victim is receiving the necessary help. This follow-up function sounds like the answer to the need for coordinating information that was discussed earlier. The Crime Service Center has begun to serve rape victims, but while the Center is aware of the problem of battered wives, it provides no special services for them at this time.[20] Perhaps it would if enough battered women from the Bronx applied to the Center for help.

In Fort Lauderdale, Florida, the Victim Advocate Project, sponsored by the police department, provides on-the-scene emergency help, liaison services, and transportation to responsible agencies. Joanne Richter of this project has been actively encouraging battered women to respond to the Project's offer of aid.[21] Victim Advocates have been successful in helping to integrate services and have even turned up available services that had not been well publicized before. In an evaluation report on integrated services for victims prepared for the National Association of Counties Research Foundation, Mary Baluss commends the project: "Victim Advocates are available 24 hours a day and their clearly marked vans have aroused both interest and a rare positive response to law enforcement personnel in the high-crime, low-income areas of the city. . . . At the same time, the victim gets sure directions, an advocate rather than a bureaucratic run-around, and a service source that is available on more than a 9 to 5 basis." Baluss says that the project has elicited an impressive response from the community: off-duty nurses volunteer home care for victims who need it, business and service clubs donate food and clothes, and a private foundation makes grants for emergency rent.[22]

Baluss also describes the Office of Victim Advocacy for Fresno County, California. This program is much more court-oriented than other victim service agencies, and seems well-suited to help the woman who chooses to prosecute her assailant. Victims may request that counselors accompany them to court. Counselors answer questions about police, prosecution, and court procedures, and will, if the victim fears for his/her safety, keep track of an offender's progress through the legal system and notify the victim if and when the offender is released from custody. Baluss notes, too, that social service agencies are found to be more responsive when a victim counselor accompanies the victim for the initial interviews.[23]

Unique among existing victim services is the Aid to Victims of Crime Project in St. Louis, Missouri. This project is independent of any government agency and is largely staffed by volunteers. While the project maintains contact with and makes referrals to regular city and private agencies, the staff has no direct ties with the government bureaucracy; they can therefore overcome more easily victim suspicion of and hostility toward the system. Volunteers undertake services that the other agencies do not provide: they call and negotiate with landlords, persuade employers to keep the victim on the payroll and allow time off for court appearances, babysit, shop for groceries, and so on. An independent center is free to take a gadfly approach to other agencies, Baluss notes in her report. Another advantage is that a citizen-run center is more likely to gain access to unreported crimes, and thus can reach victims who would otherwise be afraid to ask for help.[24]

A major function of a social agency is informing people in need that the service exists, but overworked and understaffed agencies often renege on this responsibility. They fail to inform and attract potential recipients, but they succeed in decreasing—or at least not increasing—the agency's caseload. The battered woman, as we have seen, often has to fight her own moral upbringing and a whole spectrum of social pressures in order to tell even one other person about her problem. She may be paralyzed by the idea of actively searching for help, particularly if she is not sure that help exists to be found. Therefore, above all, social agencies must make themselves visible and accessible. They must streamline their procedures so that using a social service is no longer an ordeal of endless red tape and paper work. In these respects, particularly, these newly developed victim aid programs must prove themselves.

Baluss expresses the hope that victim aid centers will "give victims of crime a share of the services that have already been offered offenders." To do their job, however, the centers will have to overcome "inertia, role confusion, community wariness and agency defensiveness," and much of their work will be in "sensitizing agencies and communities to victim problems." But, she warns, that is not enough. Social agencies, the police, and the courts have established procedures which date back hundreds of years and are not likely to change very rapidly. Once victim aid centers begin to advocate change and experience the frustration of these roadblocks, they will be inevitably "drawn into lobbying for institutional change," Baluss believes.[25] From my point of view, as an advocate for wife/victims, that development is ardently to be hoped for.

Police Training and Crisis Intervention

Many police departments continue to give marital violence calls low priority, but there is a growing trend toward "crisis intervention" training. The new programs may be educating police to the significance of their role as first contact with a family in conflict. Crisis intervention training has brought about a collaboration between law enforcement and social service agencies. Intervention specialists believe that with proper training and strong ties to social services, police can play a critical role not only in preventing crime, but also in alerting other professionals to mental health problems in the family. In these police training programs, officers learn to recognize social problems, perform screening interviews, and refer the parties to an appropriate agency for further help. Without the crisis training police merely break up a fight and leave. With it they learn to calm down the disputants, act as mediators in the dispute, and attempt to bring about a resolution.

Morton Bard, of New York City, and Donald Liebman and Jeffrey Schwartz, of San Francisco, are psychologists who act as consultants to police departments in designing "family crisis intervention training programs" for their personnel. The courses that result do give police new skills and techniques for handling family disputes, but the real motivation is to decrease danger to responding officers and to reduce the number of domestic disturbance calls in general. Training usually consists of audio-visual materials, psychodrama, reading assignments, self-study exercises, small group discussions and evaluation. Officers are taught safety measures, defusing and interviewing techniques, mediation and conflict resolution skills, and are informed of cultural and legal issues that affect intervention.

"Learning to think psychologically, to read the language of behavior was, perhaps, the major task of the group sessions," says Bard of the project he undertook in New York's West Harlem.[26] Officers learned how their moralistic attitudes could affect the situation. They were trained to repress their personal feelings in order to be more effective —to help rather than to unwittingly escalate the dispute.

Family intervention training programs vary according to the size of the police force, the amount of money available, and the particular needs of the community. The Richmond, California, police department was the first in the nation to make domestic crisis intervention part of its regular in-service training, and also the first to train its entire patrol force (eighty officers—rather small compared with the forces of larger cities). This program, developed with the help of Liebman and Schwartz, was also distinctive for being the only one of its kind to operate entirely without federal or state funding.

Each team of officers in the Richmond program was given fourteen hours of in-class training plus outside reading and practice assignments. Equally important, each officer was given a Community Resource Manual. In it were listed thirty-three city service agencies that had agreed to accept police referrals, provide immediate aid, and help indigent families. Services included alcohol- and drug-abuse, medical and dental care, psychological counseling, financial assistance, and legal aid. Unfortunately, no feedback system was built into the program because of a lack of funds, so there was no way of knowing whether a family had actually applied for and received the service needed. Nor were effective evaluation of police intervention or provisions for training new recruits made.[27]

In contrast to Richmond, Liebman and Schwartz point to the training program in Oakland, California, for which they also were consultants. In Oakland only four officers were specially trained to "man family crisis cars" and to become more psychologically sensitive to domestic situations. The liaison and referral system with service agencies was excellent. Agencies were very cooperative, and feedback was built into the program. Also, officers in at least ten percent of the cases checked back with the families themselves. More than one-third of the families referred by these officers made appointments at an agency, and 80 percent of them actually appeared. Preliminary evidence also suggested that two visits by the family crisis unit stopped further calls. This obvious show of success led the National Institute of Mental Health to grant additional funds to train ten more patrol officers and one supervisor for the unit. Nonetheless, the project was abandoned when the funding ran out. New officers presently receive an average of five hours training to deal with domestic disputes. They are given lists of referral agencies, but feedback from the agencies presumably ended with the project.

Preliminary data in the Oakland experience show that fewer arrests resulted from domestic disturbance calls than usual, and Liebman and Schwartz report this as a favorable result of the program. But I am skeptical. The danger in greatly valuing reduced arrest rates in domestic disputes is obvious given the frustration women suffer because of non-arrest policies. The counseling function of these training programs encourages police to mediate between disputants when in fact separation may be the only solution in some cases. On the other hand, a police officer who is educated to the complexities and subtleties of family disputes is certainly preferable to the one who shrugs off the incident, calling it an inconsequential marital argument.

Some police departments are trying still another strategy: the use of women on patrol. The St. Louis Housing Authority developed an in-service family crisis training program for all members of its civilian police patrol, which serves the housing projects. Louis J. Sherman, psychologist at the University of Missouri, found that the women trainees were particularly competent in handling family disturbance calls. In a family quarrel, he noted, male officers tended to "feed the fire through their own aggressive, provocative behavior"; women, on the other hand, stepped in "with greater tact and subtlety. They tended to stay longer and seemed much more concerned about getting to the root causes of the conflict." Sherman gave another explanation: enraged men "simply could not respond as angrily or violently" to the woman officer as to the man.[28]

Evaluation of female patrol officers on the Washington, D.C., and New York City police forces confirms that women police officers are often better able to defuse volatile situations.[29] And a veteran patrol officer from the Indianapolis force observed, "Some of these families will call you back two or three times a night, but I've noticed that when the women go, that's the last time we hear from the family. . . ."[30] Because of these experiences and countless others, departments which had the foresight to open employment to women are sending them or man/woman police teams to respond to domestic disturbance calls.

Intervention training may be helpful in defusing volatile situations and protecting everyone involved from immediate physical danger, but this is only a first step in confronting the problem of domestic violence. Police must get over their "family squabble" attitudes and realize that unless the family receives outside help the potential for further violence remains. Although police have been trained in intervention, family-disturbance calls have not diminished appreciably in frequency (less than 4 percent reduction was reported in one instance where records were kept). Domestic disputes continue to erupt because the underlying problem goes untreated. A working relationship between police and service agencies and a feedback system for checking referrals are critical. "Those families who lack knowledge and sophistication in matters pertaining to mental health resources may be those most likely to involve the police when family crisis approaches break down," Bard says.[31]

The family crisis intervention unit of the Hayward (California) Police Department takes the social services needs of the community very seriously. The police hire mental health professionals to accompany them on family crisis calls and to provide on-going family counseling. The program, called Project Outreach, uses an unmarked police car equipped with a radio; it is available from Fridays through Sundays between 5:00 P.M. and 1:00 A.M. to respond to DD calls along with the police officer detailed. Once the Project counselor and responding officer determine that the situation is not dangerous, the officer leaves and the counselors spends as much time as necessary with the disputants in order to resolve the problem. Also, the family may receive up to ten counseling sessions free of charge at the project headquarters. Counselors are even prepared to make return home visits if necessary. Families are encouraged to call Project Outreach directly if a problem occurs. In cases where long-term treatment is indicated or specialized services are needed (for alcoholism, drug abuse, and so forth), referrals to other agencies are made.

By the end of the project's first year, the entire patrol division of the Hayward police force had been trained in family crisis intervention, and many had become co-trainers to keep the program going. At this time, Dr. Thomas E. Whalen evaluated the program and found that repeat calls to police had been reduced by 27 percent, and total calls by 22 percent. Domestic disturbance calls took 15 percent less time for uniformed personnel, no officer injuries or deaths had resulted from DD calls at all, and no serious injuries were known to have been sustained in families that had contacted the project.

Sue Gershenson is a psychiatric social worker who goes out on DD calls for Project Outreach on weekends. At the California legislative hearings on marital violence, she reported that Hayward police have responded favorably to the program, are better able to handle domestic disputes, and are more positive in their attitudes toward the people involved. She gave a brief description of the population reached by the project: In the first year 868 persons or families were served; of these 731 required crisis intervention and counseling. Clients were from all economic and racial backgrounds. Chicanos comprised the largest minority in Hayward; they represented 20.3 percent of the project's clientele. The average family income for residents of Hayward is $11,655; for a sample of 186 Project Outreach clients the average was $12,336. According to the Hayward census, the average citizen has completed 11.8 years of school; among 283 of the project's clients 78 percent had completed high school. Gershenson felt that the project was definitely reaching a cross-section of the city's population.[32]

"As a clinician and a woman working with police, I am convinced that the combination of trained mental health professionals and police who are sensitive and trained in crisis intervention can not only help prevent marital violence, but can also provide assistance in the resolution of family disputes," Gershenson told the legislators. However, after the three-year grant from the California Council on Criminal Justice runs out in 1976, Project Outreach will need money from local sources or it will not survive. "If projects like ours are to continue beyond the grant period," said Gershenson, "the local community must assume the entire cost of the program, and this is often a burden on the local community, even though the local contribution increases over the course of the grant period. Financial assistance on the state level could insure the implementation and continuation of these kinds of programs on the local level."[33] (Since then Project Outreach has been assured of ongoing funding by the city of Hayward.)

In the meantime, if the police themselves reordered their priorities, a source of revenue would be uncovered. In most cities police spend a tremendous amount of time and energy on efforts to control victimless crime, while crimes against people are committed ever more frequently. Huge amounts of tax money are spent to control public morality (gambling, prostitution, homosexuality), while the rates of crimes involving physical injury to human beings continue to rise. "The decriminalization of certain victimless crimes would produce the greatest savings in costs or improved service to the public through the reassignment of law enforcement priorities," states Walter Quinn, budget analyst for San Francisco's Board of Supervisors.[34] Surely some of the millions of dollars spent to control our "morals" could be retrieved and used to teach police to deal humanely and sympathetically with battered women and other victims of violent crime.

The advantages and disadvantages of existing intervention training programs just about balance each other out, to my way of thinking. The real value of such programs is that a family in trouble stands a good chance of finding help before violence becomes an established pattern. To me the efficiency and thoroughness of the referral function and follow-up procedures is the measure of the usefulness of the training as a whole.

Also important is changing the behavior of the officers on the scene. If crisis training is designed to make officers more understanding, patient, and reasonable, I am all for it. On the negative side, however, the emphasis on mediation in most programs will certainly function to make non-arrest policies even more rigid. A woman who wants to press charges or have a court order enforced may find she has even less of a chance when the police are "understanding" and armed with encounter-group techniques. In any event, the new attitudes do not alter the dominant-male bias that prevails in every police department in the country. After all, the courses are designed by men for use by men, and they still countenance a certain amount of physical force as an acceptable response to anger.

One training guide for crisis intervention boldly states, "whether or not the use of such force can be considered serious depends in part on the cultural background of the people using it."[35] The implication here is that violence as an expression of anger is, for instance, a part of the Latin "machismo" and is built into the structure of the Latin family. In this context, consider the situation of a Latino woman who calls the police because she desperately needs protection. She may be confronted with a pair of responding officers who have been trained to expect and tolerate violence toward women from Latinos as part of the "cultural heritage." Such a possibility reinforces my skepticism about crisis intervention programs, but I do admit that they may represent a first step toward more liberal, and more liberated, attitudes on the part of police departments. The fact that police begin to see their function as service-oriented is in itself an encouraging change.

Mental Health Services

Though mental health service agencies do exist, there is no guarantee that they will be accessible to a battered woman when she needs them. Bess Kirven, a member of La Platica Task Force in San Jose, California, describes an incident that is all too typical[36]: "(An) alcoholic husband, who had been drinking for several weeks, stopped cold for five days. His talk and actions became bizarre; then he threatened his wife with a knife, driving her out of the house, in front of the children. The family was badly frightened because the previous year their mother had nearly died despite a week in the hospital following a beating by their father." When Kirven, a therapist who works for the Department of Social Services, arrived, she ascertained that the man needed hospitalization and treatment for delirium tremens. She contacted the police, a private mental health center, and the County Mental Health and Crisis Intervention Unit without success. In reporting the incident, she listed the various reasons they gave for refusing the case: (1) "The residence is not in our district"; (2) "We aren't the appropriate agency for alcoholics"; (3) "No one on duty speaks Spanish and we prefer not to use interpreters"; (4) "Bring him in yourself" (he was violent); (5) "It's a police matter, not a mental health problem." (The police disagreed, saying he was "not drunk and besides, we didn't see him try to use the knife." They added that old familiar refrain: "Sure, his wife says he did, but he says he didn't. It's just a family argument.")

A mental health professional herself, Kirven was not able

to convince any agency to help until the man began to drink again, and after five days—during which the family remained terrified and continually asked for help—he went berserk in the neighborhood. He was so far out of control that it took four officers and two squad cars to take him to jail. There someone saw the necessity and took him to the County Mental Health Clinic where he was held and treated for fifteen days.

So long as the violent man limited his threats to his family, no agency was willing to respond. Once more the door to the family home stood between society and the woman isolated with a dangerous man. When he finally went outside into the neighborhood, the police admitted that a problem existed and took him into custody. *Other* people were endangered then; presumably the threats the man made on his wife's life didn't count.

Exceptions do exist to the general hands-off attitude of mental health agencies. In some cities, San Francisco among them, "outreach" teams from local mental health clinics will intervene on the scene. "Reaching out" is a new trend in the service professions. The term refers to an agency's policy of actively seeking out people in need of a service rather than waiting for clients to show up and ask for help. Reaching out can go way beyond simply informing the community of the existence of services, and when it does some very tricky moral problems arise. For example, does a social worker or a police officer have the right to intervene if he or she feels a family's difficulties may erupt in violence? What are the responsibilities and the limitations of an intervening agent? Doesn't the family have the right to be left alone to settle things in their own way? Are verbal threats an exercise of free speech? If an abusive husband refuses psychiatric care, isn't that his personal privilege?

Bard and Zacker discuss these questions in their article "The Prevention of Family Violence: Dilemma of Community Intervention."[37] They delineate just how far the representative of a service agency can go when "reaching out." A policeman, for example, can make an arrest only when a crime has actually been committed, not when he fears or predicts an offense. Or, as Susan Jackson reminded me, "Equity will not enjoin a future crime." And, in keeping with the citizen's right to privacy, police officers cannot enter a home unless invited, or unless they have a warrant or reason to believe a crime has been or is being committed. A police officer who believes a crime *will be* committed has no right to enter a home in order to prevent the crime from being committed.

Mental health services may reach out into a community by setting up clinics and making services available, but they cannot force unwilling citizens to undergo psychiatric treatment or marital counseling. A mental health professional may conclude that a person is potentially violent and a real danger to his family, but unless the latter is arrested and sentenced to therapy, treatment cannot be enforced. Bard and Zacker conclude, "Individual civil rights have precedence over a behavior prediction, even if murder is the predicted outcome."

The protection of citizens' civil rights is surely a priority under any circumstances, but, as has been demonstrated almost ad absurdum, the battered woman's right to live in her own home without being molested and injured, and her right to pursue personal happiness without interference go unprotected by our criminal justice system. Even more ironic is the fact that, when it comes to mental health services, battered women themselves turn out to be recipients far more often than irrationally violent men.

Mental hospitals, overcrowded and understaffed as they are, may not welcome the idea of taking on a man who "is liable to be intractable, disruptive, and dangerous," in Pizzey's words. And it is not likely that any court will detain a wildly violent husband in a mental hospital just because he has caused injury to his wife. A far simpler solution to the domestic violence problem is teaching women to be more compliant and accepting of their lot. As Pizzey points out, far more wife/victims wind up in mental hospitals than do assailant/husbands. When a wife finds that she is unable to change her home situation, she may fall into depression and despair. The majority of women who sought refuge at Chiswick Women's Aid had spent time in mental institutions for depression and/or suicide attempts.[38] In fact, some women will commit themselves to institutions because there is no other refuge from their oppressive marital situations.

Women in the feminist movement often complain, as does Pizzey, that the mental "health" approach to women far too often consists of prescribing massive doses of tranquilizers to alleviate depression and anxiety rather than dealing with the causes of the symptoms. If tranquilizers don't work, doctors often decide that a troubled woman ought to be institutionalized and given a series of electric shock treatments. If she does have the bad luck to find herself in a mental hospital, the woman may lose a part of her memory from the shocks—permanently sometimes—and she will undoubtedly be drugged continually. As a final solution to a stubborn case of depression, "the psychiatrist, bored with her crying, decides sometimes that the most useful move would be to perform a leucotomy and remove the anxiety," Pizzey says.

This possibility may sound extreme or unbelievable to some, but in his article in *Medical Opinion*, Peter Breggin gives evidence to show that the use of psychosurgery is on the increase.[39] Breggin calls the current practice "a crime against humanity, a crime that cannot be condoned on medical, ethical, or legal grounds." He charges that all forms of psychosurgery represent "a partial abortion of a living human being." Originally such surgery was only used in severe cases in which a patient was so violent that other types of treatment had no effect. It is now being directed toward a different target population, Breggin says: those with anxiety neuroses, obsessive neuroses, personality disorders, and reactive depressions. The people who suffer most from these disorders—or, more precisely, those in whom these disorders are diagnosed most frequently—are women. According to Breggin, "Dr. Peter Lindstrom of Children's Hospital in San Francisco, who uses a beam of sound to irradiate the frontal lobes, reports that 80 percent of his neurotic patients are female; so are 72 percent of psychotic patients who get the same treatment." Breggin also notes that Dr. Robert Hetherington, of Kingston Psychiatric Hospital in Ontario, "was refused permission to do lobotomies on male patients because of the adverse publicity the technique had received in Canada. But he was allowed to operate on 17 women!"

The danger is obvious. Women who become deeply depressed about their home lives may not have the will to resist these inhumane "medical" procedures. Pizzey reports that such victims turned up at Chiswick Women's Aid—mindless women who put up with their husbands' beatings with "cheerful indifference," and others whose children had been taken from them because they had lost their memory and all sense of responsibility.

If a woman tries to have her husband committed to a mental institution because of his violent behavior, however, no one talks about pills to tranquilize him or electric shocks and lobotomies to relieve him of his violent rage. Instead, mental health professionals recommend psychotherapy and say that nothing can be done unless the man comes in voluntarily. Still, women should know that legally at least they may take measures to have their husbands involuntarily committed.

A booklet prepared by the League of Women Voters states that California law presently allows involuntary treatment if "a person is a *danger to himself, or others, or gravely disabled*" (League of Women Voters' emphasis). If a woman's husband is dangerously violent and she wants to have him hospitalized, she must go to court to show reasonable cause. The involuntary custody period for evaluation and treatment is not more than 72 hours. If after the 72-hour detention period the man is still considered to be dangerous, and if he will not accept voluntary treatment, he can be certified for intensive treatment for a period not exceeding 14 days. He could be confined up to 90 days longer if diagnosed as *"imminently dangerous."* But again a court hearing must be held, and the man naturally has the right to hire an attorney and to request a jury trial contesting the decision to hospitalize.[40]

We already know how battered women are treated when criminal charges are at issue, so there is little reason to believe that a judge will more readily detain a violent husband for hospital care than he would in the case of a criminal complaint. Furthermore, mental health authorities would not be likely to conclude that a man is "dangerous," let alone "imminently dangerous," if wife-beating is his only "symptom."

Mental health workers with the best intentions in the world may be totally unable to comprehend the urgency of the problem if they have not experienced, or at least observed, a domestic conflict close at hand. George Kirkham, in an article in *Human Behavior*, pinpoints the difference between police and social service response to domestic violence: "Police deal with other people at their worst day in and day out. They mediate interpersonal conflict in situations where the disputants were crying, kicking, screaming, threatening, bleeding, drunk or enraged. Let me assure you that it is quite a different thing to discuss Jones's chronic temper outbursts in a counseling setting and to face the same man after he just smashed his wife's face with a fist and is angrily proclaiming his readiness to do the same to you!"[41]

Social workers, psychiatrists, and correctional workers are almost invariably removed in time and space from the context in which a violent incident occurred. Usually, by the time a mental health worker becomes involved in a case, the latest round in an on-going marital contest is already a week or ten days in the past. By that time, wounds are already healing and tempers have cooled; the very complex psychological adjustments that have enabled a couple to maintain their marriage in the face of occasional violence have already been made. The calm, contemplative setting of the office may even add to the general feeling that things went momentarily awry but are all right now—even in a marriage that has a steady history of violent outbursts.

One more caution is necessary here. Even in the seemingly ideal event that a husband agrees to therapy, the battered woman must protect herself against bad advice. A therapist may assist the victim and assailant in recognizing the patterns that lead to their violent altercations, but the identification of dangerous patterns and habits is no guarantee that the relationship will mend itself. Nor is it a foregone conclusion that the marriage should continue. Sometimes successful therapy results in separation and divorce; such action would surely represent a positive improvement in the wife whose will was paralyzed by dependency and despair.

In his book *Psychotherapy,* Dr. Donald J. Holmes addresses his colleagues in the psychiatric profession: "We are charged with no obligation whatever to conserve the nuclear family, foster monogamy, or to save marriages. Our assignment is to save people. . . ."[42] Again, that may be true ideally, but the view that reconciliation is the only answer is, as we have seen, all too prevalent among representatives of the social system. A particularly common variation on this theme is that a marriage should be preserved at all costs "for the sake of the children." People who subscribe to this view tend to forget that exposure to violence can be more traumatic for children than a clean break between their parents would be.

The services offered by our society reflect the most deeply engrained moral attitudes of a culture that often sacrifices the woman to protect the man as well as the image of the family. If reconciliation is regarded as the only solution or goal, wife-beating will only be perpetuated. Even if a battered woman can overcome her sense of isolation and shame to actually ask for help, so far as the criminal justice and social service systems are concerned, her efforts may be wasted.

8

SURVIVAL TACTICS

In the preceding two chapters I examined the ostensible solutions offered to the battered wife by society at large. Although several of these courses of action seemed designed to help battered women, a closer look reveals that they actually exert pressure on her to endure her lot in the name of "reconciliation." The criminal justice system and the social services in this country must be made more responsive to women's needs in general. As a beginning, these institutions must formally acknowledge the existence of wife-beating as a social problem.

These are huge demands, which will not be met overnight. Hopefully, change will occur incrementally as the consciousness of the entire country is raised to encompass a feminist perspective. Social change of any sort is a long and complex process. Once a segment of the population comprehends and accepts a new insight, months and even years go by before the new way of thinking is reflected in the inertia-bound institutions of society at large. But women trapped in violent domestic situations cannot wait for society to favor their cause. They must be encouraged to take every action possible to protect themselves from harm and to escape from their trap.

Above all, and a factor to be considered before any other, the battered woman must take precautions against isolation. Although a battered woman's reasons for keeping her problem to herself may be deeply rooted, she must fight against secrecy and the isolation that results from living a lie. If the reader is a battered woman, I say directly to her: don't keep secrets; don't worry about protecting your, or your husband's, reputation. Make contact with a woman you can trust and to whom you can run in time of need. Anticipate the worst and prepare for it. Remember that if you have nowhere to go when things get rough, you may end up reconciling with your husband, not because you want to continue living with him, but because you feel there is no other alternative. If you have reason to expect trouble, figure out ahead of time where you and your children can go. You will need a place where you can think about what to do next and find support from someone who understands your problem and *believes* you.

Physical Fitness

In *The Second Sex*, Simone de Beauvoir discussed the differences between the way girls and boys are conditioned to live in the world. Of the young boy she said, "Against any insult, any attempt to reduce him to the status of an object, the male has recourse to his fists, to exposure of himself to blows: he does not let himself be transcended by others, he is himself at the heart of his subjectivity. Violence is the authentic proof of each one's loyalty to himself, to his passions, to his own will."[1] But of the girl, she has this to say: "Such masterful behavior is not for young girls, especially when it involves violence[2]. . . . [The girl] simply submits; the world is defined without reference to her, and its aspect is immutable as far as she is concerned. This lack of physical power leads to a more general timidity: she has no faith in a force she has not experienced in her body; she does not dare to be enterprising, to revolt, to invent; doomed to docility, to resignation, she can take in society only a place already made for her."[3]

Times have changed just enough since de Beauvoir wrote *The Second Sex* for us to say with confidence that women are not inevitably "doomed to docility, to resignation. . . ." Women are reclaiming their bodies and beginning to learn their own physical potential. Slowly this trend is radiating outward from the women's movement into the community at large. As a result, more opportunities are arising—self-defense classes, martial arts training programs, and so on—for women to build up their strength and thereby develop confidence in the power of their bodies. A woman who has never tested herself physically and is unaware of her own strength will not dare to defend herself from attack. The ability to make that gesture, even against an opponent

150

of superior strength, may signal a battered woman's desire to take an active stand against her fate. I do not mean to encourage women to risk serious injury for the sake of a symbolic gesture. But when a woman *does* make a gesture of resistance, even against impossible odds, she may have at that moment turned from the "docility" and "resignation" that de Beauvoir saw to take an active interest in changing her circumstances. Physical fitness can help, if not inspire, a woman to take responsibility for her own life.

In a series of articles written for *The Furies,* Lee Schwing discussed the value of physical fitness. To be strong is to have some idea of what it means to be in control of your life, said Schwing. "Being physically weak makes women think that men are naturally stronger. If you are weak, intimidation is easier and the constant fear of rape and other forms of physical violence keeps you in place. Physical weakness relates directly to women's traditional passivity. As we were forced to accept the weaker role, especially in the middle class, so we also accepted the idea that being strong or aggressive in any way was a man's role. Our role was acting weak, submissive and quiet."[4]

Thus physical weakness in women tends to confirm for many people the myth that traditional patriarchal sex roles are based on biological realities. Many women as well as men accept this assumption. As a result, a dangerous myth lives on. Women *are* capable of great strength and great physical endurance. Even when a man is physically larger and stronger, a healthy and self-confident woman, if she knows what she is doing, can put up a formidable defense. Cynthia Hales, who teaches a Karate-based form of self-defense at Glide Church in San Francisco, has found that women are almost always stronger than they think they are. She notes that many women carry children and heavy grocery bags; these exertions contribute to muscle tone. Lessons in self-defense develop that strength as well as the self-confidence and self-respect necessary to put up a fight. Much of what Hales teaches is aimed at building her students' self-confidence and helping them to express it through their bodies.

According to Susan Murdock, who teaches at the Womens' Martial Arts Center in New York City, "Fear of men turns women into victims." As a homework assignment she asks her students to look at men on the street, to note their physical condition, and to size them up as possible opponents. Having completed a course at the Center, Murdock contends, a woman will be in better physical shape than three-quarters of the men in New York City.[5]

Courses like those Hales and Murdock teach are really designed for street-fighting, specifically for combating a would-be rapist or attacker. "Most women teach a Karate-based form of offensive self-defense, with added variations of their own—anything they know will work," Hales told me. "We teach a woman how to stop somebody and immobilize him temporarily, so she can escape. We give her a sense of what to do, where to hit or kick, how to ward off a blow or break a choking block." Hales also said that since a woman is usually smaller than a male opponent, she has to be quicker and more accurate.

Some standard techniques taught in these classes include punching, elbowing, knife-handling, kneeing, kicking, and yelling—not the traditional scream for help but a ferocious, blood-curdling "KEEEAAAIII!" This Karate-type yell is meant to startle the attacker, giving the woman a chance to get in a good jab or Karate chop and run. Translating the techniques of street-fighting into defenses inside the home poses some problems. Outdoors a woman has more space and is free to run once she has immobilized her attacker. In the home space is limited by four walls and narrow hallways. But the main difficulty is that the battered woman's attacker is not a stranger, but someone with whom she shares an intimate relationship. She may feel squeamish about deliberately trying to hurt her husband, even if he has repeatedly injured her. At that point she must put herself into what Murdock calls "the fighter mentality." It may save her life. (My friend, mentioned earlier, who interceded when she saw a man beating his wife on the street, managed to get the man down and sit on him until the police arrived. Her training in the martial arts gave her the knowledge and strength needed in a time of crisis.)

Schwing observes that women's fashions contribute to keeping women "in their place."[6] High heels, clunky heels, and now platform shoes make running almost impossible, and most skirts hamper a woman's ability to move freely. A woman should wear comfortable clothes that allow her the most freedom of movement. But, above all, Schwing insists, she should have a plan of action in her mind in case of attack.[7]

I am reminded here of the experience, described in Chapter 2, of my daughter and grandson who were caught in the crossfire of an angry, drunken husband threatening his wife. The man wound up by striking my daughter in view of her young son. When they finally reached my house, my daughter and grandson were still afraid that the man might show up looking for his wife, so we pulled out the materials I had collected on self-defense and tried to work out a plan. We read that feet are good weapons, that stomping hard on the opponent's foot is effective, and so is a well-placed kick. Without time for practicing the more specialized techniques, we decided that a good swift kick in the shins would be the best we could do. All four of us (my twelve-year-old granddaughter had been home with me) began making short fast kicks, putting as much strength behind them as we could muster. "But if we all begin kicking him at once, we'll probably wind up kicking each other," my granddaughter pointed out. We burst into laughter as we visualized ourselves immobilizing each other instead of an attacker. Then I looked down at our feet: my daughter and grandson had on tennis shoes, my granddaughter was barefoot, and I had on slippers. We obviously needed another plan of action. We were so worked up by the incident and the fear of attack that we hadn't realized until then that we outnumbered our supposed opponent four to one. We could surround him. I looked up the telephone number of the police and wrote it down on a card by the phone. My grandson was assigned to make the call if it was necessary. And then we all went to bed, but my daughter slept with her boots on that night.

If physical fitness helps individual women to become aware of their own strength, it also adds to the potential of group efforts. Anti-rape squads have been formed in some cities across the country. These squads are composed of women who band together for the purpose of punishing men who have raped or attacked women. I do not advocate this eye-for-an-eye philosophy, which seems to contribute to already soaring crime rates. But a Japanese version of the female brigade appeals to me very much. In Tokyo a group of feminists are on the alert for situations in which women are victimized by men. These women don pink helmets and march into the man's office, carrying placards proclaiming, "We will not condone the tyranny of the husband!" If the man is present, the women shout at him through bullhorns so that all can hear, warning him to mend his evil ways. If he is not there, they demand that the company executives justify themselves for hiring such a heel. Misako Enoki,

153

who heads the Tokyo brigade, says that the tactics used by her group get results. "It works because of loss of face. The demonstrations cause shame and embarrassment to the husbands." But not all cases require a full demonstration. There are times when the group meets with both the husband and wife. They find that the husbands are very polite under these circumstances. "We have become so famous they are afraid of us," explains Enoki.[8]

Mental Fitness

The corollary to physical fitness is, of course, mental health. A woman who is periodically abused by her husband and feels she is trapped may start to believe that she deserves what she gets. At such a point, she feels little self-esteem or motivation to change her situation. Such despair is intensified by loneliness. Women who suffer the indignity and physical pain of beatings often do so alone and in silence. Up to now these secrets have been locked inside the family home. Sisters may not even tell sisters that they have been beaten; daughters may not tell their mothers. Violent and frightening sounds in the night remain mysteries to children.

The phrase "bears her shame alone" accurately reflects a social reality, but actually the battered wife bears her *husband's* shame at giving way to his childish and dangerous need to exercise power over another person. As we have seen, society allows a man to behave violently in his own home and often assumes that his wife deserves to be beaten. When *she* begins to believe she deserves abuse, a woman is in real trouble. But she still might see her way clear to ask for help. Her options could include psychotherapy on a one-to-one basis, a women's movement consciousness-raising group, or an assertiveness-training class.

Any or all of these alternatives can help a troubled woman to regain a sense of her own identity and individuality as a person, and not as an adjunct to her husband. They can also help to restore her sense of self-worth and give her the support she needs to make a lasting change in her life. Still, the woman looking for help must consider with care which method is best for her. And she must "shop around" with the same caution she would use when planning any investment of time and money.

The world of clinical psychology or psychiatry is traditionally conservative and no more reflects sexual equality than do our criminal justice system and social service institutions. The clinician often adheres to the patriarchal myths that form our cultural heritage. If the woman seeking psychotherapy does not shop around and proceed with skepticism, she may find herself in the care of a therapist who subscribes to the theories of female inferiority and innate masochism and actually *believes* that a battered woman provokes or deserves the abuse she gets.

Naomi Weisstein is the author of a classic piece on this subject called " 'Kinder, Kuche, Kirche' As Scientific Law: Psychology Constructs the Female." The basic problem, she says, is that "[p]sychology has nothing to say about what women are really like, what they need and what they want, essentially because psychology does not know." She contends that "the kind of psychology which has addressed itself to how people act and who they are" fails to understand *why* they act the way they do and what might make them act differently. Psychiatrists and clinical psychologists have drawn theories from their practice based on "stuff so flimsy and transparently biased as to have absolutely no standing as empirical evidence." Years of clinical experience is no substitute for empirical evidence, Weisstein claims. The problem with a discipline which rests its findings on "insight, sensitivity, and intuition is that it can confirm for all time the biases that one started with."[9] In other words, if a psychiatrist believes, as Freud did, that all women are born with an innate streak of masochistic self-destructiveness, any and all clinical experience that a psychiatrist has with women will confirm that belief. If a psychiatrist believes that a battered wife or a rape victim somehow precipitated the crime against her, he will interpret her words and actions—and even her dreams—to support that theory.

Nobody likes to be beaten. Karen Horney said in *The Neurotic Personality of Our Time,* "We have to tackle a misunderstanding, which consists in confounding actual suffering with the tendency to suffer. There is no warrant for jumping to the conclusion that since suffering exists, there is therefore, a tendency to incur it or enjoy it."[10] Elizabeth Truninger agrees with Horney and suggests that the pattern and frequency of wife-beating merely demonstrates that some women *tolerate* violence (for whatever reasons), not that they invite it.[11] And Letty Cottin Pogrebin says, "To claim that women provoke the violence of which they are so often victim is to argue that Jewish passivity invited genocide or that the exploited poor are to blame for the corruption of the rich."[12]

Nevertheless, some elaborate theories on provocation have developed out of the social sciences; they fall under the general heading of "victimology." Victims are treated as if they created the situation in which they find themselves and are held responsible for their own problems, irrespective of other contributing factors. Researchers arrive on the scene with personality and motivation tests to determine what is in the individual's psychological history and behavior that causes or contributes to his or her victimization.

According to Stephen Schafer in *The Victim and His Criminal,* the victim-precipitation theory requires the victim "to do nothing to provoke others" and to attempt actively to prevent a crime in order to escape responsibility.[13] In the case of marital violence, where assailant and victim live together intimately, however, I cannot see how it is possible *never* to annoy or anger one's partner at some time or other. Implicit in the theory, as Schafer describes it, is the warning "Stay in your place. Do what your husband bids, and he won't beat you."

Menachem Amir elaborates another aspect of the problem in *Patterns in Forcible Rape.* He says that "victim precipitation of rape means that in a particular situation the behavior of the victim is *interpreted by the offender* either as a direct invitation for sexual relations or as a sign that she will be available for sexual contact if he will persist in demanding it. . . ."[14] Again, where marital violence is concerned, it seems to me that the husband can as easily misinterpret his wife's words, gestures, actions or motives as the rapist can. When provocation is ascribed to the victim, it may really exist only in the offender's mind.

Nathan Caplan and Stephen D. Nelson complain in *Psychology Today* that a "person-blame" bias arises from too much concentration on victims' behavior and not enough on the offenders'. They say this bias is the result of erroneous definitions of the problem, and that impartial empirical research is badly needed. The alternative to studying individual psyches is a "situation-centered" examination of the powerful physical, social, and economic forces that influence individuals. Person-centered research may have its own validity, these writers say, but it vastly oversimplifies the situation and "reinforces negative labeling of groups already socially, politically and economically vulnerable."[15] A study deliberately designed to be "situation-centered" is currently being conducted by Russell and Rebecca Dobash, who are studying battered women in refuges in Edinburgh and Glasgow. In addition to considering the social variables investigated by Gelles and others (alcohol use, unemployment, and so forth), the Dobashes are also taking into account the institutional history of the families, the lack of effective sanctions by relevant social agencies, and the general status of women in Scotland.[16]

Sociologists Lynda Holmstrom and Ann Burgess have challenged the usefulness, as well as the sexist bias, of the victim-precipitation theory directly. They suggest that the emphasis on the theory within the mental health profession serves only to limit our understanding of attack and victimization. They point out that if rape victims are seen to cause the crimes committed against them, then only by changing the victims' behavior will rape be eliminated. The same, of course, applies to wife-beating. By placing the emphasis on the victim, sociologists and psychologists fail to ask more relevant (and obvious) questions: Why do men rape? Why do husbands beat their wives? Under what social conditions is this behavior encouraged or discouraged? What can be done to change the *assailant's* behavior? Seeing the victim as responsible adds to her oppression and in no way contributes to a solution. In fact, such an attitude implies that, under certain circumstances at least, a man has the right to abuse or attack a woman. Anyone who allows that assumption to go unchallenged by supporting the victim-precipitation theory is committing, in effect, a political act.[17]

Politics are concerned with power. Claude Steiner, in *Issues in Radical Therapy*, sums up the relationship between power and psychotherapy very neatly: "Oppression can only be perpetuated through the use of power. We cannot oppress others if we have no power over them. . . . We consider all psychiatric activity to be political in nature. This is because in every instance, psychiatric intervention affects the structure of the power relationship between people. Psychiatrists deal constantly with situations in which people are victims of abuses of power. Psychiatric intervention invariably affects those situations, either by changing them or leaving them alone in which case psychiatric intervention, by default, supports the oppressive *status quo,* and becomes once again, political."[18]

Wife-beating is, without question, an example of power-abuse. A therapist who believes that the man should be wielder of power in a relationship and the woman should be subordinate will only validate the man's right to express his power over his wife. Such a therapist may encourage the husband to develop less explicit, physically injurious expressions of power, but still supports "the oppressive *status quo.*" A woman who expects help from such a person may as well stay home.

The now classic Broverman study, published in 1969, demonstrated that not just some, but *many* professional therapists hold sexist notions of what constitutes mental health in the adult male, the adult female, and the adult per se. In this study clinical psychologists were asked to describe male and female behavior and also to indicate what they considered to be "normal, adult behavior" (sex unspecified). Not surprisingly, their descriptions of typical male and female behavior matched commonly accepted sex-role stereotypes. Also, the therapists equated characteristics of the male with what is "normal" and "adult." Women were viewed as "more emotional," "less objective," "more submissive," and "less competitive" than men. The "typical" behavior of women was not considered to be consistent with that of "normal adults."[19]

It is no wonder that the woman who expresses her personhood and tries to act like a "normal adult" is often called unfeminine, masculine, or a Lesbian if she succeeds. Feminist therapists Ruth Pancoast and Lynda Weston say that men experience no dichotomy between adulthood and manhood because society says that the two are identical. Women, however, have two conflicting ideals: woman and adult. . . . "A woman who tries to be a healthy adult does so at the expense of being a healthy woman, and vice versa. . . . Society then has constructed a no-win situation for women."[20]

Within the professions of psychiatry, psychology, and social work, women are raising their voices to protest the power imbalances and genuinely sexist interpretations of mental health supported by their colleagues. At the American Orthopsychiatric Association conference in San Francisco in 1974, Pancoast and Weston, as members of the

Feminist Counseling Collective in Washington, D.C., flatly refused to accept the official line: "As we see it, if women continue trying to reconcile the unreconcilable, we just can't win. We must realize that as long as sexist standards exist and women try to live up to them, women will be oppressed. But women can win. We can repudiate the contradictory demands and change the nature of the goals we are trying to achieve."[21] The Feminist Counseling Collective, they said, outlines for itself four major goals and directions: (1) a non-sexist alternative to traditional therapy; (2) training of new feminist counselors to continue the service; (3) raising the growing feminist consciousness of the professions by organizing workshops and discussion groups and by speaking at conferences, universities, and agency staff meetings; and (4) developing a feminist theory of psychotherapy and the psychology of women to help them achieve self-actualization and a sense of self-worth.[22]

Basic to the notion of feminist counseling is the integration of what were previously known as "masculine" and "feminine" qualities, and the recognition that they are really "human" traits possessed by every individual to greater or lesser degrees and at various times. The woman is encouraged to be centered in herself, to acknowledge her own strength, and to recognize her own capabilities. She is taught that labels on her behavior such as "unfeminine" are meaningless. She is helped to become aware of the options open to her and hopefully convinced that whatever she chooses to do is an expression of her own nature and her own needs at a given time. Feminist therapy offers a pathway to womanhood, personhood, and self-respect.

It bears emphasizing that the Feminist Counseling Collective represents a radical minority in a basically conservative profession. The trend toward feminist counseling and radical therapy (which incorporates a feminist viewpoint) among mental health professionals is gradually taking hold, but a woman should take great care in selecting a therapist. Professionals may have all the proper letters after their names, but there is no guarantee that their services are enlightened or even in the client's best interest.

I strongly encourage battered women to seek out a feminist therapist—a professional who understands the bias in our prevailing value system and will help women to become autonomous in defiance of that system. Unfortunately, such people are rare. Not all women therapists are feminist therapists; female clinicians in the Broverman study were no less sexist than their male colleagues. In fact, not all those who claim to be feminists really are. Their commitment may only be superficial because feminism has become chic in certain professional circles.

A woman searching for a feminist therapist may have to rely solely on referrals. Recommendations can generally be obtained through local women's centers or other women's organizations. Therapists on such referral lists usually have been screened to some extent. But these lists are not foolproof. The woman seeking therapy is well advised to interview a prospective therapist, sort out her feelings about the interaction, and consciously try to determine whether the goals and approach of the therapist are compatible with her own. Does the therapist try to maintain "neutrality" (as if that were possible!) or is she willing to discuss her feelings and admit to personal biases? Does the therapist believe that saving a marriage is a top priority, or does she encourage women who choose to make it on their own? How does the therapist react to the word feminism? A client has the right to know the answers to these questions before investing her trust, time and energy—not to mention money—in a course of therapy.

For more specific information along these lines, invest a dollar and send for a *Therapy Information Packet for Women*, available from Women in Transition, 4634 Chester Avenue, Philadelphia, Pennsylvania 19143. This packet includes articles on how to choose a therapist and how to evaluate a therapy experience. A woman contemplating going into therapy should understand her role as a consumer and be prepared to evaluate the services offered.

Consciousness-Raising Groups

In the late 1940s, after Mao Tse-tung's Revolutionary Army had purged the villages of North China of enemy control, political workers called the townswomen to the village square to testify to the crimes that had been committed against them. Slowly, painfully, and sometimes inarticulately, the women spoke of their oppression: of being sold as concubines by their fathers, of being raped by landlords, of being beaten by their husbands and fathers-in-law. The process of venting anger became personally liberating, and out of these "Speak Bitterness" meetings, as they came to be called, local Women's Associations were formed. In these associations the women found the strength and sup-

160

port they needed to confront their oppressors and demand equality. In *Woman's Fate,* Claudia Dreifus calls the Speak Bitterness meetings "the first consciousness-raising groups, the first known attempt to convert womankind's private laments into political acts. . . . Through public recitations, women discovered their situations were not isolated. They developed self-confidence. From self-confidence came consciousness. From consciousness grew action."[23]

Consciousness-raising in the United States is a small-group process which evolved within the Women's Liberation movement to give women what Pamela Allen calls "Free Space." The small group brings women out of their isolation, makes them aware that other women share the same experiences, helps them to recognize and interpret their feelings, and gives them the self-confidence to make changes in their lives. The group fosters a feeling of intimacy and trust, allowing the individual woman to open up and discuss her personal fears and problems, perhaps for the first time in her life, in an atmosphere of sharing and understanding. "What we have found is that painful 'personal' problems can be common to many women present. Thus attention can turn to finding the real causes of these problems rather than merely emphasizing one's own inadequacies."[24] Out of their own experience women begin to establish priorities, invent their own approaches to problem-solving, forge a feminist ideology, and take action. The group helps a woman to "gain perspective on her life and the possible solutions to her problems," but would never tell her what choices she ought to make. Rather, the small group serves as a reference point from which the woman can operate, using it as a "stimulus to self growth."[25]

"So here we are: eight women, simultaneously common and uncommon, articulate and inarticulate, separate and the same," Dreifus says of her consciousness-raising group. "We have all lived the female experience and don't know what to make of it. The only thing we know for certain is that female is the bottom of the life ladder, and that hurts. In our own varied ways, we search for a freedom we are not sure exists. . . . We stumble, we plod, we are awkward, uncertain, vulnerable, yet we are a surprisingly tough bunch. . . . At each session, we are amazed at the similarity of our experiences, at the closeness we feel for each other —we, who started out total strangers."[26]

"Consciousness-raising is many things," Dreifus says, "but one thing it is *not* is psychotherapy, or any other kind of therapy. Therapeutic processes have been employed mostly to encourage participants to adjust to the social order. CR seeks to invite rebellion. . . . Psychotherapy frequently forces the individual to think her problems are private and personal. CR, through group discussions and analysis, shows women that most female problems stem from a patriarchal societal structure. Freudian psychoanalysis, as a matter of fact, is defined as part of the problem—not the solution."[27]

Allen says, "The total group process is not therapy because we try to find the social causes for our experiences and the possible programs for changing these. But the therapeutic experience of momentarily relieving the individual of all responsibility for her situation does occur and is necessary if women are to be free to act. This takes place in both the opening up and sharing phases of the group activity and gives us the courage to look objectively at our predicament, accepting what are realistically our responsibilities to change and understanding what must be confronted societally."[28]

An advantage of a consciousness-raising group for the battered woman in particular is that in addition to helping her confront her domestic situation truthfully, it automatically puts her in touch with other women who understand her circumstances and can offer her shelter in times of need. For one who "has borne her shame alone," there is no more positive encouragement toward self-confidence and self-respect than the realization that others have suffered in the same way and that collectively they can find answers to their problems.

But the battered woman who joins a small group and fails to share her secret (as I have learned some have done, for fear of rejection) is cheating herself and her sisters. She not only passes up the chance to articulate her predicament and get some feedback, but she also denies herself the joyful experience of being honest, of learning to trust, and of sharing with other women. Also, she impedes the progress of the group by blocking the trust relationship which is basic to the objectives and functions of the total group, and prevents the others from experiencing and analyzing wife-beating as a part of women's oppression.

Assertiveness Training

Ironically, male psychiatrists often characterize the battered wife as a domineering, overbearing shrew. Yet those

162

who operate shelters for battered wives have learned that these women are generally passive, inhibited, and helpless. "In anxiety-provoking situations, many women feel unable to act. They find themselves at a loss to come up with an effective response, or any response at all," state Stanlee Phelps and Nancy Austin.[29] These writers lead workshops combining assertiveness training with consciousness raising for women at community health centers in Southern California. In their book *The Assertive Woman*, Phelps and Austin define assertiveness as "behavior that allows a person to express honest feelings comfortably, to be direct and straightforward, and to exercise personal rights without denying the rights of others and without experiencing undue anxiety and guilt."[30] Through assertiveness training, women can learn to express the awareness they gain in consciousness raising.

Phelps and Austin explain that there are several ways for people to react to any given situation—passively, indirectly, aggressively, or assertively. They make a distinction between aggressiveness and assertiveness, and object to putting them on a continuum, even at opposite ends of the scale. They see aggressiveness as negative and assertiveness as positive behavior. Pam Butler and Portia Shapiro, who gave a two-day workshop for the University of California Extension, agree that the two concepts should not be confused. Assertiveness means expressing oneself directly, honestly, and spontaneously, they say, whereas, aggressiveness involves attacking another person or infringing on the rights of others.[31]

In a chapter called "The Anger in You," Phelps and Austin say that an assertive expression of anger has the "potential to prevent violence."[32] People who find it difficult to express their anger honestly allow it to build up and fester until they lose control and overreact to something trivial. Such people need to learn to deal with anger appropriately and realistically. Once they do, these writers contend, much unnecessary violence will disappear. Women in particular often have difficulty expressing, and even acknowledging, their anger. The depression many experience may be an extension of their passivity, as some argue, but it may also be anger that has been turned inward. This anger needs to be redirected and expressed as what it is. Phelps and Austin also believe that an angry person can be disarmed by what the listener says in response; active listening alone can have an impressive effect. Their book offers many suggestions and techniques, both for expressing anger and dealing with it in other people.

Beverly Stephen, in an article on assertiveness training for the *San Francisco Chronicle,* states: "Obviously assertiveness wouldn't have worked very well for slaves and it probably wouldn't work very well for underdog groups today. It works for people who have real options."[33] I agree that in chronic situations, where the wife is a "slave" and is beaten habitually, assertiveness on her part might aggravate her husband all the more. But new communication skills might help the battered woman to attain self-confidence, and realize that she does have options. Equally important, they could enable her to cope with the agency personnel on whom she must rely if she decides to seek aid. She certainly won't get anywhere with the legal or social service systems unless she knows how to assert herself.

Divorce

For women who have been brought up to believe in the necessity of conventional marriage, deciding to get a divorce is a revolutionary step. A woman who comes to this decision effectively chooses to live on her own, to manage her own domestic and financial affairs, and, if she has children, to take full responsibility for their upbringing. For a person with no experience in living alone and relying on her own resources, the life of a "single woman" may appear to be an unattractive alternative to her troubled marriage. But once a pattern of violence has been established, and she admits to herself that it will repeat itself no matter what she does, a battered woman must face the fact that she would be better off on her own. If she has involved herself in therapy or consciousness raising in order to develop her self-respect, she should use that outside support to strengthen her resolve to strike out on her own, rather than waste time and energy in vain attempts to patch up a hopeless marriage.

Choosing an attorney to handle a divorce is as important as selecting a therapist. Many attorneys do not want to be bothered with wife-battering cases because of the paperwork and court appearances involved in obtaining restraining orders and the problems arising from protecting the client while the case is pending. Some lawyers who are willing to take such a case may lack the specialized experience required and overlook protective procedures. Others, who cannot comprehend the danger to the woman and the urgency of her case, or who believe that all efforts toward reconciliation must be exhausted first, may delay rather than try to obtain an early court date. For these and other reasons—not the least of which is the individual attorney's fee schedule—a woman must be very careful in selecting an attorney. She needs an advocate who understands her plight and will represent her best interests. Again she should obtain referrals and check them out. Many cities have a Women's Law Center which offers legal advice and makes referrals.

Having handled 2,500 divorce cases, of which 800 involved violence, in her first three years at Brooklyn Legal Services, Marjory Fields understands the needs of her battered clients. First, she arranges for the wife and children to leave the family home immediately, and go to an address that is unknown to the husband so that he cannot continue to harass or harm them. Then she tries to demystify and speed up the legal processes, while involving the client as much as possible—such as arranging for the summons to be served on the husband by a friend or relative. Fields has found that several critical time factors apply in wife-beating cases. If no action takes place by one week from the time of the beating, the woman is liable to rationalize her situation and change her mind. Also, women who have experienced periodic beatings consistently for over a year are more likely to pursue a divorce or leave home permanently than those who have been beaten for a shorter time. Many women who have not received counseling and who have been beaten only once are apt to back down. But after a year or more of such beatings these same women return to follow through.

Sad to say, once the battered woman has hired an attorney, she faces yet another ordeal in convincing the court that she deserves a divorce. Though most states consider physical cruelty (also called cruel and inhuman treatment) to be grounds for divorce, the record shows that wife-beating does not automatically qualify as physical cruelty in the opinion of some judges. This fact is not really surprising, since the same system which refuses to prosecute the wife-beater as a criminal has the power to grant and withhold divorces.

Barbara Hirsch, author of *Divorce: What a Woman Needs to Know,* describes marriage as a contract entered into by three parties: the wife, the husband, and the state.[34] But power is not divided equally among the three parties. The state has the controlling interest in every marriage, with its exclusive jurisdiction over the marriage status, divorce, and all other domestic-relations proceedings. That means that the court has complete control over the behavior of the other two parties to the marriage; in fact, those parties must apply to the state in order to make *any* change in their legal relations with each other. The state issues protective orders, grants annulments or separate-maintenance decrees, can order the husband and wife to a marriage counselor before granting divorce, grants or denies divorce, decides under what conditions a divorce may be allowed, and determines who shall have physical custody of the children.

The state also determines the particulars in a divorce settlement, effectively determining certain basic aspects of the other two parties' lives after the divorce is final. The state can demand an accounting of the financial assets of the man and woman, determines the amounts of child support and/or alimony to be paid, and divides community property. The state can also send the offending party to jail for failure to comply with its orders. In fact, the state can enforce whatever it deems best for the other two parties in the marriage. Furthermore, through the Internal Revenue Service and other revenue sources, the state exacts payment from the other two parties for the above services rendered, whether or not those decisions have favored their interests. The decisions of this third party are binding, though they may be revised from time to time by an appeal for re-hearing or by legislation—again, at the discretion of the state. Applying for a divorce is a solemn business, then, and assurance that the divorce will be granted is by no means guaranteed in states that do not have no-fault dissolution. Consider the following case:

The wife of a prominent Washington, D.C., attorney left her husband permanently after he beat her severely, inflicting wounds that required thirty-seven stitches. The woman expected to get a divorce with no trouble, but the couple lived in Virginia where physical cruelty is not recognized as a ground for divorce. Only abandonment, desertion, adultery, impotency, imprisonment for a felony conviction, pregnancy by another, sodomy, and voluntary separation are legal grounds in Virginia. Therefore, though the woman presented credible medical evidence to prove her case, the *husband* was granted a divorce from her on grounds of desertion since it was she who had left the family home. Prior to the separation and divorce, the couple had lived affluently, but since the wife was found to be legally "at fault," she received a poor property settlement and no alimony. She was sixty-two years old and without work experience. At present she works as a domestic.[35]

This woman could have chosen to use voluntary separation as a means of obtaining divorce. Voluntary separation provides that if a husband and wife live apart for a specified period (the time varies from state to state and ranges from six months to seven years), one or the other party may apply for divorce. This is a no-fault procedure; it makes no difference who left or who asks for the divorce. A husband could beat up his wife and leave her, wait out the required time, and then divorce her for voluntary separation. But the Virginia wife expected to be granted a divorce on the basis of her medical evidence as well as a substantial property settlement because of the couple's economic status. She probably never even considered voluntary separation. First, she would have had no means of support to rely on while she waited out the required period of time. Second, she probably never dreamed a court would require her to remain married to a man who had injured her severely, and therefore never considered she might be risking the settlement she had a right to expect. The moral here is never rely on common sense, not to mention common decency, in matters of domestic law.

Most states do allow physical cruelty as a legal ground for divorce (the exceptions are the District of Columbia, Louisiana, Maryland, North Carolina, and Virginia). The snag, of course, is determining what constitutes physical cruelty. In 1966, beating—as cruel and inhuman treatment—became a ground for divorce in New York state. Even so, the plaintiff must establish that a "sufficient" number of beatings have taken place. As Marjory Fields puts it, "One or two slaps will not do, but if you have four attempted chokings, you're in."[36]

Fields sent me the briefs on a case in progress—the *Echevarria* case—which she feels could be a test for future wife-beating cases. According to the Statement of Facts in this case, the wife had been beaten about the "head, face, and all over her body" within the first month of her marriage. She did nothing about the beating at that time, but four years later her husband beat her again, this time even

167

more cruelly. She sought and was granted an order of protection, left her husband, moved in with her parents, and, with legal services counsel, sued for a divorce and alimony. The judge dismissed the case, however. He ruled that as a matter of law, "if a husband beats a wife two times and there is a hiatus of four years between each beating, that is not sufficient ground for a judgment of divorce." The judge held that New York law requires a "continual course of [cruel] conduct." Although the wife claimed that she was unable to work because of continual harassment from her husband, which made her fearful and nervous, the judge also denied her support payment. He suggested that perhaps after one year she could file for divorce on the ground of constructive abandonment, since she had been forced to flee from the marital home for her safety.

Throughout the proceedings, by the way, the husband did not have an attorney; he chose to represent himself. As it turned out, he was quite right not to incur the expense of legal counsel, since he did not even have to defend his violent behavior during the hearing.

The case was appealed and the Appellate Division upheld the dismissal, though one judge did dissent and voted to grant a new trial. The case has now been submitted to the New York State Court of Appeals. The brief for the plaintiff raises two questions. Are two beatings sufficient basis for a divorce on the ground of cruel and inhuman treatment? Is a wife of four years, without income or assets, entitled to alimony?

Fields states in the brief that "case law has established what is insufficient conduct for a divorce based on cruel and inhuman treatment," but the issue of how much cruelty a wife must suffer to qualify for a divorce has never been clarified in court. But since the court held that the two beatings in this case were insufficient basis for divorce, they contend, the court therefore requires that a plaintiff be subjected to "a continual course of [cruel] conduct" in order that a divorce be granted on grounds of cruel and inhuman treatment.

By the time a decision is made on this appeal, the time period will have matured for action on a constructive abandonment ground for divorce. But Fields is doubtful that this cause of action can be established in this case in which the facts indicate cruelty. Fields is a fighter; she has handled too many divorce cases in which physical abuse was a factor to let this one go by. She wants a determination once and for all on just how much cruelty a wife must endure before the court will allow her to terminate her marriage. The outcome of this case will be of vast importance to battered wives everywhere, but particularly in New York state.

A statement from *Women in Transition: A Feminist Handbook on Separation and Divorce* attests to the universality of the problem. New York judges are not the only ones who have to be convinced that wife-beating constitutes physical cruelty. "Mere hitting and slapping, even if it resulted in a broken nose, will not qualify for physical cruelty (although it could be part of a charge of 'indignities' or 'mental cruelty,' and would certainly be good evidence of 'incompatibility'). Nor can you use merely accidental injuries as evidence of physical cruelty. You must show that the physical acts indicated either an uncontrollable and dangerous tendency to violence on the part of your spouse, or that his feeling toward you was manifested in the physical cruelty."[37] To prove physical cruelty, a woman must produce medical records as evidence of the severity and frequency of the offense.

"Mental cruelty," on the other hand, covers a wide range of grievances from insults in public to "minor" physical assaults and threats of violence—any course of conduct that causes mental anguish or endangers health. If a woman suffers from nervousness, migraines, or sleepless nights as a result of her husband's behavior, she can claim mental cruelty. If she has seen a doctor or therapist and has been put on tranquilizers, she can use that as more evidence of the serious harm done to her health and well-being. The hitch is that "a course of conduct" must be established. The wife must prove that her husband's pattern of obnoxious behavior has persisted over a fairly long period of time. "Obviously, legislatures and courts are not going to allow divorces for the normal stresses involved in a marriage," the *Women in Transition* handbook says.[38] Furthermore, not all states allow mental cruelty as a ground for divorce. Those which do not are Louisiana, Maryland, North Carolina, South Carolina, Virginia, Arkansas, and the District of Columbia.

Though as a rule violent husbands apparently do not need to prepare a careful defense against the charge of physical cruelty, certain standard defenses do exist. Presumably, self-defense does *not* constitute an adequate one. If a wife strikes first and the husband has to defend himself, he is justified only insofar as his action fends off the

169

immediate threat, though judges have been known to "consider height, weight, and relative strength of the parties in deciding the question of self-defense," says Barbara Hirsch.[39]

Laches (delays in exercising the right to sue) or statutes of limitations apply in divorce cases; if a specified amount of time (different from state to state) has passed between the beating and the charge, the beating is not admissible as ground for divorce. *Women in Transition* clarifies: "This does not mean, however, that you cannot get a divorce at the end of twenty-five years of continuous mental or physical cruelty. You can always say, 'I've tried and tried, and now I know it just won't work.' (Or—'I just don't think I'll last much longer.') What you *cannot* do is wait an unreasonably long time after the last incident on which you base your complaint."[40]

One familiar line of defense is known as "condonation." If the husband/defendant can prove that his wife forgave him and so "condoned" the offense, divorce is not granted. The legal definition of condonation is "full and free forgiveness, expressed or implied, of an antecedent matrimonial offense on condition that it shall not be repeated and that the offending party shall treat the other with conjugal kindness." In fact, if the wife voluntarily has intercourse with her husband at any time after the beating she cites, legally at least (and probably without knowing it) she condones his violent act.[41] Says Hirsch, "condonation is automatically *implied*" from just one act of sexual intercourse.

Happily, the defense of condonation has undergone some recent changes. The Missouri Court of Appeals granted a woman a divorce even though she had sexual relations with her husband. The court decided that her indulgence was an "unintentional adventure resulting from propinquity of person and the opportunity it afforded" and did not imply forgiveness. A Superior Court granted another woman a divorce because her husband had acted "premeditatively and fraudulently" with the express purpose of nullifying her chances for a divorce when he teased and cajoled her back into the conjugal bed. A few years ago the Vermont legislature abolished condonation as a defense, and Texas will only allow it if indeed there is a very real chance that the couple might reconcile. Illinois came up with a unique idea. Since the state is forever trying to hold the couple together and it is feared that condonation is a deterrent to "reconciliation," the legislature passed a law allowing copulation during litigation. The case is temporarily suspended while the husband and wife give it the old college try, and during the life of the order condonation does not apply.[42]

Recrimination is another defense against a divorce action. The battered wife who seeks special relief must be blameless herself. If her husband can make a retaliatory charge against his accuser, she may not be granted a divorce. The courts still speak of making *equitable* judgments under the circumstances of the case. "If you seek a divorce decree, you must not have been guilty of grounds for divorce yourself. No matter how badly your husband may have treated you, if you sue him for divorce, he may contend that you are not entitled to the equitable relief of a divorce decree because you also have been guilty of misconduct amounting to grounds for divorce," Hirsch warns.[43] It is not enough that a victim/wife be a martyr and put up with repeated beatings; she must be a saint as well.

"While recrimination has a logical basis in the historical context of the equity courts, it just isn't a realistic approach to marital problems, and certainly does not provide a solution," Hirsch contends. "Keeping a man and woman under the same roof when at least one wants a divorce and both are guilty of grounds for divorce is, at best, an exercise in futility and, at worst, an invitation to open warfare and let the children be damned."[44]

Vermont and Texas have abolished recrimination as a defense against a divorce suit. Some states, like Oregon and Colorado, have replaced recrimination with the doctrine of "comparative rectitude," in which case the judge listens to both sides and awards the divorce decree to the partner who is the least guilty.[45] But many petitions for divorce are denied because the judge cannot fix the blame specifically on either party. The judge can dismiss the case, figuring that both errant spouses deserve each other, or he may grant a divorce to both parties, in which case most probably the wife will not fare well in the financial arrangements.

After a divorce decree is granted and the legal document is signed, sealed, and delivered, the battered wife who has children still is not home free. The court can decide where she may *not* live in order to insure the availability of the children when the father is granted visitation rights. Fathers' "visits" can, and often do, precipitate further violence, so when physical abuse is a factor in the divorce, the wife's attorney should ask the court to stipulate that the children be delivered and picked up at some neutral place, such as the paternal grandparents' home. In instances where the father has vented his violent temper on the children as well as his wife, the plaintiff's attorney might plead that visitation rights should be denied altogether. Some judges, however, feel that if the father is to pay support he cannot be denied the right to visit the children. In such a circumstance, the wife's attorney should argue for the stipulation that visits take place only in the presence of another adult.

A mother who seeks a divorce may be awarded custody of the children, but support payments may be negligible. The judge determines monthly child support based on the husband's income and ability to pay. Child support is always minimal; it rarely even begins to meet expenses. Collecting the payments is often a problem. As protection—both physical and financial—the wife's attorney can ask that the husband be instructed to pay child support checks to the court. If the husband reneges on payments, the wife may have to take him to court. This means more legal fees and expenses, with little chance of recovering back payments. Courts consider the case closed when *one* payment is made, according to Elizabeth Spalding, who made a study of the enforcement of support orders in the state of Connecticut for NOW's National Task Force on Marriage, Divorce, and Family Relations. Of 29,489 cases of non-support handled by the Connecticut judicial system in fiscal year 1972-73 only 48 percent were "closed"; 772 of the delinquent fathers were convicted on warrants for non-payment.[46] Another study by William Goode showed that 35 percent of divorced husbands always paid child support, another 14 percent usually paid, 11 percent came through once in a while, and 40 percent rarely or never paid.

Despite the myths, alimony is rarely awarded unless the couple has been married for a long time, the woman has no means of supporting herself, and the husband can afford it. Some attorneys do request one dollar a month alimony to keep the door open for renegotiation in case of illness or emergency.

Presumably an equitable settlement of community property will be made, but that cannot be counted on either. Since many battering husbands keep sole control of the family finances, wives are sometimes unaware of hidden assets and bank accounts the husband has stashed away. For a property agreement to be fair, both parties must have full knowledge of existing community property, and no settlement is valid if it was agreed to under threat. Some battered wives make concessions to the husband because they are more concerned with getting away from him and terminating the marriage than they are with haggling over each piece of community property. Few women walk away with a large settlement. The chapter on financial resources in *Women in Transition* is excellent for those women who are beginners at fending for themselves.

Divorce is a tricky business. Considering the difficulties that wife/victims can encounter in the process of filing, it is no surprise that more and more women are simply taking off. Tracers Company of America is presently, and for the first time in that company's history, searching for more runaway wives than husbands. On the other hand, a 1974 Census Bureau survey recorded 925,000 divorces over a twelve-month period—up 200,000 from 1972.[47]

Because of the differing laws and precedents across the nation, the most I have been able to do is point out some possible pitfalls in the divorce process and warn the battered woman not to expect an easy time of it in states that do not have no-fault dissolution. For women who wish to learn about the laws and regulations affecting divorce in their own states, I strongly recommend Barbara Hirsch's book *Divorce: What a Woman Needs to Know*. For an account of personal process—what happens to the individual before, during, and after separation and divorce—read *Women in Transition: A Feminist Handbook on Separation and Divorce*. "We believe that separation and divorce can be a positive, creative process rather than the draining, debilitating trauma it usually is," say the authors, and that statement alone is enough to recommend their book. The manual includes many personal accounts and just about all the factual information a woman needs to become acquainted with the process. The emphasis is not on how to change the system, but on how the existing system operates and how one can cope with it successfully.

For some women divorce is not an acceptable alternative. Because of religious or other considerations, they may wish instead to sue for separate maintenance. If granted, the marriage remains intact, but the spouses live apart. Community property is not divided up, and neither party can claim sole ownership of house or furnishings. The judge can award use of the house and belongings to the wife and children and order the father to continue supporting the

173

family. But in granting separate maintenance, the judge will not offer any protection to the woman or the couple's jointly owned property. The property, after all is said and done, really belongs to the husband. He can even destroy it if he wishes to keep his wife from using it. He would not be able to collect on the insurance policy, though, if that's any consolation.

Self-survival means taking action to protect oneself. The first thing a battered woman must do is look to her physical and mental health. Who is she and what does she want out of life for herself and for her children? Then she should realize that hope remains, not necessarily for her husband to change, but to free herself to begin a better life. Tish Sommers, who heads NOW's National Task Force for Older Women, says in *The Not-So-Helpless Female*, "*I can* is the best cage-breaker of them all. Tattoo it on your soul."[48] If the despairing wife/victim would say it to herself, or even scream it out loud, over and over again—"I can, *I can*, I CAN!"—she could begin to break out of her cage of helplessness and take some of the steps toward self-survival suggested in this chapter. Community volunteer organizations, especially those growing out of the women's movement, often offer the help and support that tradition-bound agencies fail to provide: understanding, self-help training, counseling, job rehabilitation, and referrals to therapists and lawyers. Making critical changes in one's life is a big step, and often a difficult one. But hope, and help, exists for the battered woman who will but recognize and accept it.

9

REMEDIAL LEGISLATION

"You can't legislate attitudes" is a truism in political circles. But I disagree; I think that legislation very often effects changes in public attitudes over time. The activity preceding the passage of a bill contributes to the process. The public must be educated to the issue and legislators must be actively pressured into dealing with the problem. Even enlightened legislators need the support of their constituents before they will stick their necks out on a controversial issue. Thus the public sector is often flooded with information when a bill on a new subject is drafted.

Once a law is passed, however, another kind of attitude-change is inevitable. When a bill becomes a law, the die-hards have to learn to accept its existence. Under threat of prosecution, they have to begin acting publicly *as if* they believed in the attitudes expressed by the law. After the civil rights legislation was passed, for example, bigots were forced to tolerate minorities as their equals and act out changes in attitudes, even if they did not feel them at gut level. But though the Archie Bunkers of this world did not really change, a lot of other people did. Many found it necessary to reassess inherited beliefs about minorities when civil rights issues were raised. Ignorance and fear, the sources of bigotry, were confronted publicly, and prevailing attitudes in society at large began to change.

Still, social change is not instantaneous. It is a complex process that can be accelerated by legislation. Given the force of law and the necessary funding for programs that will realize its original intent, behavior and, subsequently, attitudes, can be modified. When a law is enforced, it eventually becomes a part of the social fabric, a given in the daily lives of citizens. Only then does the collective change in attitudes have a lasting effect.

Throughout this book I have tried to demonstrate that the problem of wife-beating will never be solved until a radical change is effected in prevailing attitudes about women and marriage. To some extent such changes are already taking place, but only in areas affected by legislation. For example, certain inroads have been made in equal opportunity for women in employment and education as the result of new civil rights laws. But change has not been automatic; whatever progress we can claim in "legislating attitudes" has resulted from enforcement of new laws, not the laws themselves. Women's rights groups have watch-dogged federal compliance offices and brought suits resulting in court orders when discrimination occurred. Many men still resist the changes that have, for example, allowed women to become police officers or members of boards of directors in large corporations, but no one denies any longer that our society is in a period of transition, or that the changes now visible are significant and inevitable.

I believe that remedial legislation—laws making wife-assault a crime, correcting inequities in marriage and divorce laws, and equalizing opportunity of all sorts—will truly change behavior and eventually attitudes toward women and marriage, but only if such legislation is enforced. To solve the immediate problems battered wives suffer, legislation is necessary to change the legal situation in which wife-beaters currently escape prosecution more often than not. To effect a permanent change in attitudes legislation making women equal with men in every respect is a necessity.

Time and again I have pointed out the discrepancy between theory and practice with regard to the battered woman's options and the legal relief she can expect from the social system. In theory a wife who is beaten by her husband can leave him and get a divorce. In reality she must go to extremes to prove she deserves a divorce, and very often her suit is denied. In theory a wife-beater, as with anyone else who commits physical assault, is apprehended, prosecuted, and punished. In practice the offender is above the law because of his marital status and is seldom held responsible for his criminal acts. For the sake of sanity, if not human decency, our social institutions must translate these theoretical options into practice through legislation. Existing laws that do not accomplish their purposes must be thrown out or revised. Situations which are not accounted for under the law must be attended to. And, perhaps most important of all, inequities in the laws on our books must be corrected. Finally, as an active expression of these legal reforms, family-violence prevention and treatment programs must be created, funded, and put into operation.

Legislators and attorneys tell me that we have enough laws on the books to deal with wife-battering. The problem, they contend, is that the laws are not enforced because authorities refuse to recognize and deal with wife-assault as a crime. I disagree. I think that laws which do apply to wife-battering are ambiguous or not explicit. As a result, buck-passing occurs: conflicts arise between criminal and civil law, and different branches of the criminal justice system squabble endlessly over who has primary jurisdiction in individual cases. Giving wife-beating cases low priority obviously reflects a problem in police attitudes, but conflicts between criminal and family courts and debates over enforcement of protection orders reflect defects in the laws and in the legal system generally. When law enforcers are able to keep a "family man" out of jail even though he has injured his wife and children, something is wrong with the law. Police, district attorneys, and judges use weaknesses in the laws to excuse their own inaction and to discourage wife/victims from prosecuting.

The newly formed National Task Force on Battered Women/Household Violence of the National Organization for Women, coordinated by Nancy Kirk-Gormley and myself, proposes to tackle the problem of wife-battering by (1) launching a massive education program to make the public more aware of the prevalence of marital violence; (2) forming coalitions with other women's organizations and civic groups to establish emergency shelters for victims; (3) lobbying for remedial legislation. We hope that mobilizing public support will enable us to find funding for the refuges. Public concern will also help us convince legislators to review existing laws and to institute programs that will have greater long-term efficacy in eradicating violence of all kinds. As a society we must declare forthrightly and unequivocally that we will no longer tolerate marital violence, that no man has a right to beat his wife, and that offenders will be prosecuted. We must support this resolve with the dual commitment to see that victims are protected and the legal and social service systems in our country are renovated. Initiating legislation is one phase of the total effort to accomplish these goals.

177

Revising the Laws

Police must make arrests in cases of marital violence. If overcoming police reluctance to arrest requires that legal conditions for arrest be changed, then so be it. Some states do permit an officer to make an arrest for probable cause in misdemeanor cases, but most states do not. Because of media attention to police inaction, legislators are becoming more sensitive to this problem. In 1976 a bill was introduced in the Florida State Legislature "authorizing a peace officer to arrest a person without a warrant if the officer reasonably believes that the person has committed an assault or battery upon the person's spouse."

Either this probable-cause policy should be adopted nationwide or citizen's arrests should be made easier. The San Francisco Women's Litigation Unit has prepared a draft statute that would simplify the citizen's arrest procedure by allowing the citizen to merely "indicate to the police that he or she is making the arrest, describe the crime committed, describe and/or name the alleged offender, indicate where the alleged offender may be found, and describe the reasonable cause for believing the alleged offender has committed the crime."[1]

Reform in arrest policies relating to the violation of protection orders is equally necessary. If such orders are indeed to be "protective," the police must be required, by legislation if necessary, to take immediate action when a violation occurs. The buck-passing situation whereby police advise a woman to get a restraining order, but send her back to her attorney when the husband violates the order, has no protective effect at all.

Up to now, Pennsylvania has had no legal procedure for forcing abusive husbands to leave the home and refrain from further contact with the family. Therefore, the recently drafted "Protection from Abuse Act," proposed by Laurence Mass of Community Legal Services in Philadelphia, affords us the opportunity of examining a brand-new piece of proposed legislation presumably designed to meet the needs of the present day. One feature of the act is especially welcome. It would give the court "jurisdiction over all proceedings in which one adult is alleged to be or to have been abusive to another adult or minor child with whom the respondent lives."[2] Usually only married spouses are granted injunctive relief and then, very often, only after filing for divorce. Unmarried cohabitants rarely manage to obtain protective orders against each other. Therefore, if this act were passed, *all* battered women—unmarried women, women who have filed for divorce, and women who have not—would be granted equal protection under the law.

The proposed act, which failed in the lower house in 1975, said nothing about penalties for violation of a restraining order. It was reintroduced in 1976 in the Senate with this omission corrected. In most states enforcement is left solely to the discretion of the judge who grants the order. In California, under Penal Code Section 166.4, violation of a court order is a misdemeanor, but as has already been stated, police seldom make arrests under this provision. To me a protection order under these conditions functions at best as a warning rather than an order; and a warning, when the potential for violence continues to exist, has no legal value at all. Perhaps the real solution here is to make violation of a restraining order a felony so that police can arrest without seeing the violation occur, given probable cause. How else, except through explicit legislation, can enforcement be guaranteed?

The police, too, abuse their power of discretion when they refuse or neglect to respond to domestic disturbance calls (refer to the Bunnell case cited in Chapter 6 in which the woman died). Why shouldn't police officers be held legally responsible for their own negligence or poor judgment? The California Government Code presently exempts a public employee from liability for an injury "resulting from his act or omission where the act or omission was the result of the discretion vested in him, whether or not such discretion be abused."[3] At the California Senate subcommittee hearings on marital violence, the Women's Litigation Unit proposed an amendment to this section that would delete the phrase "whether or not such discretion be abused" and substitute "except for gross abuse of discretion resulting in substantial injury or death to a citizen."[4] This amendment would give the possibility of redress to a victim who has been injured as a direct result of a public employee's abuse of discretion. Perhaps such legislation would put the fear of God into those who believe they are exempt from all responsibility, even the results of their own actions.

Reform is also critically needed in legal procedures that

179

are followed once a battered wife brings criminal charges against her assailant/husband. As noted in Chapter 6, district attorneys often abuse their discretionary powers—that is, their right to make choices within certain legal bounds. A victim has a right to justice. A wife-beating case should be treated like any other criminal case. The victim should have access to an attorney who can inform her of her legal rights as in *Miranda* vs. *Arizona* and aid her in following through with her case. Giving assistants who have little or no legal training authority to decide the merits of a criminal case appears to me to be an unlawful delegation of the district attorney's power. The victim has a right to expect an attorney to review her case and to evaluate it on the basis of law, not the conciliatory precepts of social work. Prosecution of crimes should be given priority over crimes against property and victimless crimes. The victim of marital violence should have the right to prosecute, and district attorneys should be directed to take "high risk" cases. Likewise the wife/victim should have the right to prosecute the case as a felony if she wishes; she should be consulted on her case at all times and allowed decision-making power in the plea-bargaining process.[5] Convictions are the means by which offenders are put on notice that their anti-social behavior will not be tolerated. With practice prosecutors might learn how to get convictions in marital violence cases.

Legislators must review practices within the criminal justice system and provide the necessary guidelines to correct its deficiencies. In the prosecution of a crime of violence, the whereabouts of the victim should not be divulged to the defense. If a wife/complainant fears further attack from the accused, certainly the rule of disclosure should be waived. Since district attorneys and judges fail to exercise their power of discretion in such instances, legislation is obviously needed to explicitly permit victims of violence to withhold information that would endanger them.

The Family Court, where "reconciliation" is the primary concern, serves the husband's interest by decriminalizing his behavior. In states where Family Court has jurisdiction over marital violence cases, legislatures should take immediate steps to return such cases to the criminal courts where they belong. The criminal court's function is to adjudicate, not conciliate. Coercing a victim into reconciling and living with her assailant/husband is not only a miscarriage of justice, but an absurdity. The next time she could wind up on a slab in the morgue.

Reform is needed at every stage of the legal process. If a man is prosecuted on the charge of battering his wife and is actually convicted, at the discretion of the judge he can get off with a suspended sentence and a warning. Naturally, everyone, including the wife, hopes that the guilty husband will not repeat the offense, but experience shows that more often than not he does. The judge's warning does no good at all. In the case of a first offense where injury is not severe, I believe that at the very least the husband should be remanded to some sort of psychological or psychiatric counseling. A reprimand is not enough. If the batterer receives help at the outset, his erratic behavior might be corrected; he might even learn to control his rage. Since most batterers refuse to seek therapy voluntarily, the court must mandate therapy. Follow-up is also required of the court to protect against the Framingham experience—where clinicians followed the line of least resistance and wound up counseling the wives instead of the battering husbands. If the offender refuses therapy, he should be sentenced to jail. And repeat offenders should be sentenced to jail automatically.

Many people object to sending a violent husband to jail; they believe that he will not be rehabilitated in jail and will only return to vent his pent-up rage against his wife. Others reject the concept of enforced therapy, arguing that unless a client initiates therapy out of the desire to change, the treatment will be ineffective. But what are the alternatives? How else is the cycle of marital violence to be broken? I am aware that the alternatives have shortcomings, but the risk of failure is preferable to doing nothing at all and allowing husbands to beat their wives with impunity.

Nor can we allow the men who control our legislatures to continue to exempt husbands from prosecution for rape when the women they rape are their wives. Rape is another crime of violence that goes unpunished when it happens within the sanctity of marriage and the home. To date our society has refused to acknowledge even the possibility that a wife can be raped by her husband. As a matter of fact, under the terms of the unwritten marriage contract, American law protects the husband's right to sexual intercourse with his wife on demand. The husband's marital "right" is the wife's marital "duty." If a wife reneges and her husband uses force to exert his conjugal rights, she has no legal recourse.

By contrast, a husband in Russia is answerable under the laws on rape. According to William Mandel in *Soviet Women,* a husband can get two weeks in jail for "gross behavior" towards his wife—simply on her word. He can also draw a sentence of from three to seven years for rape on his wife's complaint—with no witnesses needed. Mandel says this does not mean that Russian courts fail to weigh the credibility of testimony given by both parties. But a woman's so-called "enticing" behavior—the usual defense for rape in the United States—does not excuse the man for acting against her will. A Russian prosecutor told Mandel that the victim's behavior does have significance, "but it does not eliminate responsibility for the use of violence." Also, drunkenness does not mitigate, but rather increases, responsibility. The Russian approach to rape in marriage may be due to the fact that at least one-third of the prosecutors, judges, and lawyers and one-half of the jurors are women.[6] The criminal codes of Sweden and Denmark, as well as countries in the Communist block, also proscribe rape in marriage.[7]

Rape is rape. The identity of the rapist does not alter the fact of his act, nor lessen its traumatic effects on his victim. The marital status of the parties involved should have no bearing on the definition of the crime of rape any more than it should on the crime of battery. In some states legislators are redefining the conditions under which rape is prosecuted, but none have as yet dared to address the issue of rape within marriage. They need to be confronted with the deleterious effects of their omission not only on the institution of marriage, but also on society as a whole.

To me the double standard is the basis for our most serious social problems. One set of rules operates in society at large, while another set, informed by the "home-is-a-man's-castle" philosophy, applies to behavior in the home. I believe that our society is now plagued with violence because it is allowed to run rampant in the family home. Behind that sacrosanct door, men are allowed to rape and beat their wives. Children learn these lessons from their parents first-hand. It is really not surprising, therefore, that the elderly people in our cities presently must be protected against teenagers who beat and rob them. Children who literally have been educated to violence eventually become inured to it. Their behavior results from the tacit agreement by law enforcement officials to look the other way while some people express their violent tempers however they wish.

One means of intercepting crimes of marital violence is through a better reporting system among public agencies contacted by victims. The police, district attorney, doctors and hospital emergency attendants, family and social service agencies, and mental health clinics should be required, by law if necessary, to keep records of such cases and send them to a designated central registry for compilation. Researchers could then determine trends and patterns in the use of these agencies and pinpoint trouble areas, including identification of repeat calls. For instance, an act relating specifically to spouse-abuse was introduced in the Florida legislature requiring personnel of public agencies to report cases of such maltreatment to the Department of Health and Rehabilitative Services. The bill provides immunity from liability to reporting agents or agencies and denies physician-patient and husband-wife privilege "in any civil or criminal litigation in which the abuse of a person by his or her spouse is an issue."

Legal reform that will criminalize marital violence is only a beginning. Other aspects of family law must be reviewed and evaluated in terms of sexual equality, particularly those statutes and case-law precedents that empower a husband to control his wife's finances. We need explicit legislation to correct the grave inequalities that exist in marriage. Federal, state, and local government must provide leadership and appropriate funds to initiate and implement any or all of these legal remedies.

Gun Control

Gun control legislation would go a long way toward reducing the atmosphere of violence of which wife-battering is a single expression. In Chapter 2 I discussed the high rate of killings that occur between intimates and noted the fact that guns have top billing as the weapons used in these homicides. According to Goode in his section of a lengthy report from the National Commission on the Cause and Prevention of Violence, "every serious analysis shows that a reduction of gun ownership would substantially reduce the rate of homicide."[8] It would also deescalate the atmosphere of violence, he says, as would the gradual elimination of guns from the hands of the police. "The tools of violence increase the potential of violence" in today's society just as they did in the Old West.

Reliable estimates indicate that guns can be found in approximately half of the total number of American homes. The increasing availability of these weapons not only heightens the potential for more murders, but also generates an atmosphere of tension and anxiety and a greater readiness for violent solutions to problems. The National Rifle Association and other lobbyists have managed to block legislation for strong gun control up to now. Donald Lunde, professor of psychiatry at Stanford University, who has researched the high murder rate in the United States as compared to other countries, claims that because so many guns are already in the public's hands, stopping their sale now would have little effect. He suggests a far more effective solution would be ammunition control. As the "close to home" aspect of the gun issue becomes increasingly clear, I believe that the women's movement and other human-rights groups will take on the issue of gun and ammunition control as their own. Any legislation that might affect the atmosphere of violence in our country deserves our full support.

British Proposals for Legal Reform

Following the publication of Erin Pizzey's book and other related articles, the House of Commons in Britain appointed the Select Committee on Violence in Marriage to investigate the problem. Members of the committee concluded the report on their findings by proposing legislation expressly designed to meet the needs of battered wives. This expression of official concern is certainly worth the attention of American legislators, since the proposals themselves are directly relevant to the shortcomings in our own legal system. We might even use the committee's proposals as models for revising our own procedures.

In its 1975 report, the committee stated that "assaults in the home are just as serious as assaults in other places and that citizens who call the police to their aid at a time when they are being assaulted are entitled to the full protection of the law. . . . It must be stressed that certainly where there is evidence of any injury the police should be ready to arrest the man there and then, subsequently to

184

charge him and either keep him in custody until his appearance in court or, should this not be feasible, escort the woman and children to a Women's Aid refuge or other safe place. We deprecate the use of summonses in this situation, which leaves the man free until his court appearance. It may well be that, given this initial protection and if referred to a solicitor, the woman will prefer to pursue a civil remedy rather than a criminal one or there may be a reconciliation. Neither should be seen as proof that the police action was a mistake. Rather the reverse. This is not the kind of case where a conviction rate can be a justification of the initial action. We believe that effective police intervention in this area would do a great deal to reduce the problem of violence in this country and contribute to the prevention of a number of homicides."[9]

The committee suggested that when an injunction is served on the husband a copy should be sent to the superintendent of the local police station. (See Chapter 6 for a similar suggestion regarding American police.) This procedure "would confer power on the police to arrest the man should it appear that he has either entered (or attempted to enter) the matrimonial home when he has been ordered to keep away, or (where the injunction restrains the husband from assault) that he has committed an assault upon his wife or that there is immediate danger of assault." The committee added that it recognized "the arguments against involving the police in civil law," but considered this "the only way to make enforcement effective." Furthermore, its members concluded that "the problem of battered women is exceptional enough to require an exceptional remedy."[10]

The committee objected to the requirement that divorce or separation proceedings be initiated before an injunction will be granted (a common requirement in United States jurisdictions as well). The power to issue an injunction is presently limited in England to the High Court or Divorce County Court. These courts are not immediately accessible, but the Magistrates' Court is. The committee therefore recommended that Magistrates' Court be allowed to issue injunctions restraining a husband from assaulting his wife and excluding him temporarily from the family home.[11]

Much of the committee's research was conducted in Scotland, where wife-battering is also known to be severe. When a criminal charge of assault is brought, Scottish law requires that the charge be corroborated by a witness. Evidence of injuries is not enough. This requirement is analogous to the common requirement by American district attorneys that witnesses other than children be available to testify before a case is considered worthy of prosecution. The Select Committee recommended that this condition be amended in instances of marital violence. Such a rule may be generally justifiable protection for the accused in other cases, the committee conceded, but "it makes it too difficult for the law to protect the battered wife." Assaults on wives generally take place in the privacy of the home where there are no witnesses other than the children, and judges are unwilling to subject children to the rigor of court hearings.[12]

The committee noted other disadvantages suffered by battered women under Scottish law which have their counterparts in many United States jurisdictions. For example, a wife cannot start divorce or judicial separation proceedings based on cruelty and thus obtain an interdict [injunction] while she is still living with her husband as his wife, but she does not have the right to occupy the family dwelling pending a divorce, and she cannot prevent her husband from selling the property even if it is in her name.[13] The Select Committee consequently recommended that reform of Scottish divorce law be given a high priority.

Models for Social Reform

The 1975 hearings on marital and family violence held by the California Senate's Subcommittee on Nutrition and Human Needs represented a gesture of public concern that might serve, at least in their intent, as a prototype for expressions of interest by other state legislatures. During these hearings, the Women's Litigation Unit proposed a statute that would create a California Center for the Prevention and Treatment of Family Violence, to be maintained under the direction of the Secretary of Health and Welfare.[14] The Women's Litigation Unit's draft described the center as a clearinghouse for information. The center staff would compile and analyze statistics on family violence and determine the extent of wife-beating in particular. It would encourage and publish new research on family violence, and develop training materials for personnel engaged in family crisis intervention. Also, the center would provide financial and technical assistance to public and nonprofit private agencies and organizations that created promising programs for identifying, preventing, and treating the causes of family violence.

The eventual result of the proposed statute would be the establishment of local centers serving defined geographic areas throughout California and staffed by interdisciplinary teams to provide a range of services related to family violence. Services would include the support of shelters for battered women and their children, crisis switchboards, rap groups, and drop-in centers. Programs for the prevention and treatment of alcoholism and drug-abuse as they relate to family violence would also qualify. Self-help organizations designed to prevent or treat family violence would receive priority for funding, and steps would be taken to preserve the confidentiality of all personal records.

To qualify for supplemental state funds, local governments would have to have a local ordinance on family violence and a means of recording and reporting the incidence of family violence in their jurisdiction. This provision is extremely important. Hard data on reported incidents of wife-beating would not only confirm the prevalence of this crime, but would furnish a means of measuring the effectiveness of projected remedies. Another significant provision of the act is that local governments would be required to unify the efforts of law enforcement and local public service agencies and guarantee prompt service to victims.

A similar bill was introduced in the Florida legislature in 1976. And such a program could be adapted to a national scale. Hard-pressed state and local governments could receive revenue-sharing funds from the federal government under the administration of the Department of Health, Education and Welfare. To date, one United States senator, Birch Bayh, has expressed interest in introducing federal legislation on family violence through the Senate Judiciary Committee on which he serves.

The recommendations for social service reform made by the British Select Committee on Violence in Marriage and those of California and Florida are strikingly similar. The Select Committee recommends that Britain's initial goal be the establishment of twenty-four-hour emergency services in family crisis centers in all towns and cities with a population over 50,000. Simultaneously, committee members want to see one specialized refuge for battered women established for every 10,000 people.[15] The recommendations were based on evidence gathered over a five-month period from the testimony of government officials, professional experts from related fields, and victims themselves. Committee members also paid visits to refuges already established in England and Scotland. "What is clear is that the number of battered wives is large—much larger than may be thought—and the demand for places in the refuges which have opened reflects the pent up need,"[16] the committee report stated. Committee members felt that ongoing research would now be necessary to determine cause (which they had difficulty distinguishing from effect) and to discover measures that would prevent violence in marriage.

The committee's research was reassuringly thorough and its recommendations were far-reaching. The report expressed the need for programs in the school system that would focus on domestic conflict, the roles of partners in marriage, parent/child relations, family law, and the value and use of social services. The committee was also quick to note that children who live in refuges need special nursery and other educational provisions. The report suggested that nursing and medical schools include courses on social dynamics of family life in their curricula. And, as an over-all approach, they proposed that special conferences be set up all over Britain to encourage and help each area to determine for itself the best local response to the problem.

Some of the recommended services already exist in our social service system, but they are not now easily accessible or specially adapted to the needs of female victims. Intrinsic in the California and British proposals is the integration and special adaptation of these services. Time and money will be saved in the long run if the delivery system for social services is adapted to the special needs of clients. For example, twenty-four-hour staffing may not require extra personnel; it may only necessitate a rescheduling of shifts.

The Select Committee was explicit in its report as to the value of taking action. "It is worth repeating our awareness that some of our suggestions involve the spending of public money at a time of great financial stringency. We have made these recommendations, however, in the confident belief that the long term saving, in cash terms as well as in terms of greater human happiness, will amply justify the expenditure incurred."[17] Legislators in this country would do well to realize that postponement of appropriations for victim service centers and shelters could result in situations far more costly.

Legislation on Employment Opportunity

Many battered women remain in violent domestic situations because they are totally dependent financially on their husbands. Recently two bills have been introduced in Congress which, if passed, could change this situation drastically. The first is the Equal Opportunity for Displaced Homemakers Act, introduced in 1975 by California Representative Yvonne Brathwaite Burke. This bill, now in the House Committee on Labor and Education, would establish multipurpose service programs for persons who have worked solely in the home and who are therefore unable to collect health, retirement, social security, or unemployment benefits as a result of their labor. Under the terms of this act, the individual who has worked for "a substantial number of years providing unpaid household service" for the family, is no longer supported by the income of a family member, and experiences difficulty in finding employment because of the "lack of recent paid work experience" is eligible for job counseling, training, and placement. A similar program, established by the California legislature and now operating in Alameda County as a two-year pilot project, limits eligibility to people over thirty-five, but the federal act does not specify age. Both programs deal specifically with the homemaker's economic insecurity should she be divorced or widowed. The battered woman who needs to become self-supporting in order to make good her escape would also be eligible for the program.

The other federal bill, perhaps a more "pie in the sky" measure because of its sweeping and total approach, is the Equal Opportunity and Full Employment Act of 1976, introduced by California Representative Gus Hawkins. This bill could provide the opportunity to an economically dependent woman to earn her way to independence. But even more useful in the long run, it might eradicate the circumstances that contribute to female dependence in the first place. The Hawkins Act declares that all adult Americans able and willing to work have the right to equal opportunities for useful full employment at fair rates of compensation. It elaborates an ambitious program involving everyone from Local Planning Councils to the President

189

in developing programs and jobs in both the public and private sector. The goal of the act is to insure full employment within five years. It would create a federal Job Guarantee Office and a Standby Job Corps that would provide temporary placement on public service projects if no suitable jobs were available. Any person who felt deprived of his or her job rights would have the opportunity to seek redress by suing through the United States Court.

This legislation would not only provide full employment opportunity to all citizens, but would also pave the way for new attitudes towards women, marriage, and family relations. Women who can attain independence and be self-sustaining make better partners in the mutual venture of marriage and family. Also, provisions in the bill for part-time work and flexible work schedules would allow couples more options in structuring their marriages and dividing family responsibilities. The husband and wife could take turns working full time, for example, or they could both work part time and take turns caring for the children and performing necessary household chores. They could move away from narrowly defined roles and eliminate some of the pressure and anxieties both might feel in maintaining such roles. The right to full employment could put both spouses on an equal footing and give them equal responsibility for their shared household. The balance of power has long been a principle in international relations where it serves to prevent strong industrialized nations from taking over weaker underdeveloped countries and to stave off war. By analogy, the balance of economic power between marital partners might be seen as a means of preventing the tension that leads to domestic violence in the first place.

The Equal Rights Amendment

The proposed Equal Rights Amendment to the United States Constitution provides that, "(e)quality of rights under the law shall not be denied or abridged by the United States or by any state on account of sex." The other two provisions of the proposed amendment give Congress the power to enforce the amendment and charge that the amendment will go into effect two years after ratification, thereby giving the states time to comply. At the time of this writing, the ERA has been ratified by thirty-four states; to secure passage of the amendment thirty-eight states must ratify. The sixteen states that have failed to ratify the amendment are Alabama, Arizona, Arkansas, Florida, Georgia, Illinois, Indiana, Louisiana, Mississippi, Missouri, Nevada, North Carolina, Oklahoma, South Carolina, Utah, and Virginia.

By law, married women are presently entitled to little more than bed and board as reward and compensation for their work as homemakers. Although they would benefit greatly by the passage of the Equal Rights Amendment, they are often among the most vociferous opponents of ratification. Such women object to the ERA on erroneous grounds which indicate their misunderstanding of the nature and effect of the amendment. They argue, for example, that the ERA will undermine the structure of the family, that the wife will have to work outside the home in order to provide fifty percent of the family income, and that upon dissolution of the marriage the wife would no longer be entitled to alimony.

On March 22, 1972, Senator Birch Bayh read into the *Congressional Record* excerpts from the Senate Judiciary Committee report explaining some of the ramifications of the ERA. In domestic relations, as elsewhere, the amendment would prohibit discrimination based on sex. "This will mean that State domestic relations' laws will have to be based on individual circumstances and needs, and not on sexual stereotypes. . . . It is clear that the Amendment would not require both a husband and wife to contribute identical amounts of money to a marriage. The support obligation of each spouse would be defined in functional terms based, for example, on each spouse's earning power, current resources and nonmonetary contributions to the family welfare. . . . [U]pon the dissolution of marriage, both husbands and wives would be entitled to fairer treatment on the basis of individual circumstances rather than sex. Thus alimony laws could be drafted to take into consideration the spouse who had been out of the labor market for a period of years in order to make a noncompensated contribution to the family in the form of domestic tasks and/or child care. . . . In sum, there is no reason to fear that the Equal Rights Amendment will have undesirable effects on the rights of men and women under State domestic relations laws."[18]

The ERA would also insure an equitable division of community property. Presently, in some states the wife is not entitled to her half of the shared property when the husband dies; he may will away as much as two-thirds of the estate. Even in states where community property laws do exist, the husband generally has sole right to control the family finances and can make transactions without his wife's consent. A man can buy a house in his name and sell it without his wife's knowledge. The Equal Rights Amendment would also nullify state laws that place special restrictions on the right of married women to establish credit, to enter into contracts, to establish a business, or to become a guarantor or a surety.

Laws that were originally enacted to "protect" women often function now to restrict their economic freedom and keep them dependent. Protective labor laws, for example, limiting the number of hours women may work have "protected" them from earning premium overtime pay and from being promoted to higher paying jobs. Protective laws have been manipulated and twisted to legally justify job segregation, differential wages, and discrimination with respect to seniority. As a result, women have traditionally worked in menial jobs at the lowest pay. The Equal Rights Amendment would make such discrimination illegal and give all women the opportunity to become economically independent. The amendment would therefore afford battered women and mothers alone working to support their families the assurance that their rights to fair pay and equal job opportunity were guaranteed by the United States Constitution.

A well-financed campaign designed to defeat the ERA has been misrepresenting the nature and intent of the amendment in states that have not yet ratified. Who is behind this campaign and where is the money coming from? The answer, obviously, is whoever has the most to gain by continuing to discriminate against women. In *Majority Report*, Sandra Roth writes about her attempt to identify these people: "In states like Illinois, Nebraska, and Oklahoma, where ERA ratification has faced overwhelming opposition, the insurance industry has particularly powerful lobbies."[19] She goes on to name leaders of the anti-ERA forces and their connections with various insurance companies. In another article, *Majority Report* states that "the vast bulk of the multibillion dollar industry's profits comes from large policies sold to married men. And, as men retreat from the role of sole provider for the family, women will probably not take up the slack in life insurance coverage. . . . The average policy taken by a married man [according to the industry's 1972 statistics] was $21,430, compared with $8,010, the average policy sold to a woman head of household. . . . If married men were no more susceptible to insurance salespeople's guilt tripping than women heads of household, 2,381,191 fewer policies would be sold in a year. The loss would amount to $51,028 billion."[20] And yet another article in *Majority Report* states: "In the sale of life insurance, sex discrimination takes the form of ignoring the statistical differential in favor of women; while in health insurance, women frequently pay up to 150 percent of what men pay for equivalent coverage. Though they pay more, women usually wind up with less inclusive coverage than do men: benefits are of shorter duration, premiums are higher, and pregnancy-related illnesses as well as 'female disorders' are usually excluded."[21]

Obviously, insurance companies are not the only large corporations that benefit from sex discrimination. Married women who oppose the Equal Rights Amendment would do well to consider the apparent wealth of the anti-ERA campaign and to investigate the motivation behind it. The proponents of the amendment are relatively poor; as victims of the economic discrimination they are fighting, their financial resources are notably small. Nevertheless, pamphlets on the Equal Rights Amendment that will help to clarify the provisions of the ERA and to distinguish fable from fact are available at any branch office of the League of Women Voters.

The Self-Negotiated Marriage Contract

The Equal Rights Amendment would correct discrimination based on sex expressed in statutes and case law presently governing marriage, divorce, and family relations. But many people nowadays are questioning the viability of marriage altogether and are trying to create alternatives that could exist as legal entities. Lenore Weitzman begins her thoughtful consideration of alternatives to marriage by analyzing the pitfalls of the conventional "unwritten" marriage contract. She writes that the state's interests in controlling marriage include promoting public morality, ensuring family stability, assuring support obligations, and assigning responsibility for the care of children.[22] Most opponents of marriage consider the state's interest in public morality to be the most objectionable. They argue that questions of morality are personal and religious, and not the business of the state in a free and diverse society. Given the separation of church and state, a principle basic to our understanding of democracy, the state's only concern should be ensuring fairness to and safety of the persons involved in legal or quasi-legal marital relationships. These individuals, and not the state, should define their own relationships and roles within marriage.

Weitzman suggests that couples be allowed to negotiate their own contract according to their own needs and lifestyles. "A man and woman could decide, in advance, on the duration and terms of their relationship, as well as the conditions for its dissolution. They could specify their respective rights and obligations for the financial aspects of marriage (support, living expenses, property, debts, and so forth) as well as those for their more personal relations (such as responsibility for birth control, the division of household tasks, child-care responsibilities). Further, they could make some decisions before entering the relationship (such as their intentions with regard to procreation or adoption), while reserving others for later (such as domicile changes). They could also specify the process of making a later decision, such as an agreement to use an arbitrator in the event of disputes."[23]

Weitzman also envisions contracts in lieu of marriage that would allow the legalization of relationships which presently exist outside the structure of state-regulated marriage: extended families, communes, group marriages, and homosexual marriages. Although many of these "marital and family forms do not seem to create any 'societal problems,' the courts have been slow to grant them recognition," Weitzman says. "Contracts in lieu of marriage would provide a flexible alternative for those who wanted to join together in a non-traditional legal relationship."[24]

Drawing up alternative contracts is one thing; as might be expected, enforcement is quite another. Courts are apparently adamant about the "essential obligations" of the husband to support the wife and of the wife to serve the husband. Attempts to alter these roles have been declared null and void by judges "on the theory that a party cannot contract to perform that which she or he is legally bound to do."[25] Weitzman argues that such decisions are "questionable under recent developments in the law of equal protection, and surely would be in violation of the proposed Equal Rights Amendment."[26] Some California courts have recognized prenuptial agreements making personal property community property, but most courts "will not enforce contracts in contemplation of divorce"—that is, provisions for property division, support, or child custody in the event of a divorce.[27]

Judges apparently fear that such agreements tend to encourage divorce (again, failing to admit that some marriages are disasters and should be terminated). But the real problem with existing marriage and divorce law, as Weitzman points out, is that it favors "structure, stability and security to the exclusion of flexibility, change and individual freedom."[28] Roles which judges presently expect and require husbands and wives to adhere to are rigid, archaic, and arbitrary. They stem from material considerations and disregard personal ones. The acting out of these roles (authoritarian husband and servile wife) is largely responsible for the conditions that lead to wife-abuse. Marriage laws need to be redefined to allow the individuals involved to determine and agree upon their own obligations to each other and to define their own roles and living arrangements. These agreements should not be the business of the state; the state's business should be to adjudicate disagreements. Until such time as marital roles and the state's role are redefined, either the written marriage contract or the contract in lieu of marriage appears best to meet the needs of modern society. Such contracts can forge the way to new concepts that will equalize the marital relationship and allow more flexibility and individual freedom.

"Reformulating the legal structure of marriage may provide a unique opportunity for lawyers and social scientists to work together and to share their professional expertise" in arriving at a more balanced and judicious combination of individual and societal needs, Weitzman concludes.[29] Such change is imperative. Without it we only perpetuate the conditions that foster family violence.

Several other proposals relating to marriage should be noted in passing. The NOW Marriage, Divorce and Family Relations Task Force suggests that child support orders should have cost-of-living escalation clauses and be backed up by federal legislation enabling the Social Security and/or the Internal Revenue Service to locate missing spouses.[30] (According to Herma Hill Kay, professor at Boalt Law School of the University of California at Berkeley, a new parent locator service is now being established by the

Health, Education and Welfare Department.) And Virginia Cowan, a lawyer and member of the Nashville chapter of NOW, is the author of the proposed "Bonnie Plan" regarding income tax splitting. Under this plan partners using this method of computing their taxes would be required to attest to an oath "that he or she does in fact have equal ownership, management and control of the income, assets and liabilities of the marriage partnership, with penalties for perjury and fraud inhering in the oath."[31] Thus a husband could not exploit his marriage for tax benefits without affording his wife her due.

Clearly the time has come for legislators and courts to review and revise old laws which reflect sexual inequality and an obsolete system of values. Such activity could have profound effects on the overall problem of domestic violence and on wife-battering specifically. Not only do men presently take advantage of their favored position in marriage by bullying their wives, but women are intimidated by the lack of support they can expect from the law. Equality and the protection of equality must be key concerns in all legislation concerning marriage, divorce, and family relations.

10

REFUGES FOR
BATTERED WOMEN

After having reviewed all the supposed options open to battered women, I have reached the conclusion that the creation of shelters designed specifically for battered women is the only direct, immediate, and satisfactory solution to the problem of wife-abuse. Victims and their children need refuge from further abuse; any other consideration —such as the need for counseling or legal advice—is of secondary importance. As I have repeatedly tried to show in this book, the battered woman's safety is not even *considered* by the service and legal professions, let alone guaranteed.

"But you can't just run from violence and find peace," writes Erin Pizzey. "Our goal is to provide a warm, supportive situation where we can help these women figure out what they want to do. For some of them it's the first time in their lives they've ever had any psychological or emotional support. Here they have other relationships to cling to—relationships with other women and children sharing the same problem."[1] In the few such refuges that already exist, battered women find solace and support. These houses are havens where she can recuperate from her wounds, recover her sense of self, and re-evaluate her situation. At houses run by feminists the battered woman becomes fully aware of all the possibilities open to her—a service no representative of the conventional social service system is permitted to perform. The need for more such shelters becomes apparent every time someone begins to investigate the problem of marital violence. Whenever a new refuge is opened, whether in this country or elsewhere, it is filled to capacity almost immediately and remains full, though the turnover of residents may be rapid.

A very brief overview of activity will bring us up to date. Some shelters for women and children did exist in the United States before Pizzey's book broke the habit of secrecy that kept battered women from leaving home and seeking help. The original Haven House in Pasadena, California, was started in 1965 by women from Al-Anon, a self-help group for families of alcoholics. This shelter housed a total of six hundred women and two thousand children before it was forced to close in 1972. New fire regulations would have required $50,000 worth of work on the building; Haven House simply could not afford to meet the code. Another refuge was operated in Maine from 1967 to 1969 by a group called Ingraham Volunteers. This house was closed when federal funds were cut off.

With the rebirth of the feminist movement in the late 1960s, women began to use the newly established women's centers, the homes of their new-found sisters, or women's communes as emergency facilities. But the establishment of Chiswick Women's Aid in 1971 was the starting point for the current international trend to create shelters specifically for battered women. Today refuges exist all over England, in Ireland, Scotland, Holland, India, Canada, Australia, and the United States. Some were modeled after Chiswick; others were created in response to local problems by groups that had never heard of Women's Aid. These refuges have now been operating long enough for us to learn from their experiences. In this chapter I will briefly describe the creation of each refuge and try to summarize the lessons learned, particularly regarding house policies and fund raising.

Refuges in the United States

Women's House—St. Paul, Minnesota

Women's House is the best-known refuge in the United States. It was created by the Women's Advocates collective in St. Paul, Minnesota, which had evolved out of a consciousness-raising group. Action-minded members of the group decided that local women needed access to legal information relating specifically to their own concerns, and in March 1972 they started a phone service for women in

198

the county Legal Aid office in St. Paul. Their effort was financed by contributions and monthly pledges made by concerned women in the community. The collective was astonished to discover that the overwhelming majority of calls came from women who had been assaulted in their own homes by their husbands. It did not take long to discover that the local public welfare and social services network (which the group considers to be the best in the country) did not provide emergency shelter for battered women, and that the women/victims were essentially trapped in their homes for lack of options. "So we housed women and children on our living room floors for two years," wrote Sharon Vaughn, a member of Women's Advocates, "while continuing to operate the phone service, helping to provide necessary legal services."[2]

In February 1973, Women's Advocates moved their office to a one-bedroom apartment, so that they could offer at least minimal shelter for a few women while continuing to conduct their phone service. Here they officially launched a campaign for a real shelter, to be called Women's House. In May they started a newsletter to keep their supporters informed of their progress. By that time they had received $750 in one-time contributions and $430 in monthly pledges, some of which were as little as 75 cents per month—gestures of support by women who could not afford more. In August Women's Advocates left their office/apartment rather unceremoniously. The apartment manager gave them the boot because of the steady stream of strangers—victims seeking shelter—who kept showing up there. The group then took occupancy in the dining room of a private home. Not until April 1974—over a year after they had begun to seek funds—did these stubborn women manage to obtain outside funding that would enable them to buy a house. By July they were painting, sanding floors, and tracking down furniture and supplies. Getting the place ready took longer than they had expected. During a five o'clock board meeting on October 11, 1974, women in need of shelter just started moving in, ready or not. By the time the meeting had ended, Women's House was filled to capacity—twelve women and their children. During the first month of "trial-by-group-fire" the house accommodated a total of twenty-two women and fifteen children.

Women's House, which sits high on a hill, has a living room, dining room, five bedrooms, a couple of kitchens, two and a half bathrooms, and an assortment of nooks and crannies. Special features include two splendid fireplaces, a paved parking area, and a large basement for a children's play area. The gigantic attic on the third floor was originally meant to be the Women's Advocates office, but the need for housing space was the first priority, so part of it was converted into living quarters.

During its first year and a half in operation Women's House has had its share of security problems. Although most refuges for battered women try to keep their addresses secret for as long as they can, their location is bound to become known eventually. Women's Advocates installed a $12,000 security system with two panic buttons designed to set off alarms at the police department. Despite these elaborate precautions, the St. Paul police took thirty minutes to respond one night when a husband of one of the residents broke into the house and ended up stabbing himself. In other midnight incidents windows were broken and glass shattered over the beds in which children were sleeping. Luckily no one was hurt. Women's Advocates decided to keep the outside of the house well-lighted at night and to replace window panes with plexiglass or cover them with rock-proof screen. Having done what they could at home, all thirty-four residents and staff (fourteen women and twenty children) descended upon Mayor Lawrence Cohen's office one afternoon to complain that police were ignoring their alarms. The visit brought the desired results, and police are now responding promptly to calls from Women's House.[3]

Women's House has caught the attention of the national television news media. Those who visit the house to film the women in action respond to the warm and loving atmosphere and the collective spirit among the residents and staff. The house has received both national and local publicity, and now occasionally gets calls from people who simply want to help. Still, most calls come from battered women in need of shelter. Women's House is filled beyond its capacity, and has a waiting list. The success of the project has its price; the need to expand is now unavoidable. Women's Advocates are therefore taking on the added responsibility of buying the house next door, which they hope to refurbish with a Community Development grant from St. Paul's Housing and Redevelopment Authority (HRA).

I want to backtrack here to consider Women's Advocates' funding experience. The collective had conducted a year-long publicity campaign and had made the rounds of agencies, both public and private, to little avail. The turning point came when the St. Paul-Ramsey Area Mental Health Program Board endorsed their proposal for a refuge "in concept" and appointed a committee to study the project and investigate possible funding. Comments from the board members were very encouraging. "I don't know of any agency that could do the kinds of things you're talking about," admitted one. Another pointed out that the police and welfare department hesitated to get involved because of the high risk, adding, "I'm for it if they've got the courage to take it on." A staff psychiatrist noted, "This is one of the few services we can offer that's potentially life-saving." And a medical director indicated that most agencies are too slow in reacting to emergencies, stressing that the main advantage of Women's Advocates was their quick response and flexibility. Only one sour note was sounded. An ex-officio board member reminded the board that residents often objected strongly when crisis homes and other service facilities were established in their neighborhoods. A number of studies were then being planned to avoid high concentrations of service centers in residential areas.[4]

The results of the board's meeting were most unusual. Usually agency boards take so much time studying a project and deciding whether to fund it that the instigators become discouraged and drop it. By the very next month, however, Women's Advocates was assured of a $29,000 grant from the Ramsey County Mental Health Board. Furthermore, the Bush Foundation agreed to make a down payment on a house in the amount of $10,000 as well as to provide an additional two-year matching grant of $25,000 for running the house and paying staff salaries. This good fortune whisked Women's Advocates "into the big-time agency stratosphere." Once they reached that lofty height, their troubles really began. The Bush Foundation, for example, stipulated that none of the money to match their grant could come from either the Mental Health funds or pledges and contributions accrued before April 1974. But the problem of how to match the Bush grant was nothing compared with the trials and tribulations the women suffered when they tried to finance the property.

The house they wanted to buy cost $34,000. Prior to the promise of funds Women's Advocates had consulted an attorney and bankers about methods of buying. They investigated the option of purchasing the house as a nonprofit corporation, and then considered buying through an individual on the basis of either long-term lease or buyback terms. They compared the merits of a mortgage with those of a contract for deed, and they studied the possibility of renting with an option to buy. They talked with a banker about the feasibility of a low-interest loan as a down payment and other funding alternatives. They investigated potential insurance costs and the probable tax status of the house.

The women discovered that the problem of non-homestead tax status (which would push normal tax rates up by about 70 percent) would be solved by buying the house as a non-profit corporation. This they decided to do. But corporations are often charged higher interest rates than individuals, and usually have a harder time getting a mortgage. When the time finally came to negotiate a mortgage, Women's Advocates Inc. drew a blank with the numerous banks and savings and loan institutions in the Twin Cities (St. Paul-Minneapolis) area. They finally had to settle for a 15 percent two-year commercial bank loan of $24,000. The interest alone on this loan is $300 per month. In two years, after paying out $7,200 in interest, Women's Advocates would still not be one cent closer to owning the house. Undaunted and resolved to meet the need for Women's House, the group devised a plan for meeting their unconventional "mortgage." They presented the following proposal to their constituents in the newsletter: "What we are asking is for people to participate in our self-help community. Here's how it works: You and 239 other people each lend us $100. With this $24,000 we pay off Commercial State Bank (there's no prepayment penalty on the loan). Each month after that we pay back our present $300 payment to lenders, saving thousands of dollars in interest. In six and two-thirds years, at the very most, we will have the entire amount paid off. If you need your money paid back, it can be paid back within 30 days after your request for payment. Do you lose interest by investing your money in this way? No. Self-reliance is your return, and no bank will come up with a gimmick or percent to approach that. The interest you have in supporting a house that belongs to the women of this community is already yours. Women by themselves have no financial power, but pooling financial resources gives all of us power . . ." If the women in the community responded and made the outright purchase of Women's House a reality, the experience would serve as a model for needed houses elsewhere and an important talking point when other groups approach foundations for matching grants. Above all, Women's Advocates reasoned, success in this venture would help make women aware of their collective financial power.

As of November 1975, ten months before the bank loan is due, Women's Advocates reported that the total "mortgage fund account" collecting interest in the bank was $7,109.58. Although a long way from the $24,000 needed, the women were nonetheless buoyed up by the spirit of the response—"the spirit of concern and responsible love behind the one and two dollars from women on welfare; behind the $25 check from a woman taking home less than $2 an hour and paying out $30 a week for a baby sitter!"

The hurriedly scribbled notes often tucked into the envelopes with the checks are a strong source of encouragement:

- Elaine L., "You weren't there eight years ago when I needed a place to go with my baby. Thank God you're there now for those in need!"
- Cheri R., "I hope this will help out a little bit. I haven't seen the house or your work in person, but it's such an important job to do that I can't be fussy about how you do it. I'm unemployed at the moment, but if my future starts looking brighter, I may be able to make a bigger contribution."
- Sarah D., "Little did I know when I began supporting Women's Advocates for the great idea I thought it to be, that I would be calling on you to help a friend."
- Miriam M., "You are doing such wonderful work. I'm glad such loving and helpful people like you exist."
- Harriet B., "I find the newsletter a continuing source of ideas and morale-boosting—especially as a model of how to write a newsletter that generates a sense of involvement in readers, (I want to write to you every time I get one.)"

"The struggle has always been one of survival. The irony of 'alternative' service groups," Vaughn wrote to me, "is that we provide a service not provided by the regular social service network, and making it work, we end up devoting an obscene amount of time and energy convincing the same straight system, that uses us as a dumping ground, to give us money to exist." One factor in the continuing struggle is Women's Advocates' refusal to maintain a conventional organizational structure at the behest of potential funding agencies.

When the group first became incorporated, they did adopt fairly traditional by-laws. The Board of Directors was composed of three residents or former residents (it is becoming fashionable these days to include "consumers" on boards), three volunteers, three representatives from the community, and two staff members. But when the staff and volunteers began to take themselves seriously as a collective, they felt that these distinctions were artificial and hypocritical. In June 1975, they revised their by-laws, eliminating the separate categories of participants. Today there is only one class of members. Any adult achieves and maintains membership status in Women's Advocates by participating in an on-going work group. The membership equals the Board of Directors and the Board of Directors equals the membership. "This unorthodox structure has already presented problems with funding," Vaughn wrote. "United Way turned us down, presumably because we have staff as voting members on our board, but we were told by one member of their board that our application was never taken seriously anyway."

Women's House operates "on the premise of respect, trust, and women supporting women as *women* rather than as professionals 'helping' clients find solutions to problems," Vaughn wrote to me. "I have spoken to professional groups and been asked to define the 'modality of treatment for the phenomenon of battered women,' and have always strongly rejected this type of syntax as automatically creating a barrier which only serves to further isolate and dehumanize the woman who is a victim not only of her husband or lover, but of society itself."

Once a battered woman's physical needs are met, Women's Advocates contend that peer counseling is the crucial factor. The strength she sees in others like herself allows the battered woman to see her own strength. She no longer feels isolated knowing that even if she decides to return home, there is a bond between herself and other women.

One of the few rules of Women's House is that if a woman is there because of physical abuse, she must not let the person responsible know where she is. A woman, who had been beaten previously, came to Women's House because of threatened violence; she had not actually been hurt this time, and decided to inform her husband of her whereabouts. He sent her a dozen long-stemmed roses and arrived the next day to take her home. Another resident was upset and asked a staff member, "Do you tell women who go back that they are making a big mistake?" The staff member replied, "No, I might like to, but I watch her go and feel sick with my own sadness and powerlessness. To tell her she's making a mistake is to increase her sense of failure—she already knows in her gut what she's doing. My job is to make it possible for her to be able to come back. What *you* tell her is much more valid than what I tell her anyway. I just work here."

Collective decision-making and the therapy of shared experience is not readily understood by conventional agencies and funding sources. The banding together of interested professionals into a Consortium on Battered Women for the Twin Cities area has been of inestimable value in bridging the communication gap. Women's House provides a much needed service for the community and in turn needs the support of the community and its various service and funding agencies. Ideally the various agencies would mesh their services with those of Women's House in response to the victim's self-determination of her needs.

As of February 1976 the purchase of both houses was assured. Women's Advocates joined with two other groups that provide emergency housing and presented a city-wide $96,000 proposal to the St. Paul City Council. When the recommended Community Development grant was cut in half, the three groups held a press conference, lobbied individual Council members, and finally succeeded in getting the Council to allocate the full amount. Women's House received $36,000—$24,000 to pay off the mortgage and $12,000 for repairs and alterations, leaving the mortgage fund for the house next door which has twelve apartments. Because of its run-down condition, the place was up for sale for $10,000, with $5,000 owing in back taxes. With a $2,000 bequest from an estate Women's Advocates were able to put $1,000 down and buy the place on a contract for deed. They are seeking $30,000 from St. Paul's Housing and Redevelopment Authority to refurbish the property and are negotiating with the State to have all or part of the back taxes forgiven because of the public service nature of their operation.

The new "annex" will allow Women's House to expand its capacity without having to double its staff. Women's Advocates are asking Community Design Center, a non-profit agency, to lend them an architect to plan the use of the two houses to best advantage. At present they are considering a walkway between the houses, a large kitchen in one house, one large play area for children, rooms for office and meeting space, and living quarters.

The patience and hard work of the collective had paid off—or so it seemed. But on March 25th came the news that HUD (Housing and Urban Development) had issued a federal regulation disqualifying city-wide programs for Community Development money. Ironically, it was at the urging of the local CD staff that Women's Advocates had changed their application and joined with Migrants in Action and the Urban League to make the city-wide emergency housing request. Certainly this unified approach to funding seemed logical; it eliminated unnecessary competition among worthy agencies and divided available funds more equitably. Women's Advocates, frustrated and disheartened, are now asking their Congressional representatives "why federal money designated to meet urban needs is granted, after a lengthy process, and then taken away on the basis that the need for service is shared by the whole city."

The success of Women's Advocates (past performance leaves no doubt in my mind that they will overcome this temporary setback) is a source of inspiration to other groups who are trying to establish refuges for battered women in their own communities. Withstanding pressures to conform, even at the risk of sacrificing funds, Women's Advocates have become the American pioneers in taking a stand on autonomy. Women's House is the living model which proves that enthusiasm, sincerity, and the solidarity of sisterhood are an unbeatable and powerful combination.

Because Women's House is based on the principle of sharing and because many women are interested in the details of its operation, the collective has given Sharon Vaughn a leave of absence to write a book about Women's Advocates. It will be a welcome supplement to my own overview of the problem of marital violence and, hopefully, will encourage other women to follow their example.

Rainbow Retreat—Phoenix, Arizona

The first of the now-existing refuges for abused wives in the United States was actually Rainbow Retreat, which opened its doors in Phoenix on November 1, 1973.[5] Unlike Women's House which is open to all battered women, admission to Rainbow Retreat is limited to abused or displaced families of husbands with drinking problems. One reason for this limitation is that alcohol, as noted in Chapter 4, plays a primary role in many cases of marital violence. Second, government funds are readily available for alcohol-connected treatment projects. According to Joanne Rhoads, executive director, alcoholism per se is not the criteria for admission, but rather alcohol involvement. "We stretch it a bit. But even when a woman denies that alcoholism is involved, we find that in nine out of ten cases drinking is still a factor," she told me.

Rainbow Retreat started with $50 and eleven dedicated and determined individuals. Today they have an annual budget of $110,000 and a shelter with a capacity for 13 women and children. During its first two-and-a-half years of operation, Rainbow housed more than 600 persons. Families come from as far away as New Jersey, Illinois, Texas, and Mexico. They are referred by doctors, counselors, and protective services. Some companies also send the wives of their problem-drinking executives in an effort to rehabilitate the family. But the average woman resident is thirty-five and has been married ten years; her husband's income is between $7,000 and $9,000 per year. Maximum stay is six weeks, but the average is twelve days.

The first concern of the staff is to deal with the crisis that brought the woman to the shelter—the trauma of a beating or being thrown out of the house. As soon as possible she is worked into the schedule attended in the shelter. "It sounds rigid and tiring, but when a woman is beaten and emotionally worn down, she needs to have decisions made for her at first. We try to meet the client where she is at. If she is capable of making a few simple decisions for herself, we encourage her to do so," Rhoads said. "Most of the women, when they first arrive, are not very trusting. Seeking help is totally foreign to them. The first step towards building trust is to provide a home-like setting. A pot of soup on the stove, clean sheets on the bed, a baby bottle laying around—these touches of home make a lot of difference."

Because the Phoenix shelter is accredited by the Joint Commission on Accreditation of Hospitals and funded by government agencies, the operation of Rainbow Retreat is necessarily more structured than that of Women's House. Each resident receives one-to-one counseling and is also required to participate in group therapy sessions. Emphasis is on looking at what is going on in the woman's life—examining problems of communication, sex, money, other women, discipline of the children, things that happen when the husband is drunk. "We try to get at the underlying problems," Rhoads told me. "Abuse takes many forms—not just the physical." So many wives are kept emotionally and financially dependent by their husbands that job training and placement has become another essential service provided at the retreat. "But that doesn't mean that we advocate divorce," the director quickly added. "We have found that 64 percent of the husbands get treatment"—a most promising side-effect of Rainbow Retreat's program.

During the six-month period between June and December 1974, the staff noted that they had been forced to turn away 250 people because the house was filled to capacity. To accommodate the overflow Rainbow Retreat established an outpatient program, which can offer counseling as well to abused wives who are not ready yet to leave their husbands. Rainbow Retreat thus offers a 24-hour emergency, drop-in, and telephone service.

The shelter receives $20,000 from the City of Phoenix and $25,000 from the Arizona State Health Department, Behavioral Division. Some paid staff positions are provided through the federal government's Comprehensive Employment and Training Act (CETA). Residents are charged a fee on a sliding scale depending on ability to pay, but most of the women have no money of their own. The grants are renewable each year, and because of threatened cutbacks in government spending, the board of Rainbow Retreat is considering dunning the husbands for the fees to cover their families' care. "It's a matter of survival," Rhoads said, "and we intend to survive."

Rainbow Retreat has extra insurance, however, in the form of a "God Bag" which sits on the mantle in the living room of the office and in the residence (two different locations). "It really works," Rhoads explained. "Everything we want or need, we just write on a slip of paper

208

and throw in the God Bag. He's always given it to us, maybe not what we want, but always what we need. What we need now is another residence because we have to get out of the one on Cactus Road. That's in the God Bag. I know we'll get it."[6]

Haven House—Pasadena, California

I have not visited Women's House or Rainbow Retreat, but I did make a trip to Haven House in Pasadena, accompanied by Lynda Weston of the Washington, D.C., Feminist Therapy Collective. We found that Haven House lived up to its name. A clean and pleasant place with lots of outside space and a children's playground, it is not a single building but a series of small bungalows in a court located in a well-kept residential neighborhood near downtown Pasadena. Five of the seven bungalows house women and children. One is the child care center, and another is used for offices and counseling. Usually one or two families share a bungalow, which is their home for the duration of their stay (a maximum of three weeks). Each resident group has its own kitchen, living room, bedroom, and bathroom. When more room is needed, the couches pull out into double beds. Food is distributed twice a week; women order what they need by checking off items on a shopping list form which they turn in the night before.

As with the original Haven House and Rainbow Retreat, admission is limited to abused families of alcoholic husbands. The refuge is part of the city's program for alcoholics. Prior to the establishment of the shelter in 1974, funds obtained under California's Short-Doyle Act for dealing with alcoholism were directed solely toward the treatment of alcoholics themselves; no attention was paid to the very real needs of their families. The number of residents at Haven House alone confirm those needs. During its first year of operation the shelter cared for eighty-five wives and two hundred children.

Ruth Slaughter, the director, told us that many wives show up at Haven House with black eyes, loose teeth, or broken bones. Some of the most brutal wife-abusers are drunken husbands who have "blacked out," she added. The problems that arise in the violent alcoholic's family are extremely delicate. During our visit a call came through which exemplified one common situation. A woman resident had been wavering between fear for her safety and the desire to go back home. The day before she had been afraid to return home to pick up her things. But today she was determined to go back to stay, knowing that a gun was hidden in the house somewhere. "All I can do is pray —I can't stop her," said Joan Leech, the administrative assistant who took the call. She estimates that sixty percent of the women who come to stay at Haven House return to their husbands. "Some have no intention of staying away. Others have no intention of going back." Whether they go back or not has nothing to do with the husband's physical violence, Leech claims. The wives of alcoholics usually see the drinking as the villain and not their husbands.

Slaughter believes that once a woman has spent some time at Haven House and has strengthened her self-esteem, she will be less likely to allow the situation to continue unchanged when she returns home. What happens then depends upon the husband's willingness to accept help. Almost half of the husbands whose wives seek refuge at Haven House do decide to seek treatment. Slaughter concludes from this fact that a crisis, a separation, or both may be necessary to bring the alcoholic to the point of actively seeking help.

Most refuges for battered women are staffed exclusively by women, but Haven House retains one male, Richard Del Rio, to give the children a "nice man image." Many of these children have only seen men acting like brutes, but Del Rio is a gentle, supportive man who cares about the families at Haven House.

Women's Center South—Pittsburgh, Pennsylvania

Women's Center South for women in transition began in 1973 in the home of Ellen Berliner.[7] Like Chiswick Women's Aid, the center had a Koffee Klatch beginning, the chief purpose of which was to offer the troubled woman a comfortable environment for talking out her problems with other women. Wife-beating soon surfaced as a major problem, and the Women's Center moved to a storefront location to operate a crisis center and to make the public more aware of the problem. Having received good community response and cooperation from the police, the women formed a corporation in April 1974, and opened a refuge with a $5,000 grant from the Pittsburgh Presbytery and the assurance of $400 per month in contributions and pledges from the community.

The refuge was a "learn by the seat of your pants" operation, according to Vickie Barnes who served as treasurer and fund raiser. The eight beds were filled immediately after the shelter opened its doors. Ann Steytler, a psychologist, and Berliner are the two mainstays of the Center, which is presently funded through a federal Victims of Crimes grant sponsored by the District Attorney's office. The shelter has one live-in staff person plus two other paid staff members and relies on volunteers to help with the program.

Besides the usual services for victims of marital violence, Women's Center South provides meeting space for Parents Anonymous (which relates to the corollary problem of child abuse), first offenders who have just been released from women's prison, and courses in creative listening (a prerequisite for staff and volunteers). Fathers may attend Parents Anonymous meetings, but men are not allowed in the upper part of the house. The shelter has only three bedrooms, and Women's Center South hopes to move to a larger facility in the near future.

La Casa de las Madres—San Francisco, California

Two more shelters for battered women were established in California in January, 1976: La Casa de las Madres in San Francisco, and the Women's Transitional Living Center in Fullerton. The first is modeled after Women's House and the second after Haven House (in style of operation, but not admission policy). La Casa was not funded; a coalition of thirty women just took the plunge, found a house and raised the rent. In contrast, WTLC was fortunate enough to obtain revenue-sharing funds from the Orange County government. Though both projects grew out of the same concern and are run by feminists, they differ widely in their modes of operation.

Marta Segovia Ashley, founder of the La Casa Coalition, explains the derivation of the name La Casa de las Madres or Mothers' House. When a woman leaves a violent home, she needs to "go home to mother." She needs a place where she will be safe, where she will be fed and cared for; she needs a retreat where she can grow strong again. The idea for the shelter originated in the Latino com-

211

munity of San Francisco's Mission District. Ashley, who is a feminist, has been heavily criticized by some of her Latino sisters who view La Casa as a threat. "We have to save the culture," they remind her. But Ashley argues, "Any part of a culture that depends upon or uses violence isn't worth saving. That part of our culture that is violent and oppressive needs to be amputated in the same way as an arm or leg needs to be amputated when gangrene sets in. When violence erupts in a marriage, the husband and wife need to be separated before a pattern of violence takes hold of the rest of the family. We want to preserve that part of the family and the culture that is non-violent."

As the Latino women explored San Francisco looking for a house and possible funding, they learned that marital violence was not limited to the Latino community. Other women from various backgrounds and cultural communities within the city responded readily to the project. Within a year the Coalition had grown from eight to thirty committed women with expertise in health care, counseling, children's programs, law, public relations, and fund raising. The Coalition also developed contacts with numerous feminist and community groups for additional support.

Unfortunately, the Coalition put all of its eggs in one basket in its initial efforts to raise funds. After months of trying in vain to obtain a Law Enforcement Assistance Administration (LEAA) grant through the bureaucratic maze of the Mayor's Criminal Justice Council, they became discouraged. But then the women heard that a four-story Victorian house with four kitchens, five bathrooms, and eight bedrooms was soon to become available for rent. The house is centrally located, convenient to public transportation, and near a hospital and a public park. The Coalition took one look at the house and knew this was it—La Casa de las Madres. They dug into their own pockets and came up with two weeks rent (full rent is $700 per month), and sent out a mailing that brought in the next month's rent. Then they began a massive publicity campaign asking for donations to be made through the San Francisco Women's Centers, the tax-deductible charitable agency sponsoring the project. The Coalition took possession of the house in mid-January, figuring they would need a couple of months to get it ready. But four days later, though totally unprepared, they took in their first family. Just as La Casa couldn't wait for government funding, victims of family violence can't wait for an ideal setting. Makeshift arrangements are better than none.

At present, La Casa is completely dependent on donations—contributions of money, household furnishings, office supplies, time, and energy. The house is staffed by members of the Coalition on a rotating basis twenty-four hours a day, seven days a week. Their enthusiasm, dedication, and commitment are commendable, but volunteerism has its limitations. Full-time paid staff is a necessity, not a luxury. The Coalition anticipates the need for three full-time coordinators: (1) an administrator to oversee day-to-day operations of the house (cooking, cleaning, maintenance), bookkeeping and fiscal management, fundraising, publicity, and data-gathering for research and evaluation; (2) a liaison person to oversee information and referral services, maintain ties with other service agencies, develop training programs in family crisis intervention for community agencies, and coordinate satellite houses and follow-up; and (3) a program coordinator to oversee emergency services, counseling, and other programs designed for the women, to organize children's activities, and to develop in-service training for workers and volunteers. The ambitious program proposed by the Coalition includes a twenty-four-hour hotline, peer counseling, consciousness raising, assertiveness training, self-defense and self-health training, vocational counseling, and Spanish language lessons in addition to the services outlined above.

A grant proposal has been submitted to the Child Development division of the Health, Education, and Welfare Department on the premise that services provided by the shelter will alter the structure and process of family interaction and, therefore, have a probable positive impact on the child's development. Marta Ashley and Marya Grambs, who acted as co-coordinators when La Casa first started, both came from violent homes. Their strong reaction to the violence they witnessed as children has given them a keen awareness of the trauma children experience.

The address of La Casa is kept secret to avoid the midnight escapades experienced at Women's House. Some women who came to La Casa learned a bitter lesson, however, when they enrolled their children in the school in the La Casa district. The old school transferred the student's transcript *and* phoned the father advising him not only of the transfer but of the family's new address as well. Therefore the children do not go to school. Instead, members of the Coalition go to the child's old school, explain the situation to the principal, and arrange to pick up the child's school books for special tutoring at Mother's House—address unknown. The problem that women staying at La Casa encounter when they bring criminal charges against their assailants—disclosure of their current address—is also being negotiated with the district attorney and the court system.

The Coalition expects to establish a self-sustaining business in La Casa—a telephone answering service, which would require a minimum of space and capital—to generate funds for the house. Simultaneously the service would provide vocational training and in-house paid employment for residents. Members of the Coalition also plan to raise money by serving as consultants to other community agencies or in-service training for the intervention and treatment of family violence. Toward this end the Coalition already has the beginnings of an audiovisual resource center. Ashley is also executive director of Femedia III, which has produced two videotapes. The first, "One Is for Killing, One Is for Fun," is on rape; the second, "Take Her, She's Mad," is on the mental state of the isolated housewife. Both portray society's victimization of women. Ashley is highly critical of existing family crisis intervention. She wants the police to use public service announcements on television to let battering husbands know that the City and County of San Francisco is taking a hard-line position on violence in the home as well as on the streets. Because she has learned to control her own violence (her reaction to her mother's murder by her stepfather), Ashley also plans to develop a course for battering husbands in techniques for controlling rage.

Women's Transitional Living Center— Fullerton, California

The moving force behind the Women's Transitional Living Center in Fullerton, California, was the Orange County Chapter of the National Organization for Women.[8] Karen Peters, president of the chapter in 1975, spearheaded a task force that documented existing housing facilities throughout the country to ascertain the need for a shelter, obtained letters of support, and arranged for the Orange County Community Development Council to assume overall program management and fiscal responsibility for the

Center. By October the county had been persuaded to make a grant for a ten-month pilot project out of revenue-sharing funds. The women then rented an old convalescent hospital with a big living room, four or five bedrooms on each side of a long hallway leading to a large dining room, a kitchen in the back, an enclosed patio, a parking lot, and a yard for the children to play in.

Government funding can be a mixed blessing. The proposal budget had included five full-time and one half-time staff positions; the county cut the staff down to three and a half positions, eliminating the child care specialist and the money budgeted for consultants to set up programs at the shelter. The Center was so understaffed when it opened that the two day workers had to work seven days a week. Susan Naples, the Center's cheerful but harried director, told me, "There's a lot more involved in county funding than we had expected. The reporting is horrendous—an evaluator comes in once a week, there's lots of paperwork and forms to be filled out for each agency—and I have no clerical staff!" After a month of operation the county did approve the addition of two half-time workers to relieve the women on the day shift. But because of budget cuts, program activities depend totally on volunteers, and most of the enthusiastic volunteers who had worked so hard to make the center possible disappeared when the dream was actually realized.

To make matters worse, any money from donations or outside sources is deducted from the grant by the county. This proviso makes further fund raising counterproductive; thus the Center staff has no way of supplementing the very tight budget, restoring programs rejected by the county, or meeting unforeseen needs. The women could get around the situation by setting up a non-profit auxiliary "Friends of WTLC" corporation to receive donations on behalf of the Women's Transitional Living Center. The money could then be converted into needed goods and services.

The Center accepts clients primarily through referral agencies which have been advised of admittance policies. WTLC does not admit "alcoholics, drug addicts, women and/or children who are severely mentally or physically disabled, minors who are not accompanied by their female parent or legal guardian and women coming directly out of prison." At intake the woman is required to sign a lodging agreement or promissory note, agreeing to pay one dollar for each day of occupancy plus twenty-five cents for each child or family member. This rental fee is due and payable after thirty days or on the last day of occupancy. If a family stays the full forty-five-day limit, a second payment falls due at that time. WTLC also enforces a strict 11 P.M. curfew, which has drawn some criticism from a few residents. But the staff feels this curfew is necessary for security reasons—the same reasons for which the Center was established in the first place.

B/A House—Portland, Oregon

B/A House in Portland, named after two local women who died violently—Bradley/Angle, was started by five women who saw the need to rescue women trapped in violent situations. "Most of us have come out of different lifestyles that were harmful to ourselves and have had help to get ourselves together," Dorothy Jackson, a member of the staff, wrote to me in October, 1975. "We decided to give other women the same chance to better their lives." Unlike most refuges, B/A House works with women who have drug-abuse problems (many are driven to drink and drugs by their horrible domestic situations), and with prostitutes and others who find themselves at a dead end and urgently in need of a place to stay while they rethink their lives. Most residents stay from two weeks to two months, but no set limit is enforced. B/A House can accommodate twelve women at a time.

The house has three paid staff positions, financed until December 31, 1975 by the federal CETA program, and three volunteer staff workers. Except for the three salaries, B/A House is completely dependent upon private donations. "We are rapidly running out of funds and are going to have to ask the women for $50 a month. If a woman doesn't have it, there is no pressure put on her to pay," Jackson wrote.

Emergency Housing—Boise, Idaho

In the spring of 1975, representatives from social service organizations, churches, the Legal Aid Society, and the Family Service Unit of the Idaho Department of Health and Welfare met to consider how to provide temporary shelter for women with violence-prone husbands. They founded Emergency Housing, a non-profit organization offering food and lodging in a quiet, clean, non-coercive

216

atmosphere where rest and recovery, both emotional and physical, could take place.[9]

A former parsonage and small apartment were donated by churches in the coalition. Zoning and permit changes had to be made, a stairway had to be constructed, and some refurbishing and repairs had to be done to meet fire regulations. Citizens of Boise donated goods and services and the building was soon up to code. The churches have set up on-going drives to collect food and clothing. Several retail grocers are donating canned goods regularly. A dairy gives the shelter a quantity of milk every month, and a wholesaler contributes damaged produce every week. Also, a local car dealer loaned a van to Emergency Housing until they could buy one of their own, and medical personnel have volunteered to be on call around the clock. Since it opened Emergency Housing has accommodated an average of nine people per night, though the number has been as high as nineteen at one time. Maximum stay is one week, but the average is three days. A day-care center is staffed by volunteers so that mothers are free to deal with housing and employment problems.

Emergency Housing is supervised by Brother Milton and Sister Deborah Kuolt, of the Holy Order of Mans, a non-denominational religious order based in San Francisco. With the assistance of this order, the community of Erie, Pennsylvania, has initiated a similar program. In San Francisco the Holy Order of Mans' Raphael House was the only shelter in the city to take in mothers with children prior to the establishment of La Casa de las Madres. However, residents are only allowed to stay at Raphael House for three nights; no one is allowed in the house during daytime hours. People begin lining up outside at about 5:30 or 6:00 in the evening to wait for the doors to open. These hostel-like shelters do provide emergency food and lodging, but they have their limitations not only as to length of stay, but in meeting other needs of the battered wife.

What bothers me about Emergency Housing, for instance, is that Brother Milton is the one who determines on a day-to-day basis who can be accepted for temporary shelter and who must be sent elsewhere. At a time when her life-line depends upon shedding the shackles of male domination, the woman is subjected to still another male authority who assumes control over her destiny. Feminist-run shelters are more effective in helping a woman rebuild her self-esteem and become independent. Certainly a liaison between feminist refuges and other agencies should be established so that outside agencies could handle the overflow when refuges are crowded. But most important, these agencies must be encouraged to make referrals to feminist refuges.

Other Activity in the United States

The Jane Addams House collective hopes to open a shelter for battered women in **New York City.** One possibility is an estate the size of which can be imagined from the number of bathrooms—thirteen!—to which the city currently holds title. This property could be made available as a refuge, *if* the women come up with an operational plan that is cost-free to the city of New York, presently in dire financial straits. If Jane Addams House can meet this condition, the city would be getting a real bargain. Since the mansion could serve a sizeable number of women, considerable savings in other city services would result. We can only hope the city soon realizes that the size of the mansion is well-suited to the immensity of the problem of wife-abuse.

The Ad Hoc Committee for a Women's Shelter formed in **Albuquerque, New Mexico,** has persuaded the City Council to set aside $25,000 from Community Development funds for a refuge.[10] The women are worried, however, that the money may go to the County Mental Health Center as contractor rather than to the Women's Shelter Committee.

The Women's Union of the **Minneapolis, Minnesota,** Housing and Redevelopment Authority (HRA) went to the Board and demanded funding for a shelter to be used for temporarily homeless (and battered) women. After a series of hearings, which included testimony from Women's House in neighboring St. Paul, the board voted them $50,000: $35,000 to buy and refurbish a house and $15,000 to hire a coordinator.[11]

"Despite poverty, isolation, large families, minimal education, health problems, and the traditional *machismo* of the mountain male, the women of Appalachia are moving to get it together," Jacqueline Bernard reported in *Ms.* magazine.[12] In 1975, they founded the Appalachian Women's Rights Organization, which grew out of a meeting of health workers and clients at the community-controlled Mud Creek Clinic of **Floyd County,** in eastern **Kentucky.** During a subsequent meeting in **Hindman, Kentucky,** the group discussed plans for obtaining federal funding for child care homes in low-income areas and for shelters to take in women and children fleeing from their abusive, drunken husbands. Drinking is the traditional escape from frustration and poverty for mountain men, and the women could predict that the men would react violently to the establishment of a permanent shelter. They decided that a *known* shelter would be too obvious a target and might be shot at or burned down, and a roving shelter would be too difficult for some women to find. The group agreed on several solutions which they are currently working to implement. These proposals include creating shelters in town where they could get police protection, organizing a special AWRO patrol, and (or) developing alternative programs for families of alcoholic husbands through Alcoholics Anonymous.

In **Somerville, Massachusetts,** a group called RESPOND also wishes to open a refuge for women in crisis.[13] One of its founders, Maureen Varney, suffered two mental breakdowns before divorcing her husband. During her stays at Massachusetts General Hospital and West-Borough State Mental Hospital she met many battered women who had committed themselves for lack of a better alternative, according to Michelle Wasserman in the *Boston Phoenix.* After her release, Varney began to offer her home as a temporary shelter to these women. Although she has five children of her own and a small apartment, she has housed at least fifty women and their children during the last several years! RESPOND's refuge is still in the planning stages, but in the meantime this group, whose goal is self-help and not marriage counseling, offers battered women the usual services: a crisis phone line, group sessions, and referrals. Another facet of RESPOND's program, already in operation, is the "Independent Living Apartments" project—a house with six apartments available to young women who want to leave home and begin life on their own without getting married to do it.[14]

The Women's Project in nearby **Cambridge, Massachusetts,** is circulating a letter throughout the Boston area to raise support for a proposed Transition House for women and children in crisis.[15] The appeal, which is printed in both English and Spanish, asks women in the community to help put the project together. Anyone with skills in grant writing, counseling, carpentry, contacting organizations, compiling referrals, fund-raising, and so on is urged to participate.

The National Organization for Women chapter in **Kalamazoo, Michigan,** asked the School of Social Work at Western Michigan University to conduct a study of the problem of wife-beating in Kalamazoo County. A group of graduate students responded to the request, and evidence gathered from health centers, attorneys, police, and other agencies indicates that spouse-assault occurs in a minimum of 500 to 600 families in the county each year and that 10 percent, or over 4,000 families in Kalamazoo County, experience at least one incident of physical violence between husband and wife.[16] Armed with data from the survey and testimony from professional experts, the NOW chapter applied to the Kalamazoo Foundation for a grant to set up a shelter for battered women. The foundation did not consider the need for such a refuge to be evident and turned them down. But the NOW women have not given up and will submit their proposal elsewhere.[17]

"The Perfect Place" is a temporary residence for women located in **Saginaw, Michigan.**[18] This shelter was set up as a "retreat" for harried mothers who need a vacation from their children and has a contract with the County Receiving Home for Children. Mothers planning to spend up to three days at the place can drop their youngsters off at the receiving home and know they are in good hands. The women who run "The Perfect Place" visited Women's House in St. Paul, presumably with the intention of learning more about battered women and encouraging them to use their facility.

A drama has been unfolding for two years in **Seattle, Washington,** in which women attempting to create a shelter have been continually discouraged in their efforts.[19] In September 1974, the Seattle Women's Commission held public hearings on marital violence. Afterwards the Commission sent out a letter to more than one hundred and fifty community organizations explaining the urgency of the problem and asking for help in establishing a shelter. A convent was offered by the Immaculate Conception Catholic Church, but the present tenants would have had to be evicted. When it became available, it was in dreadful shape and would have cost a mint to bring up to code. In the meantime, because of the publicity and new-found hope for relief, community agencies such as the Salvation Army, Crisis Line, YWCA, S.O.S., community mental health centers, and Legal Aid were reporting an increase in calls from wife/victims. When these women were told that emergency housing did not yet exist, some of them just plunked themselves down, saying, "Sorry, we're not leaving."

On May 15, 1975, Jeanette Williams, chairperson of the City Council's Human Resources and Judiciary Committee, held another public hearing—this time not to discuss the need, which was by then obvious to all, but to investigate possible funding sources to assist the Women's Commission in developing a program proposal. In a news release announcing the hearings, Williams said assistance was needed to coordinate research efforts with interested agencies, conduct a survey of available buildings suitable for a shelter, survey applicable sources for grants, and prepare a grant application. She also stressed that the City of Seattle would not assume the responsibility for operating a refuge, but would help, through the Office of Women's Rights and the Women's Commission, to locate a sponsoring agency as well as an on-going funding source. At the hearing many women's groups expressed their belief that such a project should be sponsored by feminists.

Prior to the funding hearing, the Salvation Army had worked cooperatively with feminist and other community groups in making the public aware of the need for a shelter for battered women. Since then, however, the Salvation Army and the Women's Commission have disagreed bitterly over the program plan, and the Commission and feminist groups have withdrawn their support. The Commission had been willing to support the Salvation Army as the sponsoring agency provided a Sub-Advisory Committee of from nine to fifteen members (representing such groups as victims, Legal Services, Harborview Medical Center, Crisis Clinic, the Seattle Women's Commission, and helping professions) was formed to assure that the program meet the needs and basic concerns of the community as expressed at the public hearings. The Salvation Army refused to make such an agreement, chose to act unilaterally, obtained United Way funds and now plans to open in June 1976 a

221

newly purchased facility which can accommodate fifteen persons.

Hepzibah Menuhin, who has been working with the shelters in England, visited Seattle during the spring and once again fired up the groups that had been shunned by the Salvation Army. The Coalition Task Force on Women and Religion convened a meeting, and they are now considering getting a surplus house from the city. This second refuge would augment the Salvation Army facility and assure a shelter environment that would assist women in altering their self image from victim to self-actualizing person.

Feminists are worried that the Seattle experience might become a trend: Women's groups agitate for a shelter, do the leg work such as contacting agencies and gathering statistics, put on publicity drives to arouse public support, and force the city or county to deal with the issue. Then along comes the Salvation Army or some other conventional service organization, which had cooperated with the women in their preliminary efforts, to take the ball away and establish a shelter based on their own tradition-bound ideas. After all, the Salvation Army has experience and a proven track record—these factors influence the powers that be. Besides objecting to being used in this manner, feminists find it particularly disturbing that, although they document the need for housing *battered* women, the Salvation Army often envisions a shelter for women and children—period. The premises and priorities of the Salvation Army are very different from those of feminist groups and do not take into account the very specialized needs of battered wives and their families.

The experience of the National Organization for Women in Wilmington, Delaware, confirms what the Seattle feminists fear.[20] In 1973, Roslyn Rattew, head of NOW's Delaware Marriage and Divorce Task Force, bought a house so that the Wilmington Chapter could set up a refuge with minimal rent—just enough to cover mortgage payments and property taxes. With support of the Junior League, NOW submitted a proposal for revenue-sharing county funds to open a shelter for "divorcing women who are threatened with or are experiencing violence at home." But the Newcastle County Planning Council recommended funding the Salvation Army instead. Unable to raise alternative funding, the women lost their house, and the Salvation Army took the county money and established a shelter for displaced families who have been evicted or who have lost their homes in a fire. The needs of battered women in Wilmington remain unmet.

Government agencies approached with funding proposals very often insist on "feasibility studies" to determine need. In 1975, **Montgomery County, Maryland,** made a grant of $50,000 to set up a Task Force to Study a Haven for Physically Abused Persons,[21] even though the *Washington Post* and the *Washington Star* had each run a series of articles on the prevalence of wife-beating in Washington, D.C., and its suburbs. If the money Montgomery County spent on the study had gone into a refuge, battered women would be that much further ahead by now and the county would have learned what it wanted to know—namely, that the county does indeed need a shelter for battered wives. Some of the other Task Force recommendations indicate that the refuge (which appears to be assured of funding) will follow traditional lines. If the County Health Department does not assume operational responsibility, the Task Force suggested that the county consider contracting with an organization such as the Salvation Army to run the shelter, which is seen as "an alternative to remaining in danger or bringing charges." While "physically abused" persons are considered the major priority, the Task Force nonetheless hesitated to make the admission policy "exclusive," and thus leaves the door open for the Salvation Army, if granted the contract, to take over and gradually extend the admission policy. In a community with more than 4,000 known complaints of marital violence annually, unless the projected four sleeping rooms are reserved for these victims, the shelter cannot possibly fulfill its mandate: to collect data for use in studies on causes and implement programs for the prevention of physical abuse in the family.

Women Against Rape groups are becoming increasingly involved in the problem of marital violence, not necessarily by design, but because of the increased volume of calls they receive from abused wives—calls they are not yet prepared to deal with. According to Janet Hicks, Women Against Rape in **Burlington, Vermont,** is actively seeking grants and donations for a refuge for battered wives. "We need more education about marital violence and about setting up a refuge," she said. "But the need is immediate. So we'll just do it and learn as we go along."[22] The group expects to rent an apartment as a small-scale pilot project. Women Against Assault and Rape in **Portsmouth, New Hampshire,** is also overwhelmed by calls from wife/victims and is trying, too, to gain local support for a refuge. The training these women have in advocacy for rape victims qualifies them to act for abused wives. The myths, psychological reactions, and legal problems are practically the same in both instances. The difference is learning how to set up and operate a refuge.

Jan Dickey, coordinator of Women Together, in **Cleveland Heights, Ohio,** reported to me that her group is trying to set up a shelter for women in crisis. "Organizing with no money is hard enough, but even harder is hearing about women who need help and being unable to help them because we're 'still in the planning stages,'" she said.

Lois M. Hake Woman learned the hard way that "we have better laws to protect a piece of furniture."[23] She charged her husband with assault and battery and "was fined and admonished by the judge to 'Go home and mind your husband and never bring your domestic quarrels to my court again.'" Today she heads the Women's Crisis Center in **Fairfield, Ohio,** and is actively working to set up a refuge so that other women can be spared the callous treatment she received.

Many chapters of the National Organization for Women have set up Task Forces on Battered Women and are active in the movement to establish a national network of refuges for battered wives and their families. The **North Virginia** NOW task force is setting up a non-profit corporation and applying for LEAA funds under police sponsorship. Mary Ann Bridge, member of the task force, says they have found the police to be very cooperative; the hostility they have encountered has come from the professionals who provide traditional services. A group in the **Orlando— Winter Park area, Florida,** has formed an organization to help battered women. The local NOW chapter is helping them to research police training and Florida law and to write a grant proposal to set up a hot-line and other services. The **Santa Clara, California,** NOW chapter has established a liaison with the Women's Refuge Committee of **San Jose.** The **Southern Prince George's County** NOW chapter in **Maryland** is working with the County Commission on the Status of Women to meet the needs of battered women on an individual basis, while working with local police and social service agencies to understand the complexities of the issue and to develop programs to solve the problem. Prospects for funding of a temporary shelter look promising, according to Marjorie Casswell, who is on the staff of the commission. NOW and the Salvation Army are working together to arouse public support for emergency housing for battered women in **Dallas, Texas.** The **Lebanon Valley** chapter of NOW in **Pennsylvania** has joined the crusade to denounce present conciliatory practices of law enforcement and service agencies and to call for a local shelter for battered wives. "One woman beaten is one too many," Patricia Walker of the NOW task force stated. "This is what you're going to have to tell local officials and heads of organizations who might doubt the need for such a service," she told a coalition of women's groups at a YWCA meeting in **Reading.**[24] NOW and the YWCA in **Fargo, North Dakota,** are working together with Rape Victims Advocates to establish a haven.

Marcia Elayne, of the **Detroit** chapter of the National Black Feminist Organization, announced that her group hopes to open an emergency shelter just for battered wives in 1976.[25] And moves are being made by women in **Sonoma County, California,** to establish a second La Casa de las Madres in the **Santa Rosa** area.

In **Milwaukee, Wisconsin,** the 50-member Task Force on Battered Women is funded as a project of the Women's Coalition, Inc. by United Fund, Council on Women and the Church, and private donations. The task force, which has established a volunteer counseling and advocacy program, is planning a statewide conference in October 1976. The conference will focus on how to organize around the issue of woman-abuse.

The **Ann Arbor-Washtenaw County** chapter of NOW in **Michigan** has published the first of three projected manuals for peer counselors of spouse assault victims. The manual, written by social worker Mindy Resnick, does not provide exhaustive, in-depth training, but serves rather as an introduction to a practical, basic counselor-client relationship. Included is a guide to help victims in dealing with the system. Copies can be obtained by sending $1.50 to cover cost to AA NOW/Wife Assault, 1917 Washtenaw Avenue, Ann Arbor, Michigan 48104.

The need for shelters exists throughout the country, and groups are springing up all the time to goad government and other funding agencies into action. In fact, interest in the subject is growing so much and groups creating shelters are forming so rapidly that this chapter will probably be significantly incomplete soon after the book goes to press.

Refuges in Other Countries

Many existing shelters for battered women were started in condemned houses or flats by women squatting in them and demanding that the government either release the premises to them or provide other more suitable quarters. Chiswick Women's Aid got its start in a small house that had been derelict for six years and was due to be demolished. In 1971, the council of the **London borough of Hounslow** was persuaded to give Pizzey's group the keys to this rundown, shabby building for a women's center, not a shelter. At that time the group was thinking only in terms of a place where women could meet and exchange ideas. "Conditions were dreadful," wrote Pizzey. "There were rats, leaking walls, no bathrooms, outside lavatories, no hot water."[26] But within eight weeks the women of Chiswick Women's Aid, armed with paint brushes, hammers, and other paraphernalia, had made the place a comfortable base. There were two rooms upstairs; one was the office and the other had a bed in it for emergencies.

Little did the women at the new center know that the "emergency room" would be in almost constant demand. They had no idea that battered women with nowhere else to go would start coming to them for refuge as soon as they opened their doors. By 1973, Women's Aid was taking nearly one hundred telephone calls a day and accommodating as many as thirty women and children at a time by putting mattresses down on every bit of floor space, including the hall. Larger quarters were desperately needed, and another dilapidated house was located (now headquarters for Women's Aid). It had huge rooms, a large yard, a big basement area that could be converted into a playroom for the children—and three *inside* toilets! The place was totally rundown, but to Chiswick Women's Aid it was luxurious. They still had no hot water, but they did have space. As soon as they opened the doors of this second house the place filled up.

Though licensed for thirty-six people, often as many as a hundred and thirty women and children lodge in the house. There are three stoves in one communal kitchen, and sometimes eighty children in the hundred-foot yard. Children sleep four to a mattress, mothers sleep on the floor, and pregnant women sleep on the few beds. In spite of the appallingly overcrowded conditions, a marvelous atmosphere pervades the house.[27]

Pizzey's book *Scream Quietly or the Neighbors Will Hear* quickly attracted media attention throughout the British Commonwealth. Women across England took up the cause and formed Women's Aid groups. Today shelters exist throughout the country, and more are forming all the time. Shelters also sprang up in Scotland, Wales, and Ireland.

In 1974 in Glasgow, Scotland, a three-bedroom flat in an old tenement property was converted into Interval House.[28] Shortly after it opened the place was housing as many as ten women and thirty-one children at a time; they slept on mattresses everywhere except in the bathroom. Interval House is run by the residents, who are trying to buy a house for a second refuge. Maura Butterly, one of the founders, is now in Ireland working at the shelter in Dublin.

Two refuges were established in Edinburgh in 1974 by Edinburgh Women's Aid, and several others have since been created in other Scottish cities. Where no shelters exist groups are forming to pressure the Housing Corporation (the agency we would call the Housing Authority) to make dwellings available. About thirty percent of the housing in Scotland is public and falls under the Corporation's jurisdiction. Some of the houses given to Scottish Women's Aid groups were condemned and in terrible condition, but the women soon made them livable. Most Scottish refuges observe a self-help policy, leaving management of the house almost solely to the residents; local Women's Aid groups provide some volunteer assistance.

The movement spread quickly to the Continent. In January 1974, for example, six women in Amsterdam, all of them social workers, decided that the "helping" services they worked for did nothing to solve the real problems of

227

abused women. "Welfare work never begins with the woman herself, but with her relationship with a man," wrote Elisabeth Kobus. "Abuse of women, as such, thus is never discussed in welfare work."[29] Rather, it is always translated into a relational problem, the solution for which is to bring the partners together again.

The six women conducted a survey of the refuges available to women in Holland; they found that not one of the existing facilities recognized wife-abuse as a real problem. In September, the women established an alternative refuge for battered women, *"Blijf van m'n Lijf"* (Stay away from my body), to offer concrete help to wife/victims. "We decided against a 'scientific' study of the extent of the problem, and we asked for no subsidies or grants," Kobus says. "We squatted a house, spread the word about the opening of the house in all the newspapers, and waited. Within ten days there were 20 women and 35 children."

Today BvmL occupies a big house made available by the city of Amsterdam. Twelve volunteers manage the refuge, and four of them work exclusively with the children. The residents decide on policy and control activity in the house, and once a week they have a meeting to iron out all the problems. Saying "Stay away from my body," Kobus states, is the first step towards independence for the battered woman. A second house, modeled after BvmL, was opened in Zwolle a year later.

Rotterdam's first refuge was made possible in 1974 by funds from the General Aid Office of The Netherlands.[30] The house has three living units (each consisting of a sitting room and a bedroom), two kitchens, one shower, one toilet, and a children's playroom. The Rotterdam arrangement offers the women privacy, a commodity usually sacrificed in most refuges. "We want the families to lead their lives the way they want it," Huub Hodzelmans, of Algemene Hulpcentrale, wrote to me. "Therefore, we chose separate units, and not bedrooms with a common sitting-room for all of them. If they want to, it is possible, for instance, to have coffee together, but it is not necessary. So usually they serve and prepare their own food." Volunteers help by making necessary contacts with other agencies, keeping the children busy, and doing the shopping. The house is supported by small allotments from welfare for each resident and by donations.

In 1975, two more houses were rented; seven families can now be accommodated at one time in the Rotterdam refuges. In eighteen months about 1,600 people were housed there for brief periods. These houses are limited to battered women and their children, but Hodzelmans wrote that women who have been thrown out of their homes by their husbands but have not been threatened physically are badly in need of shelter. Meetings with the Official Welfare Institute of Rotterdam in December 1975, led to an offer of a larger house, with a capacity of thirty-five, for use by this latter group. The Institute also agreed to subsidize the salaries of nine helpers, since staff would be required around the clock.

At The Hague a house for ill-treated women has been in existence for more than six years. Unlike the Rotterdam living units, this house has separate bedrooms, a common sitting-room, and communal meals. The house is always full and is run by volunteers.

In Berlin a group of women, all professionals (social workers, sociologists, psychologists, and lawyers) with ties to the women's movement has drawn up a plan for a refuge.[31] Residents would be allowed to stay for a maximum of six months, and during that time they would receive counseling on practical matters such as use of public agencies, divorce, job training, and housing. A cafe/restaurant is being planned as a means of support for the house. In order to qualify for public funds, the project must be sponsored by an established organization. It has had some publicity, and the women are currently distributing a pamphlet on violence against women.

An article in *Le Monde* in November 1975 indicated that women in Paris are organizing around the issue of wife-battering.[32] Simone de Beauvoir is president of the Ligue du droit des femmes, which operates the *S.O.S. femmes-alternative* hotline. The women will try to help wife/victims find emergency housing. Another group, Librairie des femmes, also maintains a phone service. Moves are being made by these groups and others to promote a refuge for battered women in Paris.

In Copenhagen there is Kvindehuset (The Women's House). It was a rundown shell of a building that was owned by the University of Copenhagen and taken over in 1971 by the Red Stockings, the Danish Women's Liberation organization. The house is run by a commune of ten women who live in the building. Facilities include a play area for the children, a ground-floor kitchen, a Red Stockings office, mattress rooms (for sleeping or exercising), a workshop for women to do crafts or carpentry and electrical projects, and a third-floor pub with a cozy atmosphere of pillows, music, and candlelight. Any woman who needs a place to stay is welcome. Kvindehuset is a Women's Center, not a refuge per se.[33] Battered women are referred to "the social group" of the feminist movement which gives free social and legal advice to women.[34]

A number of refuges for battered women exist in **Canada:** two in **Toronto, Ontario,** one in **Saskatoon, Saskatchewan,** one in **Calgary, Alberta,** and three in **British Columbia.**

Four years ago when the Canadian Government first made funds available under Local Initiatives Program to groups and individuals who could instigate needed community projects, a woman in Calgary decided that a facility was needed for women in crisis. The government agreed to give several thousand dollars for house rent, utilities, and staff wages. There was no food budget, but in February 1972 the "Oasis" opened with facilities for twenty persons. An average six-month period will see roughly 1,000 women and children as temporary guests of the shelter. Almost 85 percent of them stay for a week or less. Those with deeper problems stay for several weeks. "We feel, however," Joyce Smith, executive director of the Calgary Women's Emergency Shelter (as it is now called) wrote to me, "that the earliest possible move from the shelter, when a woman is beginning to experience an upward trend in her life, is ideal. If she lingers once she has found a job and/or a place to stay, she is subjected to and can be depressed by the problems of the new clients as they arrive."

In 1973, two Interval Houses came into being quite independently of each other and in widely separated parts of the country. Interval House in **Toronto** opened its doors early in 1973.[35] The staff of nine members works collectively; two co-directors are elected from the membership for administrative and public-relations purposes. But as far as the residents are concerned, all staff members are equal in status—there is no boss. Every Monday night they hold a house meeting in which complaints and suggestions for the house are discussed. The children, like their mothers, have a chore chart, and occasionally the children hold their own meetings. One staff member is assigned to each family

230

in residence, and the two meet regularly to discuss future plans and actual accomplishments, and to arrange outside appointments. All staff are responsible for counseling. In February 1974, Women in Transition opened a second facility in Toronto similar to Interval House in design and operation. The two houses work very closely together in their common search for permanent funding from government and private sources.

Interval House in Saskatoon grew out of a five-month project called Women Alone, sponsored by Saskatchewan's Employment Support Program and designed to engage welfare recipients in work for the community.[36] Anne Baszucki and Karen Helstrom, who initiated the project, found themselves faced with all sorts of problems they had never anticipated, like the 300-pound woman in a wheelchair who fled with her five children when her husband beat her once too often, and the German woman who spoke no English and had lived for two years on the tiny veranda of her home because her husband refused to let her inside. When the project ended Baszucki and Helstrom found a house to harbor such women, and Our Lady of the Prairies Foundation made the $5,000 down payment. Today Interval House is operated by the Department of Social Services on a per diem per resident rate. Anyone who stays at Interval House must be approved by a social worker from the Department of Social Services or the Department of Indian Affairs. Only women who have children with them are admitted. When residents leave, they may return just once more. Children are driven to and from the school in which they were registered when their mothers came to Interval House.

Vancouver's Transition House, the first refuge in British Columbia, opened on January 1, 1974.[37] It was funded by the Provincial Government's Department of Human Resources and formed under the auspices of the advisory board of the Vancouver Status of Women Council. The House is a two-story duplex; therefore all major living areas are duplicated. After one year of operation, the government sent in a researcher to evaluate the program before committing funds to other such refuges. Today funding of Transition House is automatic and included in the yearly budget of Vancouver's Resource Board. Despite its ties to "the system," the Transition House staff still maintains autonomy over the operation and functions as a collective.

Transition House is unique in another way as well. The staff is unionized; it is an association affiliated with the

231

Service, Office and Retail Workers Union of Canada. This situation came as quite a shock to the Vancouver Resources Board, which then had to negotiate a polyparty agreement with its 1,500 plus workers as well as one with the Transition House staff. As a result the latter (a small but industrious group) is better paid and has better working conditions than most service workers in the employ of other shelters. The union, composed primarily of women, developed out of an association of working women affiliated with the original Women's Centre in Vancouver.

The houses in **Victoria** and **Aldergrove**, also in British Columbia, were initially affiliated with local Women's Centres, though the one in Victoria has since separated. Both have perpetual difficulties with funding because they receive grants from the Provincial Government's Department of Human Resources which must be renewed yearly. The Aldergrove House, also called Ishtar, has had to operate with considerable cut-backs in staff.

Auberge Transition is located in the **Montreal YWCA**, which has set aside five bedrooms at minimal rates for women in distress. The Montreal Women's Center is also trying to acquire a house where more complete services will be made available to wife/victims.[38]

In **Australia** in 1974, "Elsie," a shelter for battered women, was formed when members of Women's Liberation squatted in two abandoned houses in the Glebe section of Sydney and refused to move out.[39] Eventually the women were given a lease and a federal grant which pays the salaries of the six-member staff. The Rotary Club and other community service organizations make donations. During the first year, one thousand women and children used Elsie as their temporary home. The staff, which is chosen by a collective of twenty-four members of Women's Liberation, are all feminists and are selected on the basis of their experience rather than on traditional credentials, titles, and degrees. The house is run communally, and residents are encouraged to operate it as if it were their own home. Consciousness raising is emphasized; counseling or "therapy" is minimal, but is offered on request. Medical care and contraception are supplied by two doctors in Glebe who have been carefully screened, and by the Women's Community Health Centre (run by feminists).

Since the formation of Elsie, two sister refuges have been established in Sydney: Betsie and Bonnie. In **Melbourne**

Half Way House offers refuge to battered women; it does not admit alcoholics or retarded children. Other shelters are located in Perth, Western Australia; Brisbane, Queensland; and Hobart, Launceston, Tasmania. All are directed by Women's Liberation except for Betsie, which is run by the local government.

Evaluation

Organizations receiving grant money from foundations or government agencies must periodically prepare evaluation reports indicating the success or failure of the program. Several refuges graciously made their reports available to me. The data indicate how many people used the facility during the year and what happened as a result. Generally, the reports identify strengths and weaknesses of the programs, and make recommendations for on-going funding.

Researcher Gale Carsenat prepared a report in 1974 on Toronto's Interval House for Community and Social Services.[40] She found that Interval House served a total of 110 women during the year; another 69 women were interviewed but were not admitted. Of the 110 residents, 37 returned to their mates. Those who return, Carsenat found, tend to do so in the first four days after they leave home. Anyone who stayed for more than 26 days was able to set up an independent situation. Those who returned to their homes had been married the longest. They also had considerably less work experience and were mostly unskilled compared with the "independent" group, which did not return home. The latter group was comprised of women who had professional or skilled work backgrounds. Of those who went back home 35 percent called themselves "just a housewife." Fifteen of the 37 called back at Interval House, expressing regret at having left the House and asking for readmittance because nothing had changed at home. Of the 63 who achieved independence only six had been separated or divorced before coming to Interval House.

Janet Rosettis conducted a survey for the Department of Human Resources of the residents who had left Vancouver's Transition House.[41] The women usually told her they had lost their feelings of inadequacy while staying at the shelter. Also, they had developed a more positive self-

233

image and gained a greater awareness of community resources and how to use them. Few indicated that their previous relationships with the men they had left had changed for the better. "I'm happier without him" or "I'm not going to have any men messing me up or ruining my daughter's life" were typical responses. Rosettis also found that ethnic groups (native Indian, Greek, Italian) were significantly represented in the consumer population of Transition House. As for the staff, a major complaint was that they were forced to turn many women away without having other alternatives to suggest. They also complained of a lack of facilities for children, the need for recreational equipment, and the lack of time available to organize children's activities.

Edinburgh Women's Aid evaluated their own experience after their first year of operating two houses let to them by the Scottish Housing Corporation.[42] They reported that both houses had been fully occupied (with three families each) throughout the year. The original idea, they said, had been to run the houses on the self-help policy endorsed by the Women's Liberation Movement, with Women's Aid intervening in the day-to-day operation as little as possible. They had acquired the houses, established cooperation with appropriate service agencies, and assumed that occupants could take it from there in running the houses themselves. All members of Edinburgh Women's Aid had other full-time commitments and had expected that occasional visits and response in emergencies was all that would be required of them. Idealistically, they had assumed that once freed from their violent home environment the residents would soon regain their self-respect and, with the occasional assistance of social workers, establish a mutual support system among themselves. The Women's Aid members never dreamed that friction would develop among residents, or that the enormous emotional problems of some would threaten the very existence of the houses. Nevertheless, this is exactly what happened.

The difficulties were at their worst when one of the refuges was occupied by three families with acute problems. One woman who was a manic-depressive attempted suicide; another had five children, three of whom were delinquents; the third had just been released after a prolonged stay in a psychiatric ward and was incapable of controlling her three children. "In this situation the ideal of self-help was reduced to absurdity, and the resources of our group proved to be totally inadequate," the EWA women admitted. Given their other commitments, the EWA had never intended to accept residents with problems so severe, but they found themselves unable to send these women back to their abusive husbands. Social workers were very sympathetic and helpful, but the housing department was not quite so willing to assist. Nevertheless, all three families were eventually rehoused. However, the refuge had to be shut down temporarily while it was redecorated and re-equipped.

In evaluating this disastrous experience, the EWA women came to realize the necessity for an administrator to whom both residents and city authorities could relate. And it was apparent that someone was needed to offset the rapid turnover in the houses by providing a sense of permanence and continuity. The women also concluded that expecting people in emotional turmoil to provide each other with the necessary support was unreasonable and overly idealistic. Staff was needed to provide emotional support, counseling, mediation in household disputes, to follow-up on clients when they leave, and to keep records. The women also resolved to start a fully equipped playgroup in each house for the children and a discussion group for women who were unable or unwilling to leave their violent homes.

The EWA was thus in the position to hire staff on the promise of pay if and when funding came through from the central government. The community pitched in and helped. Local men began taking resident older boys to football matches, to the swimming pool, and so on. These outings were particularly helpful since many of the children at the refuges had never formed a stable relationship with a man. By May 1975 an Urban Aid grant was made to Edinburgh Women's Aid, assuring the project of a full-time coordinator for the next three years.

Haven House, in Pasadena, California, was evaluated after nine months of operation, at which time the facility had served 86 women and 165 children.[43] Two critical shortcomings were identified: the lack of follow-up and outreach after families left the facility, and insufficient staff for the child care center. Haven House's contract with the County of Los Angeles did not allow for follow-up services. Nevertheless, the staff noted that many of their clients had to return to the refuge, chiefly because the families of alcoholics tend to have "multiple problems." The staff felt that the addition of two family counselors would enable Haven House to provide follow-up on each client family for a year after intake. The family counselor would begin working with members of a family at the refuge and continue counseling after they had left the refuge, thereby offering a unified approach to their problems rather than the scattered aid they presently receive. Also, Haven House had one child care specialist on the staff who was responsible at any given time for 20 to 25 children from 3 to 18 years of age. While volunteers were available for assistance on a limited scale, they preferred to work under supervision. The staff concluded that one part-time evening child care worker was needed.

While child care is an essential part of any proposal for a shelter for battered wives and their families, most funding agencies are insensitive to this need. Children who use the shelter outnumber adults two and sometimes three to one. Obviously, staff is needed to supervise and schedule children's activities. Simply fixing up play areas or installing a television set is not enough. And mothers should not have to bear full responsibility for their children in the shelter, since a major purpose is to provide a place where a woman can concentrate on remaking her life. Furthermore, children from violent homes often have emotional problems and need specialized care.

In a similar vein, after just one month of operation the staff of Women's Transitional Living Center in Fullerton were harried by the ordinary problems encountered in a new venture and sadly lamenting the county's denial of their request for a child care specialist. And they hadn't even reached the full capacity of twenty-four residents! Furthermore, they were told by county officials that since the center was not licensed for child care, the staff was forbidden by law to act as babysitters while mothers went out to look for a job or an apartment.

If these refuges are to meet the goals and expectations of those who propose them, the needs of the mothers and their children must be dealt with separately and by specialists. The mother requires counseling and guidance. She has to shape a new way of life for herself and her family, and must have freedom to take advantage of the shelter. The children, too, require such special services as education

236

and tutoring, recreation and field trips, health care, diagnostic evaluation, and counseling for emotional disturbance.

House Rules

The evaluations cited here only begin to sort out a few of the more general problems encountered by some shelters. Of equal concern are the day-to-day details that tend to recur in every shelter and which must be considered and decided upon by each house staff. Length of stay, for example, is obviously of extreme importance. Most refuges for battered women allow residents to stay for three weeks to a month, giving them enough time to think things out, find accommodations of their own, and arrange for some means of financial support. Some women may need six weeks or more to protect them from having to return to a violent situation out of necessity. Length-of-stay policy will depend in part on individual shelters' facilities and staff. Presumably, experience will also make a difference. As operators of shelters obtain more help from volunteers and other community groups with in-house self-help projects, the time necessary to help a woman get on her feet may be reduced.

Haven House adheres to a three-week limit. At Women's House the average length of stay is eight days, although women are welcome to stay longer if they need to. Amsterdam's *Blijf van m'n Lijf* does not limit the length of stay at all; a woman may stay there as long as she feels it is necessary, or as long as she is in danger and has nowhere else to live. Some women leave quickly; others stay longer. Elisabeth Kobus of BvmL says, "We have *no limit on admissions*. That means that we admit every woman who is physically abused and who expresses the desire to escape that. We think it is unfair in principle to put people on a waiting list when they are in such a situation. This means that the house is very full, that everyone moves over, gives up more privacy, and makes room for the so-many women who want to escape being abused. So the house is cramfull. But that's how it is."

Kobus says that BvmL has been accused of having too many beds per room and of being too messy. Her retort: "We haven't yet heard whether they also think it's unhealthy that so many women are abused every day. Of course, it's important that you don't suffocate in your own dirt, but it is not the purpose of the house to show that women are so clean. The house exists to offer safety to women against spouses and friends who don't behave very 'cleanly.' "[44]

Some funding agencies criticize the policy of allowing the same women to return to the shelter over and over again. They claim that the facility can become a crutch or a tool in the women's relationships with others. This consideration and the fact that refuges are often overcrowded and sometimes have waiting lists have led two facilities to stipulate a one-time-only policy. Both of Toronto's shelters, Interval House and Women in Transition, after periods of trial and error, adopted the policy that when a woman leaves she cannot return. Neither shelter will admit a woman who has made use of the other facility.

Saying "Sorry, you've had your chance" is a difficult thing to do, particularly for an organization whose sole function is to provide refuge. The Toronto women evidently decided, given the limitations of their staff and facilities, that women who couldn't make the break from their husbands the first time were on their own.

I find this policy difficult to accept. Second thoughts and confused loyalties are in the nature of the battered woman's problem. Home ties are not easily broken, and many battered wives return home after a few days, as evaluation surveys have shown. Most people need time to make a final break from a job they should have quit or a personal relationship gone bad. When the battered wife makes the break, she often loses both at once: her "career" as a married woman and the most intimate relationship of her life. The reasons that operated to keep her home in the first place beckon her back once she leaves: hope that her husband will change, fear of the unknown, lack of financial resources. Vacillation is inevitable; Gayford's research on battered women in London showed that "readmissions to the hostel must be expected."[45] Gayford was referring to Chiswick, which has an open-door policy, as do most shelters. No one there has the heart to turn anyone away, for, as they say, "What if it had been me?" I cannot help but feel that the one-chance-only rule is too harsh and even a bit judgmental. Need is need, and the woman's safety has to be the prime consideration.

Pizzey faces prosecutions and a possible jail sentence for refusing to abide by regulations restricting the number of occupants at Chiswick Women's Aid. According to *The*

New York Times, Pizzey insists, "Somebody has to be responsive to the needs of these women. If they jail me for refusing to limit the number of people in this house, the staff and the mothers will run it themselves. But this door will never, never be closed."[46]

Another controversial problem to be faced by every refuge is whether or not visitors are to be allowed. Most refuges discourage visitors; others set up specific visiting hours. Male visitors are generally taboo; admitting them is just too risky and there doesn't seem to be much point to it. Residents can arrange to meet whomever they wish to see away from the shelter. At BvmL, no one, not even a woman's social worker, is allowed to come to the house. Professionals (doctors, the Council for the Protection of Children, social workers) are very critical of this policy, but the women decided to guard themselves not only against battering husbands, but also against the influence of reconciliation-minded counselors.

Other details require policy decisions as they arise. For example, the La Casa de las Madres Coalition decided that since members of the Coalition or paid staff (when they reach that point) will be held legally responsible for the operation of the house, no volunteer should ever be left alone to mind the store. A volunteer, even though she may have undergone in-service training, must always work under the supervision of a member of the staff.

Refuges usually conduct weekly house meetings to arrange schedules and deal with in-house problems. These meetings are also helpful in orienting newcomers and for discussing personal plans and problems entailed in house or job hunting. Meals are generally prepared by the residents, sometimes with the assistance of staff, and are eaten communally in many shelters. A staff person usually buys the groceries, but the residents keep lists of what is needed. Each woman is responsible for cleaning her own space and for doing her family's laundry. Cleaning chores for the house as a whole are shared on a rotating basis.

Fees, if any, are usually based on a sliding scale depending on the woman's ability to pay. If a woman is penniless, she is not pressed to pay. At Toronto's Interval House destitute women are given a small weekly cash allowance for sundries.

A house diary or log is useful for keeping track of day-to-day business, communicating messages, and maintaining a head count on residents. The diary is especially helpful to staff and volunteers coming on shift, and will also come in handy later when the program evaluation must be prepared.

Interval House in Toronto, unlike the other shelters as far as I can discover, has an official policy regarding the disciplining of resident children. If a child misbehaves, "he/she should be disciplined by the nearest adult. If you hear a staff member disciplining your child, don't think it's a reproach. You can't always be on the spot, and besides, most children go through a period of 'testing' the staff. We try to give your children lots of attention, affection and consistent disciplining to help them settle in quickly at Interval House and to feel secure."[47] Discipline may never take any form of violence, however. This taboo is adhered to by all refuges. Women who themselves engage in violent behavior are evicted. After all, the purpose of any refuge is to offer a safe environment to women and children.

Some shelters have no rules other than "No men!" Residents are expected to adjust to the shelter as they learn to relate to others in the house. On the other hand, some shelters give a new client a printed list of house rules that has been developed over a period of time to keep the place somewhat orderly. This way the newcomer knows what is expected of her and can fit in quickly.

Most refuges not only help the women to relocate when they are ready to be on their own, but also assist them in acquiring furniture and household supplies and in moving to and from the house.

Satellite Housing

The existing refuges are short-term reception centers for the battered woman, whose future is still uncertain once she leaves the shelter. Success will depend partly on the strength of her resolve and partly on blind luck. Usually even if she wants to set up a new household, she is unable to afford adequate housing for her family. She may be on welfare, in the process of training for a job, or, if she has a job, working at the minimal wages paid to trainees. For these reasons, as well as for the advantage of mutual psychological support, women leaving refuges often decide to team up and rent a house together, sometimes acquiring a place large enough to accommodate two or three families.

240

Chiswick Women's Aid believes in the safety-in-numbers policy and wants to establish residential community settlements for displaced families. In 1974 Women's Aid acquired three houses, distinct from the emergency shelter, which they set aside as the first long-term residential centers. One of these houses, a three-story Georgian building large enough to accommodate thirty people, was made available to Women's Aid by a council on the outskirts of London at a modest rent for a minimum of ten to fifteen years. The council arranged for necessary repairs on this house, and the other two buildings (one with a six-month, the other with a five-year lease) were renovated, decorated, and furnished by Women's Aid.[48]

The fate of women going off on their own after leaving the refuges interested the Select Committee on Violence in Marriage as well. In 1975, when the committee held hearings in Glasgow, members put considerable pressure on the Glasgow Housing Authority to make dwellings available for use both as refuges and as permanent housing for families after they leave the refuges. Fifty houses were actually made available for rehousing homeless people, but as of December 1975 *not one* of the residents of Glasgow's refuge had been rehoused in the fifty![49]

Needs grow out from each other like ripples in a pond. Satellite emergency housing is also needed to alleviate overcrowded conditions in existing shelters. La Casa de las Madres, even before opening its doors, began trying to line up places where the overflow could be sent while awaiting openings at La Casa. Groups currently setting up shelters can learn from their experience. Childless women can usually be placed in existing facilities temporarily. Groups should back up their efforts by encouraging the Salvation Army, the YWCA, and even private householders to provide emergency housing for battered women and their families.

How to Set Up a Refuge (and Prepare a Funding Proposal)

Toronto's Interval House, one of the first shelters for abused wives on the American continent, has been called upon so often to share information on creating refuges and obtaining funds that the staff put together a how-to list. I

241

have supplemented their list with input based on the experience of other shelters.

1. Organize a group of people who are interested in the project and hold regular meetings. People may come and go, but the meetings should be held regularly so that a core group can develop, get to know each other, and make plans. Try to make sure that the core group includes an accurate racial and cultural representation of the community.

2. Gather information about the problem of battered women. Keep newspaper clippings, magazine articles, books, book reviews, and research studies on marital violence. You will constantly be called upon to prove that the problem exists. Document the problem in your own community by gathering statistics from police, hospital emergency rooms, district attorneys, judges, doctors, lawyers, family services, and other related agencies. If they have no statistics on wife-abuse, ask them to estimate the number of marital-violence cases they see per week. Ask college students to assist you or to conduct a survey for you as part of their research on a thesis or dissertation. Check with the departments of law, criminology, social work, sociology, and psychology in the junior colleges, colleges or universities in your community to find unpublished material on the subject. Dissertations and theses describing the problem or related subjects may be on file there.

3. Check the emergency housing facilities in your area. Find out how many exist and what clientele they serve (how many beds are available for special problem groups, for men, for women, and for women with children). Determine admission and length-of-stay policies and the attitudes of the organization toward battered wives. Note any age restrictions in facilities available to mothers and children. You will be able to use this survey and the one above to assess the need for the refuge and back it up with facts.

4. Research the law. Determine the local legal situation relevant to the battered wife (arrest policies, conditions for restraining orders, legal grounds for divorce, and so on). Also, check the legal options you have regarding the proposed refuge. Check laws on immigration (where residents may have crossed national borders), tenants rights, purchase of property, non-profit corporations—anything that could conceivably be relevant to the project. Find a lawyer

who will work free if possible. Check with the National Lawyers Guild or with your local Legal Aid. They may know of public advocates, law collectives, or groups of law students who offer legal advice and referrals.

5. Visit relevant social service agencies. You will need a referral list later anyway, and you can begin to establish liaisons with appropriate agencies. Find out where your operation will fit in with the existing social service network and how to effect cooperation and mutual programs. People already involved in social service will know the local situation. They can be invaluable in providing advice, writing letters of support, and putting you in touch with other community groups.

6. Start looking for a house. Consider various neighborhoods, zoning restrictions, and rent (or selling price if you intend to buy). Then visit the neighborhood associations in areas you find suitable and do a little public relations. People in some neighborhoods are beginning to complain about being overburdened with public projects in their residential areas.

7. Find out what permits you need and what the local fire safety and public health rules are. The latter can drastically affect your budget; you could be required to double your investment in order to renovate the house you want and bring it up to code.

8. Keep detailed records of all monies you collect and how they are spent. Look for a good accountant to set up your bookkeeping system and help you with tax reports —non-profit donations, payroll, and so forth.

9. Find an insurance broker who will advise you on the types of insurance you will need (workmen's compensation, fire, auto, liability) and who will get you the best available coverage for the least amount of money.

10. Write a plan for the project and put in everything you can think of—the more details you include the better. Describe the services and programs you wish to provide, the rationale behind the project, and the staff you think you will need to accomplish your goals. Remember that a shelter needs staffing 24 hours a day, 7 days a week, 724 hours a month.

11. Put together a budget—that is, the amount of money you think the project will cost—and itemize every expenditure on it. Include everything you think you will need for the house: staff salaries (don't forget fringe benefits), rent, utilities, food, furniture, transportation

(mileage, cab fare, parking), telephone, office supplies, postage, printing, maintenance, house repairs, household supplies, and program and recreational equipment. Try to obtain a copy of a budget from a local agency comparable to the one you are projecting and find out how they arrived at their figures. If their budget makes sense to you, use it as a model in making your own estimates of costs and as a checklist of expenditures you may have forgotten.

If you combine all the elements on this list—statement of the problem, assessment of the severity of the problem locally, evaluation of local services and their failure to solve the problem, letters of support, proposed solution, plans for implementation, and budget—the sum total will constitute a funding proposal.

The overall goal or philosophy of the group seeking funds should come across in the proposal. Writing these statements sometimes calls for great diplomacy and tact; without care, your group may not stand a chance of obtaining funds. For example, in 1972 the Los Angeles chapter of the National Organization for Women decided that the government and local community should share in the responsibility for providing emergency housing. They prepared a resolution declaring that "many women have been and/or are literally trapped into continuing relationships, including marriage, which are unhappy, unrewarding and even brutal due to having no alternatives to their predicament." The members unanimously proposed that NOW in coalition with other feminist groups develop public programs to meet these women's emergency needs.[50]

In 1973 the San Pedro NOW Chapter publicized the fact that less than one percent of available emergency housing in Los Angeles County was open to women with children, and none at all was available to women with sons older than four. Since then the Momma organization for single mothers has joined with NOW in several attempts to obtain revenue sharing funds from the County Board of Supervisors. As noted in Chapter 7, despite the shocking discrimination in the policies of existing facilities, the Supervisors continually turned the women down.

Money is readily available for the rehabilitation and housing of former mental patients, for ex-prisoners, for alcoholics and drug addicts, but the well usually runs dry when women apply for funds. Women comprise fifty-three percent of the population, but groups which represent

244

women's interests rarely qualify for public monies. When the need arises, women wind up creating their own programs, volunteering their own time, and generating their own funds. Many women are trying to cope with the needs of abused wives in this manner, but the problem is too vast. It requires public money and public support—not the few hours and few dollars that volunteers can elicit from concerned citizens.

Some groups may decide that obtaining funds is of primary importance and that they will bend their proposals to soothe the prejudices of funding agencies. For example, government agencies and foundations are apt to view programs designed merely to help women as unimportant. Therefore, writers of proposals would be better off emphasizing the destructiveness of *family* crisis, the importance of saving the *children* from a violent environment, and the need to prevent domestic *homicide*. Programs whose stated goal is to help women become strong and independent threaten the establishment and frighten traditional funding sources. Consequently, many groups find it necessary to adopt two agendas: the program described to the funding agency and the "hidden agenda" to be implemented with the fees for "consultants" and "executive directors."

Other groups, however, may feel themselves strong enough or uncompromising enough to challenge the basic assumptions in which funding agencies are grounded. These groups should know what they are up against. According to Mary Jean Tully, president of NOW's Legal Defense and Education Fund, "feminist" projects (meaning any project that would improve the status of women, no matter how slightly) received "approximately $12 million of the some $7 billion of foundation monies given away from the beginning of 1972 to the fall of 1974. . . . This is almost an incalculably small figure—less than one-fifth of one percent. These funds come from about fifteen foundations, and at least half of the total is from a single source—Ford. Even at Ford, which is light-years ahead of the other major foundations, women's grants have equaled only about one and a half percent of annual giving in recent years."

Tully wrote an article in *Foundation News* in which she explained why foundations have been "so unresponsive to the needs of organizations that represent over half our population."[51] The reasons she cites are summarized here:

245

1. Ignorance abounds as to the real activities of the women's movement. The society in general often responds with dismay to some of the movement's more strident aspects but ignores the real meaning of the movement. Tully blames the media for this, but also suggests that "a bit of stridence is infinitely preferable to the destruction of life and property," tactics to which other civil rights movements have had to resort when they were pushed to the wall.

2. Foundations still look upon the women's movement as a group of discontented middle-class women who have vague yearnings for "fulfillment." They seem to live in total ignorance of the realities of women's lives and the low economic status of women in general.

3. Early proposals from the women's movement lacked the professional polish that foundation personnel were used to. Foundations therefore seriously doubted the ability of these women's groups to carry out the programs they wished to initiate. Tully does not accept this excuse. She feels that if the ideas were good and the evidence of need overwhelming, foundations had the obligation to work with the groups whatever the formal proposals looked like.

4. Many foundation executives fear social change. "Too many foundation programs are designed to provide noncontroversial solutions to noncontroversial problems." Most foundation officials are overly cautious and dedicated to the preservation and perpetuation of the status quo.

5. The foundation world fails to perceive that society's most pressing problems cannot possibly be solved without addressing the questions raised by women and without giving proper weight to the values that are important to women.

6. "Foundation executives are overwhelmingly male and are drawn from a narrow segment of society." The women with whom they spend their time are usually well-educated, socially prominent, and wealthy. These men believe that they have done their bit for women's rights when they make grants to women's colleges. And, of course, the women's movement threatens male supremacy and makes them personally uneasy.

7. Some foundations are easing their consciences by promoting women within their organizations and seeing those promotions as their contribution to the improvement

of the status of women. But few women are affected, and such tokenism cannot substitute for the broad-scale action that is necessary.

8. Funding agencies are afraid of offending the foundation "fraternity" by making grants to groups perceived to be antiestablishment.

9. Foundations argue that support for women's projects is now easy to come by—this, Tully groans, is painfully untrue.

10. Foundations argue that women's projects will be funded when they manage to fit into existing foundation programs. But Tully declares emphatically that if existing programs "do not meet the needs of so large a segment of the population, it is *they* that should change. . . . The needs of women are much too vast to be dealt with on the basis of what happens to be fashionable in foundation circles in any given year." Tully takes the foundations to task, too, for retaining the traditional male values of competition, aggressiveness, and dominance while ignoring the values promoted by feminists—compassion, sensitivity and humanistic concern.

Tully's analysis of foundations is substantiated by the lessons feminist groups have learned about writing proposals. Feminists who have consulted with others on the dos and don'ts of budget-writing discover, for instance, that they often short-change themselves drastically on salaries. Modest salary requests make proposals seem "suspect" to traditional funding agencies—that is, women making such a proposal are not considered knowledgeable or responsible enough to manage a program. At the very least these agencies expect a request for a high-salaried professional executive director.

Foundations are used to hierarchical structures and have a fetish for professionalism. Their executives do not easily take to the concept of self-help; they are suspicious of the horizontal organization of democratic collectivism where everyone involved in the project has a voice and a vote. What foundation executive or board member ever heard of a secretary with as much say as the "boss," not to mention an equal salary?

Some feminist projects in other countries—particularly in Canada, Holland, and Australia—have managed to preserve their autonomy despite the fact that they are funded by the government. Therefore, it *is* possible to obtain such grants without being co-opted. American women have yet to challenge the conventional system successfully. Women's Advocates have managed to organize as they chose, but they sacrifice certain funding options to do so. But Women's House continues to exist in spite of the sacrifices, which may mean that we are on our way to wearing down conventional attitudes within agencies and foundations. The revolution in attitudes discussed in earlier chapters must shake the very roots of the funding agencies. Otherwise, refuges will be forced by their funding sources to provide traditional services to battered women, and these will produce the traditional results: reconciliation, resignation, and despair.

Funding Sources

Your whole project rests on your ability to raise funds, so you must fly in the teeth of the dragon. Most organizing groups are strong on program development and weak on fund raising. People can often be encouraged to work at fund raising in big drives to get the refuge started or to rescue it in times of crisis, but otherwise interest in fund raising seems to lag. To counteract this inertia, your group must establish an on-going committee or task force to do nothing but conduct campaigns for donations, submit grant applications, keep abreast of all funding sources, and dream up means for making the house self-supporting.

The direction you take in seeking funds will depend on how formal you want your organization to be and how carefully your members want to protect against government or agency interference. Whatever you decide on these matters, be aware that in order to receive tax-deductible donations from *any* source (the government, corporations, foundations, or private parties), you must be incorporated as a non-profit organization. If you do not wish to incorporate, you might arrange to be sponsored by a non-profit charitable organization that agrees to assume fiscal responsibility for your project and to funnel funds to you.

Do not limit yourself to preparing grant proposals. You can obtain mailing lists from other community organizations for use in conducting periodic direct-mail campaigns asking for donations. Women's House and Women's Center South made their own mailing lists of contributors and send out monthly newsletters to sustain interest and build a constituency that brings in monthly donations. Your group should also approach any and every established organization that could conceivably have an interest in the refuge. Sororities, the Junior League, and other women's or community organizations can be asked to put on fund raising events or to make donations out of their own treasuries. Ask big corporations to help—that is where the money lies, after all. The Community Involvement Project of the Xerox Corporation provided the materials and labor for a playground with swings and slides for the children at Haven House, and plans to do the same for Women's Transitional Living Center. McDonald's Hamburgers contributed money to the Momma organization in Los Angeles for a hotline. Interval House in Toronto has received donations from such corporations as The House of Seagram, Imperial Oil, Bell Canada, Reed Paper Company, and Alcan Canada Products. You can ask businesses for donations of goods and services as well as money.

Interval House in Toronto receives funds from a variety of sources. It gets a large grant from the Canadian government's Local Initiatives Program (LIP), smaller grants from the Laidlaw and Atkinson foundations and the United Community Fund, per diem allowances from the Social Services Department for persons residing in the house, and so on. Each source has its own special rules and regulations, which are often inflexible and require a great deal of paperwork. Agencies are usually specific about the kinds of services they will fund; they make a distinction between hard services (food, beds, and so forth), and soft services (counseling and referral). Thus different agencies can fund specific programs or meet specific needs within the house.

Women's House was lucky enough to start out with two VISTA volunteers as staff members whose salaries were picked up by the federal government. You might check into both VISTA and CETA programs as a possibility for filling several of your staff positions. Other United States government sources of funding are LEAA (Law Enforcement Assistance Administration), HEW (Department of Health, Education, and Welfare), NIH (National Institutes of Health), and USOE (United States Office of Education). Under HEW are the offices of Human Development and Child Development and the Community Services Administration; under NIH are the National Institutes of Mental Health, Drug Abuse, Alcohol Abuse and Alcoholism, and Education. Marilyn Prosser, who heads a consulting firm in Sacramento, California, which supports consumer-sponsored organizations in program development and funding, prefers to go after federal monies for several reasons. (1) Duration of the grant period is usually longer. Federal projects range from 36 to 54 months, and sometimes beyond seven years, whereas local grants rarely exceed one or two years. (2) Program and fiscal audits are less frequent. Federal agencies are more business-oriented, but local agencies have a tendency to move in and interfere with day-to-day operation. (3) Grants made by the federal government are larger and can amount to hundreds of thousands of dollars. Local grants of $30,000 are atypical; they rarely exceed $10,000. In the case of revenue-sharing funds, $88,000 would be high. (4) Federal grants can escalate from the first year to the third to reflect the growth of the project. But in a two-year local grant the maximum amount would be allotted for the first year, with the expectation that funding would be phased out in the future as the project develops other more stabilized sources for ongoing funding.

Nonetheless, check with the county government about revenue-sharing funds or state programs for which the refuge might be eligible. The state Office of Criminal Justice Planning and other agencies paralleling the federal programs would be probable sources. If a grant is approved, be sure to read the fine print in the contract. Some of the provisions may be contrary to your policy (such as protecting the confidentiality of clients). You might decide your policy is more important than the money; in that case, you can refuse the grant.

Grants are made for a specific period of time (usually one to three years) and are seldom renewed. Funding agencies see themselves as serving to get a program off the ground, not as on-going sponsors. Many groups relax their search for more stable sources of funding once they receive a grant, and are therefore forced to close down after the grant runs out. One way to protect against this possibility is to invest in a business that could support the project. La Casa de las Madres plans to run a commercial answering service. A refuge in Dublin has a second-hand clothing store; another group considered operating a catering service. Ideally a commercial enterprise (such as a mail order business or an addressograph service) functioning within the shelter would enable residents to learn job skills, earn a little money for themselves, and support the operation of the refuge.

The staff of Toronto's Interval House identifies two keys to raising funds. One they call "the sourdough effect": The support of certain agencies or government departments lends credibility to your project and is often instrumental in eliciting additional support from others. This strategy can result in the proverbial chicken-and-egg waiting game, as Interval House discovered. When the refuge was proposed, many funding sources had given the project verbal support and encouragement, but the government was unwilling to commit its very considerable Local Initiatives Program (LIP) funds until other commitments were guaranteed; likewise, other agencies were unwilling to commit themselves until the government grant was guaranteed. Fortunately, the United Fund came through with seed money during the stand-off, mainly because of the second key to fund raising, enthusiasm. If you have done all your homework and can speak knowledgeably and enthusiastically about the miracles you will perform in eradicating a social injustice, you might interest someone who controls the pursestrings at a funding agency. Enthusiasm is infectious, but it falls flat if you cannot back up your proposals with facts *immediately*.

Lynn A. Zimmer, in "An Excerpt from the Pages of Interval House Herstory," described how the two keys to fund raising worked together to save the day: "LIP finally told us that they'd like us to have a house before funding us because they saw that as a big obstacle. Problem: We needed a house to get money but we had no money to get the house. We finally located a large house renting at (gasp!) $600 a month. The realtor . . . gave us a letter saying we were negotiating to rent it. We then appealed to United Fund and asked for $1,200, first and last month's rent. And we got the money! probably because of the soundness of our project, the need for it in Toronto, and our enthusiasm. We certainly did not have a very sound grasp on our finances!" Often you have to take risks to get anywhere at all, but enthusiasm can carry you a long way and can even bring in needed money.

Because so many local groups are forming all over the country and will be seeking funds from the same state and federal agencies, Prosser suggests they join in a statewide network coalition. This umbrella organization could develop an overall plan that would eliminate competition and work out a more equitable distribution of available money.

The Network

A joint effort on a national scale can often deal more effectively with social issues than isolated committees in local communities. In April 1974, nearly two hundred delegates representing groups involved in refuges from England, Scotland, and Ireland came together in London to pool their energies. The delegates shared experiences and exchanged ideas about mutual problems ranging from social security payments and the difficulties of fund-raising to the special problems faced by groups in rural areas.

At a second London conference for operating and potential Women's Aid groups held the next year, delegates heard the encouraging news that eighty-three aid groups existed and twenty-six refuges were then in operation. Besides the usual topics (causes of violence, assistance for husbands, relevance of the law), the women discussed the coordination of efforts and the development of an organizational network. Disagreements arose among the forty-two groups present as to the most effective way to operate refuges. Many groups expressed the desire to remain autonomous so they could work out their particular problems on a local basis. At the same time, however, the majority agreed that a national organization or communications network was needed for the purposes of fund-raising and lobbying for government reform. The establishment of a National Housing Association would be to provide satellite housing for women who would live separately from the refuges but still have access to and be a part of Women's Aid. Since that conference, a National Women's Aid Federation has been formed. This organization is distinct from Chiswick Women's Aid. The split between the two groups resulted from their differences regarding personal power and control, the National Federation having taken a strong feminist position for autonomy and democratic methods within each group.

Despite the unfortunate conflict within the movement to help battered women, the progress in England has been extraordinary. In November 1974, fifty-three national women's organizations issued a joint public statement calling for emergency shelters for battered women in every local jurisdiction.[52] On June 10, 1975, another coalition, the National Conference of Labor Women meeting in Swansea, urged all local councils to provide space for abused women and charged the government to investigate this situation "with a view of providing them with legal aid and protection." And, the British National Association of Probate Officers instructed the Home Office to see that police treat domestic violence the way any other assault would be treated. This pressure has prompted city councils to turn over many government-held buildings to Women's Aid groups for use as shelters for battered women.

Scottish Women's Aid Federation was also formed in 1975 to help new groups get started and to cope with the ever-pressing problems of establishing refuges and satellite housing. In a short time four houses had been acquired (in Perth, Edinburgh, and Glasgow) as a result of pressure by the Federation; applications have been submitted for even more in other cities. The Federation is presently reviewing Scottish divorce laws and coordinating lobbying and publicity.[53] Edinburgh Women's Aid suggested that a reciprocal agreement be made among the various Scottish Women's Aid groups, whereby families endangered by persistent harassment and threats could be relocated in refuges far away. This idea has merit for the United States as well. Some women in Seattle suggested to me that we needed an "underground" by which victims could be transported from one city to another as a safety measure. We know that many battering husbands become single-minded about seeking out their ex-wives, tracking them down every time they move or change jobs for years after their separation. Situations arise in which a family must disappear entirely, taking new names and carefully concealing their pasts. But at present women in the United States don't even have an "overground" network or information exchange. The few groups at work on the issue of battered wives have been working in isolation.

During my research for this book, Betsy Warrior put me in touch with various women who were either conducting research projects on marital violence or trying to establish refuges. One contact often led to another, and the seeds of a communications network began to develop. The National Task Force on Battered Women/Household Violence, newly formed by the National Organization for Women, will contribute substantially to the creation of such a network. Individuals and organizations working on the problem of marital violence are invited to contact us. Write to Betsy Warrior, c/o Houseworker's Handbook, 46 Pleasant Street, Cambridge, Massachusetts 02139, or National Organization for Women, National Task Force on Battered Women/Household Violence, c/o Del Martin, 330 Ellis Street, Room 406, San Francisco, California 94102. We plan to hold a national conference similar to those held in London and Scotland.

The American people have always been quick to respond to crises. In response to a famine we send food. In an epidemic we send medical aid and supplies. In the aftermath of disasters we search through the rubble for bodies, take care of the injured, and provide food and shelter for the homeless. Even after wars, the American people are likely to show generosity to their former enemies, helping refugees to relocate and aiding in the rebuilding of war-damaged cities.

Marital violence is a social disaster of similar proportions, and its victims have the same desperate need for relief and support. Thousands of women and children need protection from injury, food and shelter, advice, and encouragement. The American government spends millions of dollars in aid to displaced persons all over the world, but the victims of violence at home are practically ignored. The problem of wife-battering has been defined, the evidence has been presented, and one immediate solution, in the form of feminist-run shelters, has been identified. What is your response, America?

Send a CARE package home today.

1981—FIVE YEARS LATER

Delores Churchill shot point blank at her estranged husband, police officer, in broad daylight on a crowded downtown San Francisco street. She admitted taking her husband's gun and putting it in her purse beforehand. The District Attorney charged her with attempted murder and assault with a deadly weapon. It looked like a clear cut case. Yet the jury acquitted her.

Five years ago Delores Churchill probably would have been found guilty and sent to prison. Admissible evidence probably would have been limited to the immediate events leading to the incident. The jury might not have heard of the seven-year living hell she had suffered at the hands of Frank Churchill: how he had terrorized her, beaten her, raped her, threatened her with weapons, subjected her to grotesque sexual abuse, and how he continued to harass and stalk her after she had separated from him. Nor would the jury have heard the testimony of psychologist Lenore E. Walker as an expert witness on the battered woman syndrome.

A history of abuse or provocation alone does not constitute a defense. Self-defense is defined as occurring in the context of immediate danger. Traditionally the court's instruction to the jury has been based upon the "reasonable man" standard allowing a man to preserve his own life and only to take the life of another when he is in imminent danger of death or great bodily injury. He must show that the force he used to repel the danger was commensurate with that peril, and therefore justifiable.[1]

In 1977 the Supreme Court of Washington, in State v. Wanrow, held that a woman defendant's right to equal protection under the law in a murder trial was violated by instructions that require a woman's conduct be measured against that of a reasonable man finding himself in the same circumstances. This landmark decision acknowledged that the use of commensurate force and the perception of imminent danger might be different for a woman, who is entitled to have the jury consider her actions in that light. Thus came into being the "reasonable woman" standard.

255

The battered wife, who lives with persistent and cumulative terror, may act more quickly and take harsher measures in protecting her life and bodily safety. That is what the jury found in Delores Churchill's case.

Similar stories have unfolded in courtrooms throughout the country. Increasingly, charges against women who kill their abusers are being dropped from first or second degree murder to manslaughter. Judges are more apt to permit qualified researchers to give expert testimony on the battered woman syndrome, enabling jurors who may have little knowledge of the phenomenon to consider the evidence in perspective.[2]

Domestic Violence Is a Crime

More than 24 million households—almost a third of the nation—were touched by crime in 1980. A household member was the victim of assault in more than 3½ million households, according to preliminary estimates from the National Crime Survey of the U.S. Bureau of Justice Statistics, which admits the figures tend to be understated.[3]

On Valentine's Day—February 14, 1981—a day chosen at random by the *San Francisco Examiner,* crime reports in the San Francisco Bay Area revealed that 50 percent of all assaults, 40 percent of assaults with a deadly weapon, and 100 percent of attempted murders were committed by family members against family members. While this may not have been a typical day, it does demonstrate the need to impress upon the criminal justice system that domestic violence is an important crime category which should be separated from other crime statistics.[4]

Five years ago police had a "no-arrest" policy and acted mostly as referees in domestic "quarrels." Today, thanks to successful class action suits brought by battered women against police in New York City and Oakland, California, domestic violence is beginning to be treated as a crime.

A new general order, negotiated in 1980 by the Coalition for Justice for Battered Women and the San Francisco Police Department brass, radically changes both the procedure and the philosophy of law enforcement's approach to domestic violence. Under the provisions of the order, officers shall treat alleged domestic violence as alleged criminal conduct; dispute mediation shall not be used as a substitute for criminal proceedings. Officers may no longer dissuade complainants from making citizen arrests. The officer's course of action shall *not* be influenced by: marital status, whether or not the suspect lives with the complainant, existence of or lack of a temporary restraining order, potential financial consequences of arrest, complainant's history of prior complaints, verbal assurances that violence will cease, the complainant's emotional state, non-visible injuries, or speculation that the complainant may not follow through with the criminal justice system. Upon verification, restraining orders will be enforced. All incident reports of domestic disturbances involving violence shall be coded with the incident classification for both the primary offense *and* domestic violence.

Removing the Onus from the Victim

These changes in police policy have caused reassessments of the prosecutor's responsibilities in spouse abuse cases. Recognizing the victim's ambivalence about prosecution and the pressure on her to withdraw, some district attorneys (Los Angeles and Santa Barbara, California;[5] Seattle, Washington, and Westchester County, New Jersey) have adopted procedures whereby the prosecutor assumes responsibility for filing charges as a crime against the state. When the victim is relieved of that responsibility (sometimes she is formally subpoenaed as a witness) and where there is a Domestic Violence Unit within the District Attorney's Office, a remarkable reduction in case attrition and a higher rate of conviction occurs. This strategy reduces the likelihood of recrimination by the defendant, since the matter is out of the victim's hands, and increases her cooperation with the prosecution.

Judith Rowland, when she was Deputy District Attorney for San Diego County, used expert witnesses in prosecuting wife abuse cases. Expert testimony need not be limited to the defense in a murder trial, she says. In battery and assault cases the husband usually denies the charge, and it is up to the prosecutor to convince the jury that the wife is telling the truth. Having an expert dispel the many misconceptions the jury may have about battered women can increase the possibility of conviction.[6]

Other strategies include: victim/witness assistance to provide information about the criminal justice system and other sources of help available to the woman and her family during that process; the abuser's release on bail conditioned on his staying away from the victim and on his not threatening, assaulting, or otherwise intimidating her; taking care that the victim's address is not released to anyone likely to threaten her; diversion of *first offenders* into counseling programs specifically for batterers.

Careful supervision of batterers is critical to the success of any diversion program. Screening, referral and tracking are conducted by an agency, often a part of the court system, such as the Probation Department. If the offender fails to appear for counseling or otherwise violates terms of the agreement, diversion is terminated and prosecution resumed. If the batterer successfully completes the program, the charges are dropped and the abuser's arrest record is expunged.

Treatment of the Offender

Five years ago counselors focused on the wife/victim. They tried to determine what she was doing to provoke her husband and provide her with communication tools in order to avoid further violent episodes. Then couples counseling came into vogue. Perhaps it was not just "her" problem, but "their" relationship. The former failed because the victim was blamed and the batterer's responsibility was ignored. The latter failed because it was the battering that affected the relationship, not the other way around. The best therapists could do was to reduce the violence, but not to eliminate it.

Today, there are more than a hundred programs across the country that deal strictly with "his" problem, his violent responses.[7] To stop the battering requires treating the offender—not the victim, nor the relationship. Only after the batterer has learned to avoid violent behavior is relationship therapy viable.

These are the assumptions of the model program designed by Anne Ganley and Lance Harris at the American Lake Veterans Hospital, Tacoma, Washington.[8] They found that men who batter have intense, dependent relations with their victims. They fear losing the relationship and take extreme measures in controlling it. Battering men have difficulty in differentiating their emotions. Their experiences of fear, anxiety, frustration, hurt, irritation, guilt, disappointment, etc. get lumped together and are expressed as anger. Usually the target of this anger is the wife who happens to be in the batterer's immediate vicinity even though she has nothing to do with his distress. They have been violent in other relationships and will continue to batter whoever their partners are unless a major change occurs in their response patterns. Ganley and Harris contend that violence is a learned behavior and that batterers can learn new behaviors and attitudes.

Other Research Findings

Five years ago researchers who studied "family" violence avoided the specificity of wife-beating. Since then researchers like Lenore Walker, R. Emerson Dobash and Russell Dobash, and Mildred Pagelow have contributed greatly to our understanding of the battered wife syndrome.

After three years of extensive case studies, psychologist Lenore Walker formulated the three-phase cycle of violence theory and the "learned helplessness" syndrome that keeps battered women trapped in nightmare relationships.[9] The battering cycle has three distinct phases: the slow tension-building phase, which escalates until the inevitability of the explosion or acute battering incident, followed by the calm, loving respite. During the latter period of reconciliation the husband's kindness and contrite loving behavior makes the battered woman's victimization complete. He does everything he can to convince her that he truly loves her and that he will change. She wants to believe him and becomes ambivalent about leaving him. If she stays, however, the cycle begins again.

When the woman seeks help to no avail and when her coping mechanisms have no effect on her batterer, she perceives the battering as completely beyond her control. She becomes hopeless, passive, submissive and "helpless." Repeated beatings, like electrical shocks, diminish the woman's motivation to respond. She believes there is nothing she can do to change the situation and that no one can really help her. Her sense of hopelessness and helplessness becomes her reality. Walker points out that the battered woman's syndrome is the *result* of the beatings, not the *cause* of them.

Sociologist Mildred Pagelow builds a strong theoretical framework for her hypothesis that the fewer the battered women's resources, the more negative the institutional response, and the more intense the traditional ideology of the wife, the more likely she is to remain in a violent relationship and the less likely she is to try to alter her situation.[10]

The Dobashes, who conducted their research in Scotland, locate the impetus for violence in the husband's sense of possessiveness, domination and "rightful control" over his wife. They suggest that the way to dramatically reduce the number of violent marriages is to overcome the subordination, isolation and devaluation of women and to change the hierarchal family structure. The problem, these sociologists conclude, lies in the domination and control of women. The answer lies in the struggle against it.[11]

New Insight on Sex Roles

In feedback I have received from clinicians as well as the findings of the above studies, I find a common thread that appears to verify my own belief that rigid sex role stereotyping is an important factor in wife battering. Despite the volumes of literature available today on how destructive stereotypical roles are to both sexes—in stunting the emotional growth of men and in making women vulnerable to abuse—child rearing practices, for the most part, persist in encouraging and perpetuating them.

Is this due to a natural resistance to change? Is it a reluctance on the part of men to give up perceived power? Or is there some other factor operating here? Letty Cottin Pogrebin, in her book *Growing Up Free: Raising Your Child in the 80s,* suggests that the compelling force behind sex role rigidity is homophobia—fear and intolerance of homosexuality.[12] She says this fear, which inhibits pro-child attitudes in the most well intentioned parents, is based on the fear that sex roles determine sexuality, that specific ingredients make a child homosexual, and that homosexuality is one of the worst things that can happen. Pogrebin analyzes these assumptions, compares them with research findings, and concludes that they are unsubstantiated myths. She also shows how homophobia forces us into conformity, emphasizes differences and divisions between men and women, and contributes to men's contempt for everything female.

Taking Pogrebin's analysis a step further, I make the connection between homophobia and domestic violence. Homophobic men, who repress human traits that may in any way be labeled "feminine," become obsessed with "masculinity." They equate agressiveness with male identity, and power with the masculine ideal. They must constantly prove their manhood and lash out whenever they feel it is challenged. While men are socialized to be powerful, the reality is that few of them really get to exercise power in our society. Consequently many of them are like pent-up volcanoes ready to erupt. Wives, who are supposed to meet all their needs, are easy, available targets for their rage.

Pogrebin says we should stop worrying about how to raise a heterosexual child. By using stereotypes as a vaccine against homosexuality, we try to mold children into ill-fitting behavior patterns which can be psychologically damaging and sometimes inspire just what the parents are hoping to avoid. The entire system of male supremacy makes it harder to love the other sex. It actually conditions boys *against* heterosexuality because society is so relentlessly *for* "masculinity." It fosters the Battle of the Sexes—a war no one ever wins.

The Battered Women's Movement

While it is true that we have made inroads into the causes, treatment and prevention of domestic violence in the last five years, these gains are still tentative and by no means widespread. The need for emergency housing and support services for wife/victims is still of prime importance. Refuges for battered women and their children remain the only *real* protection society offers. The response I had hoped for has been heartwarming. While in 1976 I could identify less than a dozen refuges in the United States, nearly 500 exist today. They are filled to capacity and have long waiting lists.

Grass roots women's groups established most of these refuges—often a great personal sacrifice in money and labor. They conducted public awareness campaigns, networked with and provided specialized training for government and private agencies, while meeting the daily needs of victims and their families. They depended upon a few paid staff (mostly CETA positions) and a roster of volunteers. Often they were placed in the position of competing against each other for the few local, state or federal grants, private foundation monies, and public appeals for charitable donations.

Fearing that the battered women's movement could be co-opted by fierce competition for funding, and fearing that funding agencies might require a traditional approach to staffing and policy in spite of the success of the women-helping-women principle on which refuges were founded, women's groups banded together in coalitions. They organized nationally, regionally and statewide to share information, bolster support for maintaining feminist principles in the operation of their refuges, provide cooperative technical training programs, and lobby for legislation to appropriate funds for their programs and make reforms in the law.

261

Despite these safeguards some refuges found themselves making small compromises just to keep their doors open. By a gradual and insidious process, peer counseling gave way to traditional therapeutic practices; paraprofessionals, who had founded and conducted successful programs, were fired and replaced by those with professional "status." But most refuges have managed to keep their programs intact by carefully selecting their boards of directors and by rejecting funding sources which have strings attached to the monies they grant.

The National Coalition Against Domestic Violence[13] was founded in 1978 during the two-day "Consultation on Battered Women" held by the U.S. Commission on Civil Rights in Washington, D.C. The impetus was the prospect of a national Domestic Violence Prevention and Treatment Act to be introduced in the House of Representatives by Barbara Mikulski, Lindy Boggs and George Miller, and in the Senate by Alan Cranston. Representatives of women's groups met with legislative aides and with Midge Constanza, then aide to President Carter, to hammer out the details. The bill would appropriate $65 million over a three-year period for services and research and to establish a national office and clearinghouse to administer domestic violence programs.

The Carter administration, aware that the legislative process is lengthy and that passage of the bill was not guaranteed, proceeded to establish an Office on Domestic Violence in the Department of Health and Human Services. Under the auspices of this national office, regional technical assistance programs were established to assist service providers in solving funding and operational problems. Later, after extensive data collection, the National Clearinghouse on Domestic Violence was set up to disseminate information on criminal justice, research, funding, counseling, program management, prevention, medical services, community networking, etc. Address for the Clearinghouse if P.O. Box 2309, Rockville, MD 20852. The telephone number is 301/251-5172.

In 1980, after years of hearings and lobbying by the National Coalition, both the Senate and the House finally passed the Domestic Violence Prevention and Treatment Act. The victory was short lived. The conference bill passed the House, but was stymied in the Senate by right wing Republicans who threatened a filibuster in the closing days of the session. In 1981 Representative Barbara Mikulski reintroduced the bill in the House, but its chances for passage in the presently constituted Senate are remote.

While one branch of government may have reneged on its commitment to bring relief to battered women, another—the Armed Forces—took up the banner to provide services for abused wives in military families. In 1978 Captain Nancy Raiha and her co-workers in Social Work Service started the first spouse abuse program and refuge at Fort Campbell, Kentucky. Military wives played an important role in generating support on the base, which led to a directive issued by the commanding general mandating the project. At Fort Campbell, military police have a written protocol for responding to domestic violence calls: a patrol is dispatched to each call, the batterer's commander is notified of the incident, and a record is sent to the Social Work Service staff for follow-up. The batterer's commander can send the man to counseling and/or to the barracks. Also, the chaplains operate a 24-hour hotline.[14]

The most important needs in establishing spouse abuse programs in the military are to educate commanders to use constructive measures to discipline men who batter, and to dispel the victim's fear of damaging her husband's career. It is this fear that keeps many wives from reporting the abuse.

Speakers at the first national conference on "Domestic Violence in the Military Community," held in March, 1981, stressed that in order to survive frequent changes in personnel, a military domestic violence program must be institutionalized by a commanding general's directive. In this way a program's network of related military agencies and assigned responsibilities remains intact regardless of staff changes.[15]

At some installations like Fort Campbell, Fort Benning, Georgia, and V and VII Corps communities in Europe, the Army has good services available to battered wives. At others there are none. But Army Community Services is currently planning to establish similar services on most bases. In 1980 the Air Force opened an Office on Family Matters to implement a coordinated approach to family problems, including spouse abuse. The Office on Family Matters serves as a resource center for those who wish to start a domestic violence program on their installation. The Navy's Family Advocacy Program, the only service-wide program established to treat wife battering and child abuse, started in 1979. A family advocacy representative is stationed at each Navy medical facility to coordinate services on the base for the personnel and families of both the Navy and the Marine Corps. To date the Coast Guard is the only military service which has not instituted a domestic violence program.

The Politics of Funding

Because the Reagan administration has eliminated CETA and gutted other federal funding sources, and because of cutbacks in state and local government budgets, civilian refuges are in a state of financial crisis and their continued existence threatened. Most of them have been reduced to one or two paid staff in an operation that runs seven days a week, 24 hours a day. Some depend totally on volunteers, who are becoming more scarce due to today's economic crunch.

Compounding the problem is the switch by the Reagan administration to broad block grants instead of categorical grant programs (such as Title XX, CSA, etc.). States receiving block grants will have more flexibility in deciding what types of services to fund. It is likely that political clout, rather than need, will influence spending decisions. The extent to which those who are concerned about maintaining services for battered women and their children organize politically at state and local levels may determine their survival in the 80s.[16]

In many areas where state and local coalitions against domestic violence already exist, they are mainly comprised of service providers who have not been directly involved in electoral politics and in election campaigns. Domestic violence must become a campaign issue. In recent elections in San Francisco, for instance, nearly every candidate made a pledge to support La Casa de las Madres. This was done by reaching key political figures and by enlisting the aid of community policial groups and feminist organizations like the National Women's Political Caucus and the National Organization for Women.

State coalitions also need to keep up to date on legislation that has been passed or is pending in other states for law reform and for funding ideas.[17] One way to generate money is by adding a surcharge to the marriage license fee. This has been successfully enacted in a number of states. In California, instead of the $8 surcharge being collected and distributed by the state, the monies are distributed in the counties where marriage license fees are collected. This source netted

$60,000 during San Francisco's 1980-81 fiscal year, which at least paid the rent and covered basic expenditures to keep La Casa's doors open, and to make a small grant to Women, Inc., which provides back up services.

The California Alliance Against Domestic Violence conducted a poll recently on statewide use of refuge services in 1980. At this writing less than half of the returns were in, and many of these were from less populated rural areas. Nonetheless, of the 41 refuges that had reported, 38,668 crisis calls were received, 8,384 women and children were sheltered by 793 staff members (paid and volunteer), and 19,000 professional and community people received training on battered women's issues.

Such statistics demonstrate clearly that the need for refuges for women in life threatening situations is still crucial. We must find effective ways to communicate that need and ensure the continuance of the knowledge and services we have developed over the past five years.

Psycholinguistics and Domestic Violence

One way to become more effective in conveying our message is to examine the language we use. "Domestic violence" is the euphemism we first employed to attract public attention at a time when there was so much resistance to dealing with wife abuse per se. Despite our efforts to stress the *violence* of husbands against wives, news stories and police reports still refer to domestic "disputes" or "quarrels." Such references are misleading. They deny wife-beating as a crime, diminish the impact of the violence, and prevent people from coming to grips with its reality.

The diplomatic language which we employed in the past to get people to listen, or to keep from alienating those whose help we needed, no longer serves us. Now we must learn to refine our language and be more precise. We must say what we really mean, as Steven Morgan does when he refers to "conjugal terrorism."[18]

People today are all too familiar with terrorism: the taking of hostages and the threat they will be killed unless they obey their captors. Battered women are indeed held hostage in their own homes. Battering husbands wield guns or knives or fists to control their every move, isolate them, rape them and keep them captive. People understand the plight of and have empathy for hostages. They don't ask, "What did they do to provoke their captors?" They realize that the hostages hap-

265

pened to be in the right place at the wrong time. They place responsibility on the perpetrator, not the victim. And they don't ask, "Why don't the hostages just leave if they don't like it?" They are keenly aware of the danger to the hostage who makes the wrong move.

Another way to deal with "What did she do to provoke him?" is to turn the question around. The real question is, "What is it about our society that keeps a woman hostage in a violent home?" Battered women are political prisoners. Male domination and protection of the patriarchal system that breeds sexism and homophobia are the political issues at stake.

Throughout my book I have consistently used the phrase "refuge for battered women and their children." The American battered women's movement has popularized the word "shelter." While "shelters" may be easier to say than "refuges," the connotation of the former is not as precise or compelling as the latter. Phyllis Schlafly can be flip about shelters providing wives "a rest cure or vacation at taxpayer's expense," as she did during the National Women's Conference in Houston in 1977. But could she be so adamantly opposed to providing emergency housing to "refugee" women and children who have fled their homes because of "conjugal terrorism?"

We Americans deplore terrorism. We have always responded readily and generously to refugees who have been driven from their homes because of disasters over which they had no control. Can we do less for ourselves?

One Last Note

In the first chapter of this book is a "Letter from a Battered Wife." When it was originally received and published I did not know that its author was married to a prominent physician, nor that she had documented her case and placed it in the hands of the staff at the refuge for battered women in her county. She asked that her story be made public in the event something dreadful happened to her. She then returned home and told her husband what she had done.

He never laid another finger on her.

Which says to me that if a man has something to lose, he can quickly learn to change his violent behavior.

Del Martin
September, 1981

266

NOTES

Chapter 1

1. Erin Pizzey, *Scream Quietly or the Neighbors Will Hear* (London: If Books, 1974).

2. Judith Weinraub, "The Battered Wives of England: A Place to Heal Their Wounds," *The New York Times* (November 29, 1975), p. C-17.

Chapter 2

1. All figures in this paragraph from the *San Francisco Chronicle* (April 1, 1975), p.12.

2. Mary Ann Kuhn, "There's No Place Like Home for Beatings," *Washington Star* (November 11, 1975), p. 1.

3. George Gallup, "Guns Found in 44% of Homes," *San Francisco Chronicle* (July 7, 1975), p. 2.

4. Kuhn, p. A-14.

5. John Harris, "Networks Claim They've Been Toned Down but. . . ," *National Enquirer* (August 19, 1975), p.14.

6. Beth Pombeiro (Knight News Service), "Decadence Is Back—in Vogue," *San Francisco Examiner* (December 7, 1975), pp. 1, 28, and *Vogue* (December 1975), p. 149.

7. Federal Bureau of Investigation, *Unified Crime Reports* (1973), p. 14.

8. Letty Cottin Pogrebin, "Do Women Make Men Violent?" *Ms.* (November 1974), p.55.

9. Raymond Parnas, "The Police Response to Domestic Disturbances," *Wisconsin Law Review* (1967), p. 914, n. 2.

10. Raymond Parnas, "Police Discretion and Diversion of Incidents of Intra-Family Violence," *Law and Contemporary Problems*, Vol. 36, No. 4 (Autumn 1971), p. 54, n. 1.

11. Northeast Patrol Division Task Force, Kansas City Police Department, "Conflict Management: Analysis/Resolution." Taken from first draft, p. 58 (hereinafter called Kansas City Police report).

12. Commander James D. Bannon, from a speech delivered before a conference of the American Bar Association in Montreal, 1975.

13. J. C. Barden, "Wife Beaters: Few of Them Ever Appear Before a Court of Law," *The New York Times* (October 21, 1974), Sec. 2, p. 38. Figures reported as 17,277 family violence cases, of which the wife was plaintiff in 82 percent.

14. Karen Durbin, "Wife-Beating," *Ladies Home Journal* (June 1974), p. 64.

15. Laura White, "Women Organize to Protect Wives from Abusive Husbands," *Boston Herald-American* (Sunday edition, June [22 or 29] 1975).

16. Betsy Warrior, "Battered Lives," *Houseworker's Handbook* (Spring 1975), p. 25.

17. Ibid., p. 25.

18. Lois Yankowski, "Battered Women: A Study of the Situation in the Distrtict of Columbia," unpublished (1975), pp. 2-3.

19. Richard Gelles, *The Violent Home* (Beverly Hills: Sage, 1972), p. 36.

20. Ibid., p. 50.

21. Sue Eisenberg and Patricia Micklow, "The Assaulted Wife: 'Catch 22' Revisited," unpublished (University of Michigan, Ann Arbor, 1974), p. 18. A version of this study was published by *Women's Rights Law Reporter* in 1976.

22. Morton Bard, *Training Police As Specialists in Family Crisis Intervention* (Washington: U.S. Government Printing Office, 1970), p.1.

23. Barden, p. 38.

24. Yankowski, p. 3.

25. Eisenberg and Micklow, p. 16.

26. Montgomery County Council, Maryland, "A Report by the Task Force to Study a Haven for Physically Abused Persons" (1975), p. 17.

27. Kansas City Police report.

28. Ibid.

29. Ibid.

30. Ibid.

31. *California Homicides,* 1971.

32. Federal Bureau of Investigation, *Uniform Crime Reports,* 1973.

33. *Crimes of Violence,* a staff report to the National Commission on the Causes and Prevention of Violence (Washington, D.C.: U.S. Government Printing Office, 1969), p. 360.

34. San Francisco Police Department, Homicide Bureau. Statistics reviewed and evaluated with respect to marital cases by Susan Jackson and Marta Ashley.

35. Robert B. Murphy, Ed McKay, Jeffrey A. Schwartz, and Donald A. Liebman, "Training Patrolmen As Crisis Intervention Instructors," unpublished, p. 1.

36. George Levinger, "Source of Marital Dissatisfaction among Applicants for Divorce," *American Journal of Orthopsychiatry* (October 1966), pp. 804-06.

37. Eisenberg and Micklow, p. 18.

38. Warrior, p. 25.

39. Suzanne K. Steinmetz and Murray A. Straus, eds., *Violence the Family* (New York: Dodd, Mead, 1975), p. v.

40. Eleanor Emmons Maccoby and Carol Nagy Jacklin, *The sychology of Sex Differences* (Stanford: Stanford University Press, 974), p. 264.

41. Erin Pizzey, "Scream Quietly or the Neighbors Will Hear," *Manchester Daily Express* (October 29, 1974), p. 11.

42. Gelles, p. 153.

43. Ibid., p. 58.

44. Ibid., p. 136.

45. Joyce Brothers, "A Quiz on Crime," *San Francisco Sunday xaminer and Chronicle* (June 22, 1975), Sunday Scene, p. 6.

46. Bill Peterson, "System Frustrates Battered Wives," *Washingn Post* (November 2, 1974), p. 18.

47. Morton Bard, "The Study and Modification of Intra-Familial iolence," *The Control of Aggression and Violence: Cognitive and sychological* (New York: Academic Press, 1971), p. 154.

48. Sally Johnson, "What About Battered Women?" *Majority eport* (February 8, 1975), p. 4.

49. Rodney Stark and James McEvoy III, "Middle-Class Vionce," *Psychology Today* (November 1970), pp. 30-31.

50. Ibid., p. 32.

51. Gelles, p. 25.

52. Ibid., pp. 95-96.

53. Alex D. Pokorny, "Human Violence: A Comparison of Homide, Aggravated Assault, Suicide, and Attempted Suicide," *Journal f Criminal Law, Criminology and Police Science 56* (1965), pp. 488-7.

54. Marvin E. Wolfgang, *Patterns in Criminal Homicide* (New ork: John Wiley, 1958), p. 125.

55. Ibid., p. 126.

56. Gelles, p. 100.

57. Wolfgang, p. 108.

58. Gelles, pp. 104-05. D. J. Pittman and W. Handy, "Patterns in riminal Aggravated Assault," *Journal of Criminal Law, Criminolgy and Police Science 55* (1964), p. 463.

59. Kansas City Police report.

60. J. J. Gayford, "Wife Battering: A Preliminary Survey on 100 ases," *British Medical Journal* (January 25, 1975), p. 196.

61. Ibid., p. 195.

62. Bard, "The Study and Modification of Intra-Familial Vionce," p. 161.

63. Gelles, p. 173.

64. Ibid., p. 171.

65. Quoted by Judith Weinraub, "The Battered Wives of England: A Place to Heal Their Wounds," *The New York Times* (November 29, 1975), p. C-17.

66. Serapio R. Zalba, "Battered Children," *Trans-Action* (July-August, 1971), p. 59.

67. C. Henry Kempe, *Eyewitness News*, CBS Television, December 1, 1975.

68. Quoted in Kuhn, p. A-14.

Chapter 3

1. Frederick Engels, *The Origin of Family, Private Property and the State* (Moscow: Progress, 1948), p. 42.

2. Ibid., p. 49.

3. Margaret Mead, *Male and Female* (New York: Dell, 1949), pp. 77, 86-87.

4. Ibid., pp. 77, 115-16.

5. Ibid., pp. 77, 114-15.

6. Engels, p. 53.

7. Ibid., pp. 48, 53.

8. Ibid., p. 53.

9. Susan Brownmiller, *Against Our Will* (New York: Simon and Schuster, 1975), p. 16.

10. Engels, p. 57.

11. Ibid., p. 65.

12. Brownmiller, p. 17.

13. Engles, p. 58.

14. Hernán San Martín, "Machismo: Latin America's Myth-Cult of Male Supremacy," *Unesco Courier* (March 1975), p. 31.

15. *Alternative Press Digest*, "Flipside of the Japanese Miracle," No. 3 (1975), p. 66.

16. Engels, p. 64.

17. *San Francisco Chronicle*, "That Strict Arab Life" (May 1975), p. 22.

18. William Mandel, *Soviet Women* (Garden City, N.Y.: Anchor, 1975), p. 13.

19. *San Francisco Chronicle*, p. 22; William Drummond, *Boston Globe* (May 26, 1974).

20. Elizabeth Gould Davis, *The First Sex* (New York: Putnam, 1971), pp. 254-55.

21. King James Bible, Ephesians 6: 22-24.

22. Davis, p. 255.

23. King James Bible, Numbers 5.

24. Davis, p. 252.

25. Ibid., p. 253.

26. Ibid., p. 261.

27. Mandel, p. 12.

28. Ibid.

29. Ibid., p. 13.

30. Ibid., pp. 13-14.

31. Robert Calvert: "Criminal and Civil Liability in Husband-Wife ssaults," in *Violence in the Family,* Suzanne K. Steinmetz and urray A. Straus, eds. (New York: Dodd, Mead, 1975), p. 89.

32. Ibid., p. 88 (*Bradley* v. *State*).

33. Ibid., p. 89.

34. E. Lehman, "Wife-beating," unpublished (New York, 1975), 2 (*State* v. *Rhodes*).

35. Calvert, p. 89 (*State* v. *Oliver*)

36. Ibid., p. 89.

37. Lehman, pp. 2-3 (*State* v. *Edens*).

38. Ibid., p. 3 (*State* v. *Dowell*).

39. Ibid., p. 3.

40. Ibid., p. 3, n. 10 (*State* v. *Harris*).

41. Jennifer Fleming, "Wife Abuse," unpublished (Philadelphia, 75), p. 3.

42. Davis, p. 311.

43. Betsy Warrior, "Battered Lives," *Houseworker's Handbook* pring 1975), p. 38.

44. John Hess, "French Mothers to Get Equal Say in Raising hildren," *The New York Times* (April 17, 1970).

45. Warrior, p. 38.

46. Michael Arkus, "Ban on Wife Selling," *San Francisco Chron- le* (March 28, 1975).

47. *San Francisco Chronicle,* "Zulu Queen's Custody Case," ay 5, 1975), p. 24.

48. Warrior, pp. 38, 40.

49. *San Francisco Chronicle,* "Man Rapes His Wife—Jailed" ay 23, 1974).

50. Theodora Lurie, "End of Wife-Beating," *San Francisco ronicle* (May 9, 1975), p. 21.

51. James Rössel, "Women in Sweden" (Stockholm: The Swed- Institute, 1965), pp. 30-31.

52. Hess, "French Mothers to Get Equal Say."

53. Dale Ross Rubenstein, "How the Russian Revolution Failed omen," *Women's Liberation Revolution: The Class Struggle* (San ancisco: The Socialist Workship), p.4

54. Ibid., p. 9.

55. Ibid., p. 10.

56. Lenore Weitzman, "Legal Regulation of Marriage: Traditic and Change," *California Law Review*, Vol. 62, No. 4 (July-Septem ber 1974), p. 1170.

57. W. Blackstone, *Commentaries* (1765), p. 442.

58. Weitzman, p. 1172.

59. Ibid., p. 1173.

60. Karen De Crow, *Sexist Justice* (New York: Random Hous 1974), p. 164-65 *(McGuire* v. *McGuire)*.

61. Weitzman, p. 1187 *(Rucci* v. *Rucci)*.

62. Ibid., p. 1169.

63. Ibid., p. 1173, n. 16.

64. San Martín, p. 31.

65. Jessie Bernard, *The Future of Marriage* (New York: Bantar 1972), pp. 4-5.

66. Ibid., p. 41.

67. Ibid., p. 17.

68. Ibid., p. 18.

69. Ibid., p. 19.

70. Ibid., p. 20.

71. Ibid., p. 21.

72. Ibid., p. 18.

73. Ibid., p. 28.

74. Ibid., p. 29.

75. Ibid., p. 32.

76. Ibid., p. 30.

77. Ibid., p. 52.

78. Lisa Leghorn, "Women's Work," *Houseworker's Handboc* (Spring 1975), p. 11.

79. Jane Alpert, "Mother Right: A New Feminist Theory," *c our backs* (July/August 1973), p. 30.

80. U.S. Department of Labor, Women's Bureau, Washingto D.C., "Women Workers Today," July 1975.

81. Evelyne Sullerot, *Woman, Society and Change* (New Yor McGraw-Hill, 1971), p. 123.

82. Statement made by investigator at San Francisco's Equ Employment Opportunity Commission office.

83. U. S. Department of Labor, Women's Bureau, Washingto D.C., "Twenty Facts on Women Workers," June 1975.

Chapter 4

1. Erin Pizzey, "The Cultured Graduate Who Became a Thug *Manchester Daily Express* (October 29, 1974), p. 11.

2. Claudia Dreifus, *Woman's Fate* (New York: Bantam, 1973), 71.

3. Stuart Palmer, "Family Members as Murder Victims," *Violence in the Family,* Steinmetz and Straus, eds. (New York: Dodd, Lead, 1974), p. 94.

4. Erin Pizzey, "A Brute Behind That Perfect Bedside Manner," *Manchester Daily Express* (October 31, 1974).

5. *Newsweek,* October 1974, cited by Betsy Warrior in "Battered Wives," *Houseworker's Handbook* (Spring 1975), p. 38.

6. "Flipside of the Japanese Miracle," *Alternative Press Digest,* No. 3 (1975), p. 66.

7. John E. Snell, Richard J. Rosenwald, and Ames Robey, "The Wifebeater's Wife," *Archives of General Psychiatry,* Vol. 11 (August 1964), pp. 107-12.

8. Leroy G. Schultz, "The Wife Assaulter," *The Journal of Social Therapy,* Vol. 6, No. 2 (1960).

9. Richard Gelles, *The Violent Home* (Beverly Hills: Sage, 1972), p. 37-38.

10. The following account is condensed from Tracy Johnston, When He Stopped Beating His Wife," *City of San Francisco* (July 1975), p. 24. Reprinted with permission © City of San Francisco newsweekly.

11. Erin Pizzey, "Violence Begins at Home," *London Spectator* (November 23, 1974).

12. Gelles, p. 188.

13. *Practical Psychology for Physicians* (Summer 1975), p. 45.

14. Gelles, p. 52.

15. Ibid., p. 74.

16. M. Komarovsky, *Blue Collar Marriage* (New York: Vintage, 1940), p. 227.

17. J. J. Gayford, "Wife Battering: A Preliminary Survey of 100 Cases," *British Medical Journal* (January 25, 1975), p. 195.

18. William J. Goode, "Force and Violence in the Family," in *Violence in the Family,* p. 38.

19. Robert N. Whitehurst, "Violence in Husband-Wife Interaction," in *Violence in the Family,* p. 78.

20. William J. Goode, "Violence Among Intimates," *Crimes of Violence* (staff report to National Commission on the Causes and Prevention of Violence), Vol. 13, Appendix 19, p. 960.

21. Gayford, pp. 195-96.

22. Sue Eisenberg and Patricia Micklow, "The Assaulted Wife: 'Catch 22' Revisited," unpublished (University of Michigan, Ann Arbor, 1974), pp. 23-24.

23. Jeanne Wright, "Wife Beating Not Uncommon," *Kalamazoo Gazette* (December 5, 1975).

24. Eisenberg and Micklow, p. 24.

25. Gelles, p. 209.

26. Bill Peterson, "System Frustrates Battered Wives," *Washing ton Post* (November 2, 1975), p. 1.

27. Judith Weinraub, "The Battered Wives of England: A Place t Heal Their Wounds," *The New York Times* (November 29, 1975 p. C-17.

28. Gelles, p. 186.

29. Suzanne K. Steinmetz and Murray A. Straus, "General Intro duction: Social Myth and Social System in the Study of Intra-Famil Violence," *Violence in the Family,* p. 9.

30. Ibid., p. 9.

31. Whitehurst, pp. 78-79.

32. Gelles, pp. 78, 112-13.

33. Ibid., p. 117.

34. Morton Bard and Joseph Zacker, "Assaultiveness and Alco hol Use in Family Disputes," *Criminology,* Vol. 12, No. 3 (Novem ber 1974), pp. 283-84, 287-88, 291-92.

35. Gelles, p. 116-17.

36. Verbal report, Mary Vail, San Francisco Women's Litigatio Unit.

37. Gelles, p. 115.

38. Erin Pizzey, *Scream Quietly or the Neighbors Will Hea* (London: If Books, 1974), p. 85.

39. Gay Search, "London: Battered Wives," *Ms.* (June 1974 p. 24.

40. Jackson Toby, "Violence and the Masculine Ideal: Som Qualitative Data," in *Violence in the Family,* pp. 63-64.

41. Gelles, p. 83.

42. Ibid., p. 84.

43. Joan and Larry Constantine, "Jealousy—the Marriag Killer," *Penthouse Forum* (March 1974), pp. 59-60.

44. Pizzey, *London Spectator.*

45. Eisenberg and Micklow, p. 6.

46. Richard Gelles, "Violence and Pregnancy: A Note on th Extent of the Problem and Needed Services," *The Family Coordina tor* (January 1975), Vol. 24, p. 84.

47. Letter from Betsy Warrior dated February 5, 1976.

48. Toby, pp. 61-62.

49. Steinmetz and Straus, pp. 58-59.

50. Hernán San Martín, "Machismo: Latin America's Myth-C of Male Supremacy," *Unesco Courier* (March 1975), p. 30.

51. Letty Cottin Pogrebin, "Do Women Make Men Violent?" *M* (November 1974), p. 80.

52. Eleanor Emmons Maccoby and Carol Nagy Jacklin, *The Psychology of Sex Differences* (Stanford: Stanford University Press, 1974), p. 484.

53. Ibid., p. 484.

54. Pogrebin, p. 80.

55. Ibid., p. 55.

56. Both examples from Ibid., p. 55.

57. Susan Griffin, *Ramparts* (September 1971), cited by Pogrebin, 55.

58. Whitehurst, pp. 78-79.

59. Maccoby and Jacklin, p. 264.

60. Anthony Storr, *Human Aggression* (New York: Bantam, 1970), p. 39.

61. Ibid., p. 18.

62. Ibid., p. 75.

63. Ibid., p. 66.

64. Ibid., p. 70.

65. Ibid., p. 71.

66. Ibid., p. 70.

67. Ibid., p. 71.

68. Ibid., p. 77.

69. Ibid., p. 69.

70. J. C. Rheingold, *The Fear of Being a Woman* (New York: Grune and Stratton, 1964).

71. Wolfgang Lederer, *The Fear of Women* (New York: Harcourt Brace Jovanovich, 1968), p. 283.

72. Adelbert Reif, "Erich Fromm on Human Aggression," *Psychology Today* (April 1975), p. 22.

73. Ibid., p. 23.

74. Leonard Berkowitz, "The Case for Bottling Up Rage," *Psychology Today* (July 1973), pp. 24-31.

75. George R. Bach and Peter Wyden, *The Intimate Enemy* (New York: Morrow, 1969).

76. Robert N. Whitehurst, "Violently Jealous Husbands," *Sexual Behavior* (July 1971), p. 41.

Chapter 5

1. All data on the survey in this section from J. J. Gayford, "Wife Battering: A Preliminary Survey of 100 Cases," *British Medical Journal* (January 25, 1975), pp. 194-97.

2. Seth Mydans, "Group Forms to Aid Victims of Wife Beating," *Milwaukee Journal* (August 4, 1975).

3. Sue Eisenberg and Patricia Micklow, "The Assaulted Wife: 'Catch 22' Revisited," unpublished (University of Michigan, Ann Arbor, 1974) p. 30.

4. *Newsweek,* "Battered Women" (February 2, 1976), p. 47.

5. Bill Peterson, "System Frustrates Battered Wives," *Washington Post* (November 2, 1975), p. A-18.

6. Erin Pizzey, *Scream Quietly or the Neighbors Will Hear* (London: If Books, 1974), p.39.

7. From a letter to La Casa de las Madres Coalition, San Francisco. A police escort was arranged to take the woman and her family to the shelter, which is described in Chapter 10.

8. Pizzey, p. 39.

9. Eleanor Emmons Maccoby and Carol Nagy Jacklin, *The Psychology of Sex Differences* (Stanford: Stanford University Press, 1974), p. 167.

10. Claudia Dreifus, *Woman's Fate* (New York: Bantam, 1973), p. 71.

11. Barbara Richardson, "Wife beating: How prevalent is the problem?" *Dallas Times Herald* (September 21, 1975).

12. William J. Goode, "Force and Violence in the Family," in *Violence in the Family,* Suzanne K. Steinmetz and Murray A. Straus, eds. (New York: Dodd, Mead, 1975), p. 38.

13. *Practical Psychology for Physicians* (Summer 1975), p. 45.

14. Eisenberg and Micklow, p. 31.

15. Abigail Van Buren, "Dear Abby," *San Francisco Chronicle* (April 11, 1975).

16. Eisenberg and Micklow, p. 31.

17. Richardson, *Dallas Times Herald.*

Chapter 6

1. Elizabeth Truninger, "Marital Violence: The Legal Solutions," *Hastings Law Journal,* Vol. 23, No. 1 (November 1971), p. 262.

2. Sue Eisenberg and Patricia Micklow, "The Assaulted Wife: 'Catch 22' Revisited," unpublished (University of Michigan, Ann Arbor, 1974), pp. 71-73.

3. The following account is from "Indicted for Raping His Wife," *New York Post* (January 14, 1976), p. 74.

4. From a letter from Alix Foster to author dated April 18, 1975.

5. Truninger, p. 262, n. 24.

6. Susan Jackson, "Marital Violence in San Francisco," a memorandum to the Women's Litigation Unit, San Francisco Neighborhood Legal Assistance Foundation (January 1975), p. 8.

7. Truninger, p. 264.

8. Jackson, p. 9.

9. Morton Bard, *The Function of the Police in Crisis Intervention and Conflict Management,* a report prepared by Ciminal Justice Associates, Inc. on a grant from the United States Department of Justice, Law Enforcement Assistance Administration, National Institute of Law Enforcement and Criminal Justice, pp. 4.4-4.5.

10. J. C. Barden, "Wife Beaters: Few of Them Ever Appear Before a Court of Law," *The New York Times* (October 21, 1974), Sec. 2, p. 38.

11. Quoted in Eisenberg and Micklow, p. 112.

12. "Techniques of Dispute Intervention," *Training Bulletin III-J,* City of Oakland Police Services (June 19, 1975), pp. 2-3.

13. Letter from Carol Murray on the criminal prosecution of violent spouses addressed to Stanley Weiss, director of the San Francisco District Attorney's Bureau of Family Relations (1974).

14. This incident and the one following are described by *Seattle Times* reporters, Susan Schwartz and Dale Douglas Mills, "Wife-Beating: Crime and No Punishment," in "Femicide," unpublished, Carol Orlock, ed. (Seattle, 1975), pp. 6-7.

15. Eisenberg and Micklow, p. 118.

16. Elisabeth Kobus, *Vrij Nederland,* trans. Janice Weiss (July 19, 1975).

17. Truninger, p. 272.

18. Commander Bannon's remarks referred to in these paragraphs are from his address to the 1975 conference of the American Bar Association in Montreal.

19. Schwartz and Mills, p. 11.

20. Lois Yankowski, "Battered Women: A Study of the Situation in the District of Columbia," unpublished (1975), pp. 9-11, 13.

21. The following account is drawn from the written opinion in *Hartzler* v. *City of San Jose,* No. 34650 (February 18, 1975), Court of Appeal of the State of California, First Appellate District, Division Four.

22. The discussion of this statute is drawn from Truninger, pp. 263-64.

23. Dick Egner, "Dish of Legal Sauce: Judge Serves Up Surprise," *San Jose Mercury* (November 5, 1975), Sec. 4C, p. 67.

24. Emily Jane Goodman, "Abused by Her Husband—and the Law," *The New York Times* (October 7, 1975), Op-Ed page.

25. Truninger, pp. 265-66.

26. Ibid., pp. 266-67.

27. Letter from Susan Jackson to author dated February 8, 1976.

28. Truninger, p. 266.

29. Eisenberg and Micklow, p. 50, n. 18.

30. Truninger, p. 269 *(Self* v. *Self).*

31. Rita Delfiner, "Battered Wives: The 'Quiet Crime,' " *New York Post* (August 23, 1975), p. 21.

32. Goodman, *The New York Times,* Op-Ed page.

33. Liston F. Coon, "Felony Assaults in Family Court," *Criminal Law Bulletin* (May 1965).

34. E. Lehman, "Wife-beating," unpublished (New York, 1975), pp. 10-12.

35. Schwartz and Mills, p.7.

36. The account of this issue is drawn from Sigrid Peck, "Police Reluctant—Officers, Attorneys Differ on Handling of Domestic Disputes," *Sacramento Bee* (July 8, 1972).

37. Sigrid Peck, "Slighted Orders? Suit Fights Police Policy on Ex-Mates," *Sacramento Bee* (August 1, 1972).

38. William J. Goode, "Violence Among Intimates," *Crimes of Violence,* staff report to National Commission on the Causes and Prevention of Violence (December 1969), Appendix 19, p. 954.

39. Peck, "Slighted Orders?"

40. Schwartz and Mills, p. 15.

41. Murray's letter to Weiss.

42. I am grateful to the Women's Litigation Unit of the San Francisco Neighborhood Legal Assistance Foundation for allowing me access to their material on the San Francisco District Attorney's Bureau of Family Relations. This account of the Bureau was drawn from that source.

43. Eisenberg and Micklow, pp. 138, 25-27.

44. Schwartz and Mills, pp. 10-11.

45. *"Citizen Dispute Settlement—The Night Prosecutor Program of Columbus, Ohio,"* report on pilot project sponsored by Law Enforcement Assistance Administration (Washington: Superintendent of Documents, 1974).

46. The La Casa de Las Madres Coalition and the Women's Litigation Unit are holding ongoing meetings with District Attorney Joseph Freitas and Police Chief Charles Gains to iron out procedures to be followed in marital violence cases.

47. Bannon's remarks to the American Bar Association.

48. Schwartz and Mills, p. 9.

49. Quoted in Eisenberg and Micklow, p. 127.

50. Both quotes from J. C. Barden, "Physically Abused Women Are Subject of Conference," *The New York Times* (February 1, 1975), p. 20.

51. Eisenberg and Micklow, pp. 139-40.

52. Adolph W. Hart, "Thomas Promised That He Would," *The New York Times* (June 10, 1975).

53. "Even Experts Lack a Formula for Helping Battered Wives," *Reading Times* (September 18, 1975).

54. Cynthia Krolick, "Study Says No Legal Protection from Husband Assault," *Michigan Free Press* (April 14, 1975), p. 60.

55. Eisenberg and Micklow, p. 130.

56. Reported in "No Comment," *Ms.* (August 1975), p. 80.

57. Statement made during Victims of Crimes Committee meeting, part of Citizen Safety Task Force, Mayor's Criminal Justice Council, San Francisco.

58. J. J. Gayford, "Wife Battering: A Preliminary Survey of 100 Cases," *British Medical Journal* (January 25, 1975), p. 196.

Chapter 7

1. The following account summarized from Suzanne Schilz, "One Woman's Story," *Majority Report* (January 25, 1975), p. 11.

2. Women in Philadelphia may obtain copies of *Off the Beaten Track* from Women Against Abuse, 112 S. 16th St., Suite 1012, Philadelphia, Pennsylvania 19102.

3. Erin Pizzey, *Scream Quietly or the Neighbors Will Hear* (London: If Books, 1974), p. 111.

4. Letter to the author from Joanne G. Richter, Police Department's Victim Advocate Office (October 6, 1975).

5. From meeting notes and agenda supplied by Sharon Vaughn of Women's Advocates, St. Paul, Minnesota.

6. Trude Fisher, with Marion P. Winston, "The Grim Plight of Destitute Mothers Who Need Free Rooms on a Stormy Night," *Los Angeles Times* (March 12, 1973), Part II, p. 7.

7. "Family Crisis Center Feasibility Study," prepared with the aid of the National Council on Alcoholism and submitted to Santa Clara County Alcoholism Advisory Board (July 1, 1975), p. 3.

8. Reported by the women of Spectra Feminist Video to Lois Yankowski, "Battered Women: A Study of the Situation in the District of Columbia," unpublished (1975), p.19.

9. Letter from Joanne G. Richter.

10. *Off the Beaten Track*, pp. 10-11.

11. Kathleen M. Fojtik, *Wife Beating: How to Develop a Wife Assault Task Force and Project*. For copies send $1.00 to Ann Arbor-Washtenaw County NOW Wife Assault Task Force, 1917 Washtenaw Ave., Ann Arbor, Michigan 48104.

12. Sally Johnson, "Abused Wives Strike Back," *Majority Report* (May 3, 1975), p. 9.

13. *Bulletin*, Mary Elizabeth Inn, San Francisco (January 1975).

14. Sue Eisenberg and Patricia Micklow, "The Assaulted Wife: 'Catch 22' Revisited," unpublished (University of Michigan, Ann Arbor, 1974), p. 106.

15. Ibid., p. 107.

16. From the files of the Women's Litigation Unit, San Francisco Neighborhood Legal Assistance Foundation.

17. Pizzey, p. 101.

18. California Senate Subcommittee on Nutrition and Human Needs hearings on Marital Violence and Family Violence transcript (July 21, 1975), pp. 106-08.

19. California Senate Bill 149 (Behr) added to the Government Code relating to victims of crimes (Chapter 5 of Part 4 of Division 3 of Title 2, Section 13959 through Section 13969).

20. Information received from Lorraine Copeland director of Rape Victimization Study of Queen's Bench Foundation, San Francisco.

21. Margo Harakas, "Wife Beating: 'Catch 22' Trauma," *Fort Lauderdale Sun-Sentinel* (August 1975—a series of three articles).

22. Mary E. Baluss, "Integrated Services for Victims of Crime: A County-Based Approach," report prepared for the National Association for Counties Research Foundation (September 27, 1974), pp. 21-22.

23. Ibid., pp. 25-26.

24. Ibid., pp. 26-28, 38.

25. Ibid., pp. 41-42.

26. Morton Bard, *Training Police As Specialists in Family Crisis Intervention* (Washington, D.C.: U.S. Government Printing Office, 1970), p. 17.

27. Donald A. Liebman and Jeffrey A. Schwartz, "Police Programs in Domestic Disturbance Crisis Intervention: A Review," *The Urban Policeman in Transition*, J. Snibbe and Homa Snibbe, eds. (Charles C. Thomas, 1972).

28. *Time* (May 1, 1972), p. 60.

29. Peter B. Bloch and Deborah Anderson, *Policewomen on Patrol* (Washington, D.C.: Police Foundation, 1974) and Judith Greenwald, Harriet Connolly, and Peter Bloch, *New York City Policewomen on Patrol* (Washington, D.C.: Police Foundation, 1974).

30. *Time*, p. 60.

31. Bard, p. 3.

32. Gershenson's remarks are from the California legislative hearing on Marital Violence transcript, pp. 61-63.

33. Ibid., pp. 98-99.

34. "Analysis of Police Department Costs Relative to 'Victimless

Crime' " report by Walter Quinn, budget analyst, for San Francisco Board of Supervisors (October 23, 1974), p. 12.

35. Morton Bard, *The Function of the Police in Crisis Intervention and Conflict Management,* a training guide prepared under grant to Criminal Justice Associates, Inc., by the Law Enforcement Assistance Administration, U.S. Department of Justice (1975), p. 6.9.

36. From letter to the National Council on Alcoholism in Santa Clara County (June 17, 1975) attached to "Family Crisis Center Feasibility Study."

37. Morton Bard and Joseph Zacker, "The Prevention of Family Violence: Dilemmas of Community Intervention," *Journal of Marriage and the Family* (November 1971), pp. 677-82. The account of moral questions arising from "reaching out" is drawn from this article.

38. Pizzey, pp. 103-05.

39. Peter R. Breggin, "Psychosurgery Is a Crime Against Humanity," *Medical Opinion* (March 1972).

40. League of Women Voters, *Challenge of the 70's* (San Francisco, 1975), p. 8.

41. George L. Kirkham, "Doc Cop," *Human Behavior* (May, 1975).

42. Donald J. Holmes, *Psychotherapy* (Boston: Little, Brown, 1972), p. 818.

Chapter 8

1. Simone de Beauvoir, *The Second Sex,* translated and edited by H. M. Parshley (New York: Knofp, 1953), pp. 330-31.

2. Ibid., p. 330.

3. Ibid., p. 331.

4. George L. Kirkham, "Doc Cop," *Human Behavior* (May 1972), p. 5.

5. "Getting into Violence," *San Francisco Chronicle* (April 23, 1975), p. 20.

6. Lee Schwing, "Women: Weak or Strong," *The Furies* (January 1972), p. 3.

7. Schwing (May 1972), p. 5.

8. Diane Curtis, "The Divorce Furies," *San Francisco Sunday Examiner and Chronicle* (July 6, 1975), Sunday Punch section.

9. Naomi Weisstein, " 'Kinder, Kuche, Kirche' As Scientific Law: Psychology Constructs the Female," *Sisterhood Is Powerful,* Robin Morgan, ed. (New York: Random House, 1970), pp. 208-10.

10. Karen Horney, *The Neurotic Personality of Our Time* (New York: Norton, 1973), p. 261.

11. Elizabeth Truninger, "Marital Violence: The Legal Solutions," *Hastings Law Journal*, Vol. 23, p. 260.

12. Letty Cottin Pogrebin, "Do Women Make Men Violent?" *Ms.* (November 1974), p. 80. .

13. Stephen Schafer, *The Victim and His Criminal* (New York: Random House, 1968), p. 152.

14. Menachem Amir, *Patterns in Forcible Rape* (Chicago: University of Chicago Press, 1971), pp. 260-61.

15. Nathan Capland and Stephen D. Nelson, "Who's to Blame?" *Psychology Today* (November 1974), pp.101-02.

16. Russell Dobash and R. Emerson Dobash, "Violence Between Men and Women Within the Family Setting," paper presented at the VIII World Congress of Sociology, Toronto (August 1974), pp. 3-5.

17. Lynda Lytle Holmstrom and Ann Wolbert Burgess, "Rape Reconsidered: The Victim's View," paper delivered at American Sociological Association annual meeting in San Francisco (August 29, 1975).

18. Claude Steiner, "Power," *Issues in Radical Therapy* (Summer 1975), p. 7.

19. I. K. Broverman, D. M. Broverman, R. Clarkson, P. Rosenkrantz, and S. Vogel, "Sex Role Stereotypes and Clinical Judgments of Mental Health," *Journal of Consulting Psychiatry* (1969).

20. Ruth Dreiblatt Pancoast and Lynda Martin Weston, "Feminist Psychotherapy: A Method for Fighting Social Control of Women," a position statement of the Feminist Counseling Collective, Washington, D.C. (February 1974), p. 7.

21. Ibid., pp. 14-15.

22. Ibid., pp. 3-4.

23. Claudia Dreifus, *Woman's Fate* (New York: Bantam, 1973), pp. 2, 4.

24. Pamela Allen, *Free Space* (Washington, N.J.: Times Change Press, 1970), p. 26.

25. Ibid., pp. 34-36.

26. Dreifus, p. 52.

27. Ibid., pp. 7-8.

28. Allen, pp. 30-31.

29. Stanlee Phelps and Nancy Austin, *The Assertive Woman* (San Luis Obispo, California: Impact, 1975), p. 1.

30. Ibid., p. 2.

31. Beverly Stephen, "Assertiveness—Learning a Kind of Honesty," *San Francisco Chronicle* (November 10, 1975), p. 20.

32. Phelps and Austin, pp. 119-28.

33. Stephen, p. 20.

34. The fllowing account of the three-party contract is drawn from Barbara B. Hirsch, *Divorce: What a Woman Needs to Know* (New York: Bantam, 1973), pp. 9-10.

35. Lois Yankowski, "Battered Women: A Study of the Situation in the District of Columbia," unpublished (1975), p. 21.

36. Sally Johnson, "What About Battered Women?" *Majority Report* (February 8, 1975), p. 1.

37. Women in Transition, Inc., *Women in Transition: A Feminist Handbook on Separation and Divorce* (New York: Scribner's, 1975), p. 200.

38. Ibid., p. 199.

39. Hirsch, p. 54.

40. *Women in Transition*, p. 205.

41. Hirsch, p. 70.

42. Ibid., pp. 72-73.

43. Ibid., p. 78.

44. Ibid., p. 79.

45. Ibid., p. 80.

46. NOW's National Task Force on Marriage, Divorce, and Family Relations, *Newsletter,* Betty Barry, ed. (May 25, 1973), pp. 3-4.

47. Carol Pogash, "More Runaway Wives Than Ever Seek Freedom," *San Francisco Sunday Examiner and Chronicle* (March 2, 1975), Sec. A, p. 26.

48. Tish Sommers, *The Not–So–Helpless Female* (New York: David McKay, 1973), p. 15.

Chapter 9

1. California Senate Subcommittee on Nutrition and Human Needs Hearing on Marital and Family Violence transcript (July 21, 1975), p. 234.

2. Letter from Laurence D. Mass, staff attorney with Community Legal Services, Inc., Philadelphia, Pennsylvania (April 21, 1975). The Protection from Abuse Act (H.R. 1051) was introduced during the 1975 session of the Pennsylvania state legislature.

3. California Government Code Section 820.2.

4. California Senate Subcommittee Hearing transcript, p. 234.

5. A reiteration of victims' rights may be found in the "Goals and Standards" drawn up in 1975 by the Citizen Safety Task Force of the Mayor's Criminal Justice Council in San Francisco.

6. William Mandel, *Soviet Women* (Garden City, N.Y.: Anchor, 1975), p. 272.

7. Susan Brownmiller, *Against Our Will* (New York: Simon and Schuster, 1975), p. 382.

8. William J. Goode, "Violence Among Intimates," *Crimes of Violence,* staff report of the National Commission on the Causes and Prevention of Violence (December 1969), Vol. 13, Appendix 19, p. 974.

9. *Report from Select Committee on Violence in Marriage* (London: Her Majesty's Stationery Office, 1975), p. xvii.

10. Ibid., p. xviii.

11. Ibid., p. xix.

12. Ibid., p. xxii.

13. Ibid., pp. xxii-xxiii.

14. California Senate Subcommittee Hearing transcript, pp. 235-38. Copies of the proposed "Family Violence and Prevention and Treatment Act" are available on request as part of the appendices to this transcript.

15. Select Committee, pp. x, xiii.

16. Ibid., p. vi.

17. Ibid., p. xxv.

18. *Congressional Record* (March 22, 1972), S 4582, Vol. 118, No. 44.

19. Sandra Roth, "Are Insurance Giants Out to Crush ERA?" *Majority Report* (January 25, 1975), p. 1.

20. "Will Equality Destroy Life Insurance Profits?" *Majority Report* (January 25, 1975), p. 1.

21. "Why the Insurance Industry?" *Majority Report* (January 25, 1975), p. 6.

22. Lenore J. Weitzman, "Legal Regulation of Marriage: Tradition and Change," *California Law Review,* Vol. 62, No. 4 (July-September 1974), pp. 1241-45.

23. Ibid., p. 1249.

24. Ibid., p. 1250.

25. Ibid., p. 1260.

26. Ibid., p. 1262.

27. Ibid., p. 1263.

28. Ibid., p. 1277.

29. Ibid.

30. NOW's National Task Force on Marriage, Divorce, and Family Relations, *Newsletter,* Betty Barry, ed. (May 25, 1973), Vol. II, No. 1, pp. 1-2.

31. NOW's National Task Force, *Newsletter* (August 1973), Vol. II, No. 2, p. 3.

Chapter 10

1. Judith Weinraub, "The Battered Wives of England: A Place to

eal Their Wounds," *The New York Times* (November 29, 1975), C–17.

2. Most of the material on Women's House is drawn from newsletters of Women's Advocates and correspondence with Sharon aughn, a member of the collective.

3. *St. Paul Dispatch,* "Board Approves Housing" (March 8, 974).

4. *St. Paul Dispatch,* "Mayor vows quicker response to calls om Women's Advocates" (September 18, 1975).

5. Material on Rainbow Retreat was drawn from a telephone onversation with Joanne Rhoads, executive director, who also rovided me with brochures.

6. *Alive,* "Haven for spouses of alcoholics" (February 1976), . 11.

7. Material on Women's Center South was drawn from a telehone conversation with Vickie Barnes, who recently moved to San rancisco and expects to work with the La Casa de las Madres oalition.

8. Material on the Women's Transitional Living Center was drawn om their funding proposal, conversations with Karen Peters of range County NOW, and telephone conversations with Susan aples, director.

9. Material on Emergency Housing from *U.S. Family Law Reorter* (July 22, 1975), 1 FLR, pp. 2613-14.

10. From correspondence with Albuquerque NOW member, athleen Winslow.

11. From correspondence with Sharon Vaughn of Women's ouse.

12. Jacqueline Bernard, "Moving Mountains: Appalachia Women rganize," *Ms.* (September 1975), p. 21.

13. Michelle Wasserman, "Beating Up Wives: An Abuse That ociety Fails to Notice," *Boston Phoenix* (April 1, 1975).

14. From correspondence with Betsy Warrior.

15. From a copy of the letter being circulated by Women's roject.

16. Jeanne Wright, "Wife Beating Not Uncommon: Spouse Asult Doesn't Just 'Happen to Others,' " *Kalamazoo Gazette* (Deember 5, 1975).

17. From a telephone conversation with Betty Schramm, presient of Kalamazoo Area Chapter of NOW.

18. Women's Advocates *Newsletter* (July 1974), p. 2.

19. Material on efforts in Seattle drawn from meeting with the pecial Issues Committee of the Seattle Women's Commission, from ackie Griswold of Seattle NOW, and from women in the commuity.

20. NOW's National Task Force on Marriage, Divorce, and Family Relations, *Newsletter,* Betty Barry, ed. (August 1973), p. 2, and conversation with Jean Conger, member of NOW's National Board.

21. Montgomery County Council, Maryland, "A Report by the Task Force to Study a Haven for Physically Abused Persons" (November 1, 1975), and conversations with women in the community.

22. From a telephone conversation with Janet Hicks, Women Against Rape, Burlington, Vermont.

23. Lois M. Hake Woman, "Diary of a Battered Housewife," *DO IT NOW* (March 1976), p. 4.

24. *Reading Times,* "Exposed . . . wife beating is fought" (September 17, 1975).

25. Charlotte Slater, "Where can a battered wife run to?" *Detroit News* (July 27, 1975).

26. Erin Pizzey, *Scream Quietly or the Neighbors Will Hear* (London: If Books, 1974), pp. 9-10.

27. Ibid., pp. 43-45.

28. Report on activity in Scotland drawn from correspondence and materials supplied by Dr. Rebecca Dobash, Department of Sociology, University of Stirling.

29. Elisabeth Kobus, *Vrij Nederland* (July 19, 1975).

30. Material on Rotterdam and The Hague drawn from a letter to the author from Huub Hodzelmans of the Algemene Hulpcentra (February 4, 1976).

31. Letter to the author from Dagmar Schultz (October 25, 1975).

32. Bruno Frappat, "Un Fléau Social: Les femmes battues," *Le Monde* (November 4, 1975), p. 10.

33. Barbara Robin, "A Refuge for Danish Women," *San Francisco Chronicle* (June 5, 1973), p. 21.

34. From a letter to the author from Jytte Birch (November 1975).

35. Material on Interval House, Toronto, drawn from written materials supplied by Interval House, including funding proposals, house rules, and so forth.

36. Material on Interval House, Saskatoon, drawn from an article in *Chatelaine* (February 1975) and a letter to the author from Karen Wasylenka, director (January 13, 1976).

37. Material on Transition House and the other refuges in British Columbia drawn from conversations and correspondence with Susan Margaret, a member of the Transition House staff.

38. From a telephone conversation with Janet Hicks.

39. Material on activity in Australia drawn from correspondence with Dr. Anne M. Z. Walker (September 24, 1975).

40. Gale Carsenat, "Project Interval House Research Submission #1" (February 17, 1975).

41. Janet Rosettis, "Vancouver Transition House," report for the Department of Human Resources (January 1975).

42. Ruth Adler, Lea Harris, and Fran Wasoff, "Edinburgh Women's Aid: A Review of the First Year."

43. Haven House Project Proposal submitted to County of Los Angeles Department of Urban Affairs (March 12, 1975), pp. 15E-7E.

44. Kobus, *Vrij Nederland*.

45. J. J. Gayford, "Wife Battering: A Preliminary Survey of 100 Cases," *British Medical Journal* (January 25, 1975), p. 196.

46. Weinraub, *The New York Times*.

47. From the house rules, "Welcome to Interval House."

48. "Official Aid Is Essential" and "Council Gives a House," *Nemesis* (April 1974), p. 1.

49. Letter to the author from Dr. Rebecca Dobash, Department of Sociology, University of Stirling (December 4, 1975).

50. From correspondence with Eve Norman, former coordinator of California NOW and member of Los Angeles chapter.

51. Mary Jean Tully, "Funding the Feminists," *Foundation News* (March/April 1975), pp. 26, 28-31.

52. *The London Sunday Times*, "battered wives plea," News Digest (November 3, 1974), p. 1.

53. Edinburgh Women's Aid, *Newsletter*, No. 1 (February 26, 1975), p. 1.

Five Years Later—References

1. Nancy Fiora-Gormally, "Battered Wives Who Kill: Double Standard Out of Court, Single Standard In?" *Law and Human Behavior* (1978), Vol. 2, No. 2, pp. 130-165. Ann Jones, *Women Who Kill* (New York: Holt, Rinehart and Winston, 1980) pp. 286, 299.

2. Elizabeth Schneider, Susan Jordan and Christina Arguedas, "Representation of Women Who Defend Themselves in Response to Physical and Sexual Assault," *Women's Rights Law Reporter* (Spring, 1978).

3. "The Prevalence of Crime," *Bureau of Justice Statistics Bulletin*, (1981) U.S. Department of Justice, Washington, DC 20531.

4. "Domestic Violence Is a Crime," San Francisco Violence Project Distributed by Western States Shelter Network, 870 Market St., Suite 1058, San Francisco, CA 94102. Includes new general order of S.F.P.D. $5.

5. "Family Violence Prosecution Manual," Santa Barbara County District Attorney, 118 E. Figueroa St., Santa Barbara, CA 93101. $4.

6. Linda R. Insalaco Brown, "The Admissibility of Expert Test mony on the Subject of Battered Women," *Criminal Justice Journ* (1980) Vol. 4, No. 1, p. 177.

7. A list of programs for batterers is available from Center fe Women Policy Studies, 2000 P St. N.W., Suite 508, Washington, D 20036.

8. Anne Ganley and Lance Harris, "Domestic Violence: Issues Designing and Implementing Programs for Male Batterers," pap presented at American Psychological Association meeting, Toront August 29, 1978.

9. Lenore E. Walker, *The Battered Woman* (New York: Harper Row, 1979).

10. Mildred Daley Pagelow, *Woman Battering: Victims and The Experiences* (Beverly Hills: Sage, 1981)

11. R. Emerson Dobash and Russell Dobash, *Violence Again Wives* (New York: Free Press, 1979).

12. Letty Cottin Pogrebin, *Growing Up Free: Raising Your Ch in the 80s* (New York: McGraw-Hill, 1980) pp. 274-301.

13. "Handbook of Emergency and Long-Term Housing" is ava able from the National Coalition Against Domestic Violence, 1728 St. N.W., Washington, DC 20036. 202/347-7015.

14. "Battered Women Receive Help at Kentucky Army Post *Response* (July, 1980) Vol. 3, No. 11.

15. "First National Conference on Violence in Military Fam lies," *Response* (March/April 1981) Vol. 4, No. 4.

16. Special Double Issue on Funding, *SANEnews* (July, 198 Vol. 1, No. 12.

17. "State Legislation on Domestic Violence," *Respon* (August/September 1980) Vol. 3, No. 12. For legislation that delet "husband exemption" from rape laws, contact National Clearin house on Marital Rape, 2325 Oak St., Berkeley, CA 94708.

18. Steven Morgan, *Conjugal Terrorism: A Psychological a Community Treatment Model of Wife Abuse* (Palo Alto: R & Research Associates, 1981).

Note: A new film, "A Family Affair," is a model of how la enforcement response to wife abuse *could be*. VISUCOM Produ tions, P.O. Box 5472, Redwood City, CA 94063.